"Cheers to Mr. Baldassaro for mir

—**Ira Berkow**, Pulitzer Prize–winning author of *How Life Imitates Sports*

"Tony Lazzeri was one of the first Italian American sports stars, a key player of the famed Murderers' Row Yankees lineup, and an underappreciated American success story who overcame poverty and epilepsy. He is a worthy subject for this closer look at a Hall of Famer."

—**Tom Verducci**, senior baseball writer for *Sports Illustrated* and MLB TV commentator

"In real life as in baseball, how one performs in a climactic moment may unfairly obscure a multitude of other feats; Larry Baldassaro's book reveals its subject to have been not only a wonderful ballplayer but also a great pioneer on behalf of Italian Americans forevermore."

—**John Thorn**, official historian of Major League Baseball

"Who's the greatest second baseman in Yankee history? All too often, Tony Lazzeri, the Murderers' Row Hall of Famer, is left out of the debate. Lawrence Baldassaro's biography properly elevates Lazzeri's status in such discussions. This is an important contribution to Yankees literature."

—**Marty Appel**, New York Yankees historian and author of *Pinstripe Empire* and *Casey Stengel*

"More than a biography of the subtitled Yankees Legend and Baseball Pioneer, this study helps us understand how this sport affected not only a nation, but also those newcomers looking for a way to fit into the new culture. . . . Tony Lazzeri had a feel for the game that was not restricted to the fields. Beyond his move from sandlots to professional ball, from the minors to the majors, Lazzeri developed a baseball sense that he brought to life, enabling him not only to become an outstanding player but a deep thinker of the game. . . . Thanks to Baldassaro, today's generation can better appreciate what this man did for the game and his paesani in his gentlemanly and modest way."

—**Fred L. Gardaphé**, *Voices in Italian Americana*

"Baldassaro has written the definitive biography of Tony Lazzeri."

—**Jason Schott**, *Brooklyn Digest*

"In *Tony Lazzeri*, Baldassaro provides a nuanced view of Italian Americans—on and off the baseball diamond."
—**Bob D'Angelo**, *Sports Bookie*

"Lawrence Baldassaro has written the book that was long overdue. It's remarkably well researched and detailed, and holds the reader's interest from start to finish. In my opinion, it will soon be recognized as the definitive biography of this great Hall-of-Fame ballplayer, Tony Lazzeri. It's one I highly recommend to all baseball fans."
—**Gary Livacari**, *Baseball History Comes Alive!*

"Baldassaro does an excellent job describing how Lazzeri prevailed against widespread prejudice against Italian Americans, arguably paving the way for the acceptance of Joe DiMaggio and other players of Italian descent in the late 1930s. Baldassaro, a professor emeritus of Italian, uses authoritative secondary sources to deftly develop a perspective on Italian immigration and its associated prejudice in the early twentieth century."
—**Charlie Bevis**, *Bevis Baseball Research*

Tony Lazzeri

Tony Lazzeri

Yankees Legend and Baseball Pioneer

LAWRENCE BALDASSARO

University of Nebraska Press

Lincoln

The University of Nebraska Press is part of a land-
grant institution with campuses and programs on the
past, present, and future homelands of the Pawnee,
Ponca, Otoe-Missouria, Omaha, Dakota, Lakota, Kaw,
Cheyenne, and Arapaho Peoples, as well as those of the
relocated Ho-Chunk, Sac and Fox, and Iowa Peoples.

First Nebraska paperback printing: 2024
Library of Congress Cataloging-in-Publication Data
Names: Baldassaro, Lawrence, author.
Title: Tony Lazzeri: Yankees legend and baseball
pioneer / Lawrence Baldassaro.
Description: Lincoln: University of Nebraska Press,
[2021] | Includes bibliographical references and index.
Identifiers: LCCN 2020037024
ISBN 9781496216755 (hardback)
ISBN 9781496238818 (paperback)
ISBN 9781496226181 (epub)
ISBN 9781496226198 (mobi)
ISBN 9781496226204 (pdf)
Subjects: LCSH: Lazzeri, Tony, 1903–1946. | Baseball
players—United States—Biography. | Italian
American baseball players—Biography. | New York
Yankees (Baseball team)—History—20th century.
Classification: LCC GV865.L34 B35 2021 |
DDC 796.357092 [B]—dc23
LC record available at
https://lccn.loc.gov/2020037024

Set in Vesper by Mikala R. Kolander.

In memory of my parents,
Gerald and Olive Baldassaro,
who ignited my love for the game,
and to my son, Jim

Contents

Illustrations

Preface

Before there was Joe DiMaggio, there was Tony Lazzeri. A decade before the "Yankee Clipper" began his legendary career in 1936, Lazzeri paved the way for the man who would become an iconic American hero. At a time when baseball ruled the world of sports and was a major social institution, Lazzeri was one of the game's biggest stars, the de facto captain of the famed Yankees' Murderers' Row lineup and second in popularity on that team only to Babe Ruth. From 1926 through 1937 he was the second baseman for teams that won six pennants and five World Series on their way to becoming the most storied American sports franchise. He was also a mentor to DiMaggio and fellow Californians Frank Crosetti and Lefty Gomez, both of whom later joined him in the Yankees lineup.

An unwitting baseball pioneer, in 1925 the twenty-one-year-old Lazzeri became the first ballplayer to hit sixty home runs in organized baseball while playing for the Salt Lake City Bees in the Pacific Coast League. He then became one of the first middle infielders to hit with power in the big leagues. In fact his home run and RBI production in his years with the Yankees put him in the company of the most elite sluggers of that period. He was also the first major star of Italian descent in the national pastime and one of the game's first ethnic heroes. His success not only drew large numbers of first- and second-generation Italian Americans to the ballpark for the first time, but it also gave them a newfound sense of pride at a time when the stereotypical image of their group within the American consciousness was that of the bootleg mobster. Blessed with a keen baseball mind, Lazzeri was regarded as one of the smartest and most respected players in the game. In 1991 he was enshrined in the Baseball Hall of Fame.

Yet in spite of all that he achieved, Lazzeri has been largely forgotten. Over time his achievements and records were overshadowed by fellow Yankees Ruth, DiMaggio, and Lou Gehrig. And his early death in 1946 at the age of forty-two means that except at the moment of his entry into the Hall of Fame, he has been out of the public awareness for more than seven decades. Worse yet, when he is remembered, it is mainly for one moment in a fourteen-year career: his strikeout against future Hall of Fame pitcher Grover Cleveland Alexander at a crucial moment in the seventh game of the 1926 World Series, when he was a twenty-two-year-old rookie. As if to rub salt in the wound, that strikeout is even mentioned on Alexander's Hall of Fame plaque. Consequently Tony Lazzeri has become one of those ballplayers who, in spite of a career that earned him a place in baseball's shrine, is essentially relegated to the dustbin of baseball history, remembered by only the most devoted followers of the game.

Lazzeri's was an unlikely success story. Born in San Francisco to Italian immigrants, he left school at the age of fifteen to work in the same boiler factory as his father, while briefly considering a career as a professional fighter. But he beat the odds and found a way to realize the American Dream by excelling in baseball. While that in itself is a major challenge for anyone, for Lazzeri there were two additional obstacles. For one thing, he was part of an ethnic group that had been widely disparaged for decades and was not welcomed with open arms by the baseball establishment. The other obstacle was one the public was never aware of: he played his entire career while afflicted with epilepsy. A neurological disorder that not only presented the daily possibility of one's suffering a seizure, epilepsy was also so stigmatized at the time that it was best kept secret. Knowing that stress is a common trigger for seizures, a New York doctor specializing in epilepsy said of Lazzeri: "Think of a ballplayer in front of all those people, and in those times. I can't believe he played."[1]

I got a better understanding of what the doctor meant when, for a few weeks in 1992, I had the opportunity to pitch batting practice for the Milwaukee Brewers. (My pitching "career" began when I was ten and ended after one year of semi-pro ball.) I have loved the game for as long as I can remember and thought I understood it rather well. But I quickly discovered that when you're on the field with some of the best players in the world, even the relatively slow-motion activity of batting practice is an eye-opening revelation. Everything happens much faster than it looks from the stands or on television. You realize just how hard these athletes hit the ball and how quickly fielders need to react.

I learned about speed firsthand when, on one of my earliest pitches, before I got the hang of drifting behind the protective screen at the bottom of the mound as the ball is released, a batter hit a line drive straight at my head. Luckily, given my relative youth at the time, I was able to avoid the ball by flopping onto my back, much to the hilarity of the guys around the batting cage. That lesson was reinforced when I later went to the outfield to shag balls and realized how fast a baseball gets out to you, leaving little time to adjust. I came away from that experience with a much better understanding of the difficulty of playing the game at the Major League level and a much greater respect for even the average player. Such knowledge makes it all the more remarkable to me that Lazzeri was able to perform at such a high level while coping with the daily uncertainty of epilepsy.

I first became interested in the story of Tony Lazzeri when I began doing research for my previous book, *Beyond DiMaggio: Italian Americans in Baseball*. Of all the individuals I researched and wrote about in that book, none surprised or intrigued me more than Lazzeri. I had been vaguely familiar with his career, but I had no idea what a pioneer he was, nor that he was an epileptic. I wondered why I had not heard or read more about this Hall of Famer who not only had enjoyed a great career in the Majors, but had also had a significant social impact. It was then that I decided his story needed to be told. He is too important a figure to not have his achievements well documented and put into historical perspective.

It was a challenge to write this biography because of Lazzeri's strong sense of privacy. Typical of his reluctance to speak about himself was his response to a request for an interview by a San Francisco reporter: "Nothing doing," he said. "I'm not telling my life story."[2] Lazzeri was sparing with words, both about his achievements on the diamond and even more so about his private life. Consequently he left precious little in the way of anecdotes or personal reflections, and his interviews provided little if any insight into his inner life. Beyond that, given his penchant for brevity when he did speak and the common practice among some sportswriters at the time to embellish or even fabricate interviews, some of the quotations that were attributed to him are suspect as regards their accuracy or even their authenticity.

Because so little of Lazzeri's off-field life is known, even by surviving family members, it is impossible to know, for example, how the formative moments of his youth shaped his personality and life. He apparently didn't share those details with others, or if he did, there is no documentation. If this book lacks insight into his human frailties—other than making a biographer's task more difficult by his reluctance to reveal more about himself—it is only because I have found no evidence of them, either in his own words or in the accounts of others.

When Lazzeri's son, David, passed away in 2013, the only surviving family members were David's wife, Marilyn, and their three sons, none of whom, including Marilyn, had ever met Lazzeri. Early on in my research I had the good fortune of getting to know Marilyn and the oldest of the three grandchildren, Matt. In numerous phone conversations they generously shared what they knew about Lazzeri. In addition, Matt and his wife, Linda, graciously invited me to their home in Oregon, where I was given access to four large scrapbooks of clippings that had been meticulously put together by Lazzeri's immigrant father, Agostino, throughout his son's career. (Since some of the clippings are without a date or the name of the newspaper, I cite those sources as Lazzeri Scrapbooks.)

The story of Tony Lazzeri is intriguing as much for what we don't know about him as for what we do know. As the reader will see, a number of questions regarding his life, on and off the field, defy definitive answers. Even his grandson Matt told me, "There's a lot we don't know about my grandfather." I discovered that there are numerous gaps and inconsistencies in the material written about Lazzeri in the nine decades since he began his baseball career, and a fair amount of what has appeared in print is factually suspect or simply wrong. Even some basic elements of his life—where he grew up, where he went to school, where and how he died, even his first and middle names—have been subject to contradictory statements and, in some cases, mistakenly stated as fact. The absence of personal testimony by Lazzeri to confirm or contradict the words of others only adds to the dilemma of distinguishing fact from fiction. Consequently one of my primary responsibilities in writing this book was to dig up facts, both those that had never been sought and those that could correct inaccurate and conflicting information already in print. My research enabled me to correct some long-standing errors, but some issues defy easy resolution because of the lack of definitive evidence. For example, to what extent did epilepsy have an impact on Lazzeri's performance? In such instances I have laid out whatever evidence I found and, when viable, offered for the reader's consideration what seemed to me a plausible conclusion.

Most of the available information about Lazzeri is found in newspapers from his time in baseball; many of these are now digitized and available online. (Newspapers.com and ProQuest provided invaluable access to those sources.) While New York and

San Francisco–area newspapers were the most utilized and valuable sources, I also consulted papers in all cities that were home to American League teams at the time, as well as papers in the Minor League cities where Lazzeri played and managed. Other significant sources were magazine articles focused on Lazzeri, biographies of Yankee players, and histories of the Yankees and of baseball in general. Government documents and genealogical sources were helpful in tracing family history. The go-to sources for box scores, play-by-play descriptions, and statistical data were retrosheet.com and baseball-reference.com.

The one book-length study that has appeared—*Tony Lazzeri: A Baseball Biography*, by Paul Votano (2005)—is a well-researched and helpful road map of Lazzeri's career in the big leagues. However, it provides limited coverage of significant pieces of Lazzeri's life and legacy, such as his family background, his affliction with epilepsy, his post-baseball life, his rightful place in baseball history, and his social impact.

With courage, determination, and a strong competitive spirit, Lazzeri overcame the challenges he faced to become one of the best ballplayers of his era, the leader of one of baseball's greatest teams, and an inspiration to an entire new generation of fans. Given all that he achieved, he deserves to be remembered as more than a footnote on Grover Cleveland Alexander's Hall of Fame plaque. In this book I have tried to shed light on an underappreciated baseball pioneer and restore him to his rightful place in baseball history. I can only hope that I have done him justice.

Acknowledgments

I am deeply indebted to Susan Shemanske and Gary D'Amato for their meticulous reading of the manuscript and invaluable advice. They provided a great defense that saved me from numerous errors, as did Alan Kaufmann, fact checker extraordinaire. I'm also grateful to those who read and commented on various segments of the text: Michael Bauman, Fred Gardaphé, Bob Gormley, Dennis Snelling, and Mario Ziino. Special thanks to my *cara amica*, Gael Garbarino, who also reviewed parts of the manuscript and provided moral support throughout.

This book was greatly enhanced by the generous support of Marilyn Lazzeri, Tony's daughter-in-law, and her son Matt, who provided invaluable help throughout by granting access to the Lazzeri Scrapbooks and by sharing recollections and photographs. They were both unfailingly receptive and responsive to my many questions. Thanks to Matt and his wife, Linda, for graciously providing some delicious meals during my stay in Oregon.

Several people in San Francisco helped me in a variety of ways. I'm grateful to Mary Serventi Steiner of the Museo Italo-Americano for putting me in touch with the Lazzeri family. My thanks to Tom Carey and Andrea Grimes of the San Francisco History Center at the San Francisco Public Library, Gina Bardi of the San Francisco Maritime National Historical Park Research Center, Jessica Smith of the Olympic Club, and Professor Robert Elias of the University of San Francisco. Thanks also to Marc Macrae, Marlene Vogelsang, and Alan Ziajka.

I'm grateful to library staff members who went out of their way to be helpful. At the Baseball Hall of Fame Library, Cassidy Lent, Tom Shieber, and Bill Francis provided prompt and helpful answers to my inquiries. Thanks also to the staffs at the Whitefish Bay (Wisconsin) Library, the Milwaukee Public Library, and the University of Wisconsin–Milwaukee Library for promptly acquiring interlibrary loan material.

For their help in providing illustrations I thank Marilyn and Matt Lazzeri, John Horne (Baseball Hall of Fame Library), Bob Cullum (Leslie Jones Collection), Mark Rucker (Rucker Archive), Lori Hines (Bancroft Library of UC Berkeley), Rebekah Bedard (Toronto Archives), Adam Cohen (Joshua Tree Auctions), Michael Dabin, and David Eskenazi. Thanks also to Gary Livacari for his help in dating some of the photos.

My thanks to Norman Macht for sharing his expertise and guiding me to good sources of information and to Dave Smith and Adam McCalvy for generously providing detailed statistical data.

Dr. Chad Carlson, professor of neurology at the Medical College of Wisconsin who specializes in the treatment of patients with epilepsy, was most helpful in sharing his knowledge of the history and effects of epilepsy.

I'm also indebted to the following people who contributed in various ways: Dr. Piero Antuono, Bob Buege, Bill Deane, Gustavo Eydelsteyn, Larry Gerlach, Steve Gietschier, Fred Glueckstein, Ed Hartig, Michael Haupert, Dick Johnson, George Koleas, Joe Michelucci, David Schultz, Theron Schultz, Lyle Spatz, and Steve Steinberg. Apologies to anyone I may have inadvertently omitted.

Special thanks to senior acquisitions editor Rob Taylor at the University of Nebraska Press for once again having faith in me, to Courtney Ochsner, Rob's assistant, for her tireless effort to bring the book together, to senior project editor Joeth Zucco for taking the manuscript to print-ready stage, and to Bojana Ristich for her predictably stellar job of copyediting.

Tony Lazzeri

1

Growing Up in San Francisco

On a warm and humid day with thunder and lightning in the background, more than five thousand fans and thirty-one Hall of Famers gathered in Cooperstown, New York, on Sunday, July 21, 1991, to witness the Baseball Hall of Fame induction ceremony. Three players—seven-time batting champion Rod Carew and two pitchers, Ferguson Jenkins and Gaylord Perry—had been voted in by the Baseball Writers' Association of America (BBWAA). Two others had been selected posthumously by the Veterans Committee: maverick baseball executive Bill Veeck and Tony Lazzeri. It had been fifty-two years since Lazzeri had played his last Major League game and forty-five since he had passed away at the age of forty-two. But the long and unlikely journey to Cooperstown and baseball immortality by this son of immigrants had really begun in Italy before he was born.

On March 19, 1903, Agostino and Giulia (Chiesa) Lazzeri sailed from Genoa, Italy, on the SS *Trave*, bound for New York City. Soon after disembarking on April 1, they boarded a train for San Francisco, where, according to the manifest of the *Trave*, they were to join Marco Chiesa, presumably a relative of Giulia. They would spend the rest of their lives in the city by the bay.

San Francisco had been attracting Asian and European immigrants since the days of the gold rush. The Irish, Germans, Chinese, and Italians comprised the four predominant groups of immigrants, with Italians being the last to arrive. The greatest expansion of the Italian community occurred in the first two decades of the twentieth century. Between 1900 and 1924 twenty thousand Italians came to the city. The census of 1910 showed seventeen thousand Italian-born and twelve thousand Italian Americans. By 1920 there were twenty-four thousand Italian-born, making them the largest immigrant group in the city, and twenty-two thousand Italian Americans.

Unlike the great majority of Italians who migrated to the United States at the turn of the twentieth century, Tony Lazzeri's parents were not from the southern regions of Italy. In his petition for citizenship, filed in 1931, Agostino's race was listed as "Italian (North)." (Based on the "racial" profiles concocted by sociologists in the late nineteenth century, northern Italians were considered to be more desirable immigrants than southerners because they more closely exhibited the characteristics of the Nordic races.) In fact, whereas by the end of the nineteenth century most Italian conclaves in the United States were predominantly populated by immigrants from the south, in San Francisco and California as a whole, northern Italians predominated throughout the period of mass immigration from 1880 to 1924.[1]

The son of Antonio and Angela (Polonia) Lazzeri, Agostino was born on May 15, 1880, in Tresana, a small town in the Tuscan province of Massa Carrara. According to his Italian passport, he was 5 feet 4 inches tall (1.66 meters), with blond hair and brown eyes. Like most Italian immigrants at that time, he was an unskilled laborer; the ship's manifest listed his occupation as "peasant." Born on February 2, 1862, in San Colombano Certenoli (about thirty miles east of Genoa), Giulia was eighteen years older than Agostino. At the time of their marriage in Italy on March 1, 1903, she was the widow of a man named Barosso, with whom she had a son, Giovanni, born in 1884.[2] On December 6, 1903, she gave birth to a son who would be their only child. In their wildest dreams never could they have imagined that within twenty-two years that son would be an inspiration to, and the idol of, millions of immigrants like themselves.

Of the many questions regarding the details of Tony Lazzeri's life, the first regards the most elemental issue: his name. It is not surprising, given the standards of handwritten record keeping at the time, that there were many inconsistencies and gaps regarding the Lazzeri family history. As often happened with Italian immigrants and their offspring, there was confusion about the Lazzeri family names. For many, Italian names proved to be troublesome in both spelling and pronunciation. Even in print, names were spelled creatively, with little concern for accuracy—a subtle example of indifference, if not outright disdain, for the person behind the name. In various public documents such as census reports, city directories, and voter registration lists, the Lazzeri surname sometimes was spelled "Lazzari." Agostino's name appeared as Augustino, August, Agustino, Agosto, Augustine, and even Ogestine, while Giulia's name often was anglicized to Julia.

Even the name of their son, whose birth certificate was lost in the 1906 San Francisco earthquake and fire, is open to questions. From the time newspapers began covering Tony's baseball career, his given name appeared as Anthony, as it did on the contracts he signed with baseball teams. Nevertheless, the custom in Italy was to name the first-born son after the paternal grandfather. Since Lazzeri's grandfather was named Antonio, how likely is it that Agostino and Giulia, who arrived in America only eight months before their son was born, would have anglicized his name to Anthony? In fact, in the 1920 census report—the first report in which the family is listed, when they were living at 142 Missouri Street—three people were living at the Lazzeri household: August, age thirty-nine; Julia, age fifty [sic]; and "Antonio," age sixteen. Tony's name also appears as "Antonio" in the 1922 San Francisco city directory and a 1924 probate record. As for his surname, in the early years of his baseball career it would be spelled in a myriad of ways.

Lazzeri's middle name routinely appears in print as "Michael." However, on July 13, 1940, Agostino submitted to the San Francisco Recorder's Office a sworn affidavit of birth, probably to provide proof to Canadian authorities of Tony's birth, as he was about to become manager of the Toronto Maple Leafs Minor League team. In the affidavit, Agostino listed his son's name as Anthony *Marco* Lazzeri. When Lazzeri himself applied in 1941 for admission to the Olympic Club in San Francisco and again when he registered for the draft on February 14, 1942, he listed his middle name as "Mark." And in 1938, when Lazzeri was at spring training with the Chicago Cubs on Santa Catalina Island, California, the caption below his photo in the March 18 edition of the *Salinas (CA) Morning Post* identified him as Anthony *Mark* Lazzeri.

Asked about the discrepancy, Lazzeri's grandson, Matt, replied: "As for 'Marco,' my mom said all my dad was sure about was that Tony's middle name started with an M. He'd heard Mark, Michael, and Marco, and I'm not sure he ever knew."[3] (David Anthony Lazzeri was fourteen years old when his father died.) When I asked Matt's mother, Marilyn, about her father-in-law's middle name, she said that her husband had told her he didn't know what it was. "He thought maybe it was Michael," she said, "but he didn't really know."[4] The fact that the manifest of the ss *Trave* indicated that Agostino and Giulia were to join a Marco Chiesa when they arrived in San Francisco gives further credence to the possibility that his parents gave Lazzeri the middle name of Marco. Given the evidence—the Italian custom of naming the first-born son after the paternal grandfather; the appearance of "Antonio" in the documents listed above, "Marco" in the affidavit of birth, and "Mark" in his draft card and the Olympic Club application—there is good reason to believe that Lazzeri's given name was not Anthony Michael but Antonio Marco.

Another mystery concerns where in San Francisco Tony Lazzeri grew up. Most accounts that refer to his childhood indicate that he grew up in the Cow Hollow district, which is near the northern shore of the city, south of the Marina district and east of the Presidio. Others mention Telegraph Hill or North Beach. However, according to the San Francisco city directory of 1907, when

Lazzeri was four years old, the family was living on Missouri Street in the Potrero district, which is located about four miles southeast of Cow Hollow.[5] (Originally a cow-pasturing area, by the time the Lazzeris lived in the Potrero district, it had become a working-class neighborhood employing thousands in its many manufacturing plants, with more on the way thanks to the arrival of new railroads.) In the 1907 directory Agostino was listed as living at 141 Missouri Street. However, sometime prior to April 1909 Agostino had purchased the lot at 147 Missouri Street. Thomas Carey, archivist at the San Francisco History Center, suggested that "a city directory canvasser might have written '147' that looked more like '141,' so it ended up in print as 141. There were always errors in the directories."[6] It is likely, therefore, that the family was living at 147 Missouri Street in 1907. Then, on June 15, 1910, Agostino agreed to purchase the two-story house directly across the street, at 142–44 Missouri, and on June 25, 1911, the owner transferred to Agostino the property that became the Lazzeri residence until Agostino died in 1960.

There is also some evidence that the family was living in the Potrero district when Tony was born. In a 1930 profile based on an interview with Lazzeri, Harry T. Brundidge of the *St. Louis Star* wrote: "He was born on South Market Street, San Francisco, a rough and ready neighborhood."[7] While there is no San Francisco street named *South* Market, Market Street is one of the major thoroughfares of the city, originating in the Castro district and running northeast all the way to the Ferry Building on the harbor, a focal point of the city. An area more or less in the middle of Market Street's run is known as South of Market or SoMa. The Potrero Hill neighborhood is not far to the south of SoMa. It seems likely that in his interview with Brundidge, Lazzeri used the term "South of Market" to identify his neighborhood, but Brundidge understood him to say South Market Street. It may well be, then, that the Lazzeri family had been living in the South of Market area prior to the 1906 earthquake and that Lazzeri was born there.

Further evidence surfaced years later in the *San Francisco Examiner*. In the paper's issue of April 6, 1986, a column referred to Lazzeri as being from the North Beach neighborhood. Four days later the paper printed a retraction, admitting its error in identifying North Beach rather than Potrero as Lazzeri's home neighborhood: "We're surprised that so many Golden Oldies know (and phoned and lettered) that Lazzeri was born and grew up at 144 Missouri St. and first played baseball at Jackson Playground."[8] Lending credence to this claim is the fact that one of the "Golden Oldies" who wrote or called the *Examiner* was Lou Spadia, who served as president of the San Francisco 49ers from 1967 to 1976. When Spadia was a child, his family was renting the upper flat in the Lazzeri home (144 Missouri Street). By 1924, when Lou was three years old, his family had moved out to make way for Tony and his bride, who were married in 1923.

The Lazzeri home sits about one-third of the way up a classic San Francisco hill, between Seventeenth and Mariposa Streets. The adjacent building downhill was, and as of this writing still is, the home of the Monte Cristo Club, where Agostino spent his spare time playing bocce. Giulia and Agostino would live in that home until they passed away, in 1941 and 1960 respectively.

Luckily for Tony, the Lazzeri home on Missouri Street was only two blocks away from Jackson Playground at the corner of Kansas and Seventeenth Streets. It was there that he would discover his love for baseball. When Lazzeri was inducted into the Bay Area Sports Hall of Fame in 1989, the plaque commemorating him, which was placed on the Jackson Playground clubhouse, read in part: "He developed his skills at Jackson Playground in the Potrero District." On June 8, 1961, the San Francisco Recreation and Park Commission unanimously adopted a resolution calling for "the newly constructed baseball diamond at Jackson Playground [to] be named in honor of Tony Lazzeri." The resolution cited Lazzeri's national renown but also noted that he "never lost interest in imparting baseball knowledge to the youngsters at Jackson Playground after his professional retirement."[9]

Other than the family's location on Missouri Street, little is known about Lazzeri's early years, either his life at home or in school. There are even conflicting reports as to which school he attended. According to the Hall of Fame questionnaire filled out by Lazzeri's widow, Maye, he attended Saint Theresa's Catholic School through the eighth grade. However, in a 1926 "Hot Stove League" column in the *Washington Post*, Irwin Howe wrote the following of Lazzeri: "When he went to the Daniel Webster grammar school in San Francisco he aspired to be a pitcher, and he was good enough to land the championship for his mates."[10] In a 1926 article in the Lazzeri Scrapbooks, Frank Cantelmo wrote that Lazzeri "played on the open sand lots of his hometown, and later played on the nine of the Daniel Webster School which he attended." And in his 1930 *Sporting News* profile of Lazzeri, Brundidge quotes him as saying that he attended the Daniel Webster School.[11]

Lazzeri spoke to Brundidge about his ambition to be a boxer: "I guess I was a pretty tough kid. The neighborhood wasn't one in which a boy was likely to grow up a sissy, for it was always fight or get licked, and I never got licked. My early ambition was to be a prize fighter."[12] Little is known of Lazzeri's short-lived youthful aspirations to be a boxer, but two accounts of scheduled bouts provide a curious juxtaposition of reasons why both were called off at the last moment.

Brundidge cites Lazzeri's account of what was to be his first bout when he was seventeen years old; he would take on another young Italian named Pete Carlo at the Association Club. According to Lazzeri, Carlo's father wanted to examine his son's opponent before the fight. "Carlo's father came to my dressing room, felt my leg and arm muscles, and announced his Pete would not battle me that night. The manager tried to get me another fight, but failed. That ended my career as a pug."[13]

However, in the 1926 Cantelmo article cited above, the author describes a similar scenario, presumably about another scheduled bout, in which the fight was called off at the last minute but for the opposite reason. According to this account, Lazzeri was sitting in his corner waiting for the bell when a doctor stepped into the ring. After looking Lazzeri over, the doctor told him that he could not fight that match because he was not strong enough to face his opponent. Given Lazzeri's statement in the Brundidge article that the bout with Carlo was to be his first match, followed by his statement that since his manager could not get him another fight, that was the end of his "career as a pug," Cantelmo's description seems suspect. Either Lazzeri was mistaken in saying that the canceled bout with Carlo was his only scheduled fight or Cantelmo's description is inaccurate. In any case, how likely is it that two matches would be called off just before the start, one because Lazzeri was too strong for his opponent and the other because he was not strong enough? Whatever the truth about Lazzeri's limited boxing experiences, at some point he gave up any ambitions he might have had about making a living in the ring and concentrated on baseball.

The young Lazzeri was always more interested in boxing and baseball than he was in school. Well aware of his indifference to the educational process, school officials invited Tony to leave school when he reached the age of fifteen. Lazzeri's response to the authorities? "I voted all of them my thanks and good wishes. I boxed, played ball and did everything but study, and I guess I would have been kicked out of school long before I was had it not been for the fact that I pitched for the school team."[14]

At some point Agostino had begun working as a boilermaker at the Main Street Iron Works, located near the Ferry Building at the north end of Market Street, about two and a half miles north of the Lazzeri home.[15] Soon after his expulsion from school, Tony joined his father as a laborer at the factory, where he heated rivets and tossed them to the riveters. "My pitching stood me in good stead and I could toss a rivet with the best of them," he told Brundidge.[16] It was in that factory that the slender teenager developed the powerful wrists and forearms that would eventually enable him to launch baseballs over distant outfield fences. Lazzeri's destiny—to follow in his father's footsteps as a factory worker—might well have been sealed at the age of fifteen were it not for his passion for baseball.

Growing up in San Francisco would prove to be fortuitous for Lazzeri, as it was for any youngster who loved baseball. In *Nuggets on the Diamond*, a history of professional baseball in San Francisco, Oakland native Dick Dobbins wrote: "The early phenomenon of sandlot baseball—a term that originated in San Francisco—became an institution here." Dobbins concluded that, as kids, he and his friends "were growing up in the richest baseball center in the world. The game may have been 'invented' in upstate New York and played professionally for the first time in Ohio, but the true heart of American baseball is right here in the Bay Area."[17]

The city had an exceptional baseball legacy dating back to the Civil War era. By 1866 several San Francisco Bay Area teams had formed their own governing body, the Pacific Base Ball Convention. San Francisco in particular became a hotbed of amateur and semi-professional baseball. As in other cities and towns across America, businesses, churches, and civic and fraternal groups sponsored youth teams. In 1878 the semi-pro Pacific Base Ball League was established in San Francisco, and the following year the rival California League was formed in Oakland. By the mid-1880s there were two professional leagues in the state, the California League and the California State League, each with three franchises in San Francisco. The Pacific Coast League (PCL) was founded in 1903 and was recognized by Organized Baseball in 1904 as a Class A league, then was designated a Double A league in 1909, at that time the highest Minor League classification. Several of the PCL franchises had their own farm teams, enabling them to develop home-grown talent.

It was the rich pool of talent nourished first on the sandlots and later in the semi-pro leagues that enabled California's minor leagues to flourish. In San Francisco young players could take advantage of numerous baseball diamonds, a large number of amateur leagues, and a moderate climate that facilitated year-round play in order to hone their skills. Among the players who got their start on San Francisco's sandlots early in the twentieth century and made it to the big leagues were such notables as Harry Heilmann, Lefty O'Doul, Joe Cronin, and Lefty Gomez.

Many of the boys who took advantage of San Francisco's baseball richness were sons of Italian immigrants. Dario Lodigiani, who grew up in the North Beach neighborhood and played in the Major Leagues for six years beginning in 1938, was one of those kids. "We played a lot of ball," he said. "There was nothing else to do. A lot of us couldn't afford the price of going to different places, so we stuck around Funston Playground, North Beach Playground, and the different playgrounds around San Francisco. No matter what park you went to there was a ballgame going on. If you showed any kind of ability you always had a place to play. San Francisco had the best semi-pro programs in the country."[18]

Several of those kids went on to make a living playing in the PCL. Others made it to the big leagues, including Hall of Famers Joe DiMaggio and Ernie Lombardi, as well as Vince and Dom DiMaggio, Babe Pinelli, Dolph Camilli, Cookie Lavagetto, and Lodigiani. But on their way from the sandlots to the pros most, if not all, met stiff parental opposition. Much like nineteenth-century no-nonsense businessmen who expressed puritanical scorn for their peers who indulged in such a frivolous sporting activity as baseball, Italian immigrants, with little if any sporting tradition of their own and precious little leisure time, considered the game a childish waste of time. The response of Dario Lodigiani's father to his son's desire to play pro ball was typical: "You want to become a ballplayer? You'll become a bum." But also typical was his comment when Dario brought home his first paycheck in 1935: "Boy, you've got a good job."[19] Dom DiMaggio said that after his older brothers Vince and Joe had begun playing professionally, his father, who had initially opposed the idea, said to him: "And when are *you* going to start playing baseball?"[20]

No one can say with certainty that Lazzeri would not have become a Major Leaguer had he not grown up in San Francisco. However, the undeniable truth is that virtually every Italian American with a significant big league career through the 1920s and 1930s learned the game on the playgrounds of the San Francisco Bay Area. Like all of those sons of immigrants, Lazzeri got his first taste of the game on the local sandlots. In the 1926 article cited above, Cantelmo, who interviewed Lazzeri, wrote: "At first his parents objected to his playing and on many occasions Tony had to steal away to take part in his favorite pastime."[21] It would certainly be in keeping with the general attitude of Italian immigrant parents at the time if Agostino did discourage his son. However, in a 1926 article by Dan Parker, then writing for the *New York Daily Mirror*, Lazzeri is quoted as saying: "My father believed in giving me a few hours every day to play ball. If the rising generation of Italian boys put in a few hours a day at baseball or some other healthy sport, they would be better off in the long run, too. If I hadn't played ball as a kid, I suppose I'd be a common laborer now."[22] Whatever Agostino's initial attitude toward baseball may have been, there is no question that he was a proud father once his son became a professional ballplayer, meticulously assembling scrapbooks that began with Tony's first year in the Minor Leagues.

Though his primary passion was baseball, Lazzeri excelled in other sports as well. Early on, while playing at Jackson Playground, he established a reputation as a star athlete in his home town. In 1931, recounting his own path to the big leagues, future Hall of Fame shortstop Joe Cronin spoke of his boyhood idol: "Even in those early days my ambition was to be a professional ball player and my hero was not a star in the big leagues but Tony Lazzeri, who, only two years older than I, was a star athlete at the Jackson Playground. Lazzeri, who for years has been with the New York Yankees, was the best athlete in San Francisco. It was Tony who booted the ball to win the soccer match, or got the hit that won the ball game, or carried the pigskin for the winning touchdown. I was always imitating Tony."[23] Ed Linn quotes Cronin as saying of Lazzeri: "He'd come to the park around the seventh or eighth inning and always—always—hit a home run, strike everybody out, and beat us."[24]

After playing at the Jackson Playground as a youngster, Lazzeri went on to play amateur and semi-pro ball at other Bay Area diamonds. Another eyewitness to Lazzeri's exceptional athletic skill was Cookie Picetti, who was eighty-four years old when he told the story of a game in which he once played against Lazzeri:

> We were just kids, and we were playing over in San Rafael. My team was called the North Beach Merchants, or something like that. I was playing left field and Lazzeri came up to hit. They told me to get back. I got back. Lazzeri hit one over my head, way over my head. It was a home run, of course, but that wasn't the end of it. Next time Tony came up, everybody started waving and hollering at me. Get back more, they were saying, don't let this guy hit it over your head again. Well, I'm not that dumb. I got back a lot farther than I had been. He hit another wallop over my head and this one went a lot farther than the first one. Everybody was yelling at me and they took me out of the game.[25]

Lazzeri continued to pursue his passion for baseball even while working full time in the iron works mill. (He would, in fact, maintain his membership in Local Union No. 6 even while playing in the big leagues.) It was in 1922, while playing for the semi-pro Golden Gate Natives, that Lazzeri got his break: "I was soon earning $4.50 a day at the iron works and making a little money on the side playing semi-professional baseball. I gave up pitching to play shortstop. I continued working at the iron works and playing with the Golden Gate Natives until 1922, when, just as I was about to become a full-fledged boilermaker, Tim Harrington, a friend, induced Duffy Lewis, manager of the Salt Lake City team of the Pacific Coast League, to give me a tryout."[26]

From 1910 to 1915 George Edward "Duffy" Lewis, a San Francisco native, was part of the renowned trio of Boston Red Sox outfielders, playing left field alongside future Hall of Famers

Tris Speaker and Harry Hooper. As the left fielder in Fenway Park, Lewis had an unusual obstacle to navigate. When Fenway opened in 1912, a ten-foot slope ran the length of the left-field wall. At the time it was not uncommon to place standing-room-only fans on the playing field. The slope was a convenience for those along the left-field wall, enabling them to see the game over the heads of those in front of them. But for the left fielders who had to negotiate the slope, it was anything but convenient. Lewis became so proficient at dealing with the obstacle that in time it became known as "Duffy's Cliff." When his thirteen-year big league career ended in 1921, he completed the season with the Salt Lake City Bees, hitting .403 in 105 games. In 1922 Lewis was in his first year as player-manager when he agreed to invite Lazzeri to a tryout. He was impressed enough by the eighteen-year-old shortstop that he signed him to a contract for $250 a month. The would-be boxer and boilermaker was about to begin a new life away from San Francisco.

2

The Agony and the Ecstasy of the Minor Leagues

N ow a professional ballplayer, Tony Lazzeri left his job at the Main Street Iron Works and headed for Modesto, California, where the Salt Lake City Bees' spring training camp opened on March 2. As it turned out, his experience with the Bees in the 1922 season may have convinced him that he had been wise to hold on to his iron workers' union card. He soon learned that for all his success and renown as one of the best sandlot and semi-pro players in San Francisco, he was not yet ready for life in baseball's fast lane.

The PCL was one of only three Double A leagues and was the stepping stone to the big leagues for many West Coast players. In fact, dozens of PCL players moved up to the Majors in the 1920s alone, including nine future Hall of Famers. In his history of the PCL in the 1920s, R. Scott Mackey asserts that "it is hard to imagine another time or place in minor league history filled with as many great stars, teams or characters."[1] Some players who were sought by big league teams chose to stay in the PCL, where they were close to home and could make almost as much money as they would out east in the Majors. Five of the eight teams were based in California (Los Angeles, San Francisco, Oakland, Sacramento, and Vernon) and the other three in Utah, Oregon, and Washington.

At eighteen, Lazzeri was the youngest player on the Bees' roster by five years, his teammates ranging in age from the midtwenties to the midthirties. In fact the average age of batters in the PCL that year was twenty-nine. Some, like Duffy Lewis, Oscar "Ossie" Vitt, and Rudy Kallio, had returned to the Minors after playing Major League ball. The young rookie's performance quickly exposed his limitations. A utility player, he was used primarily at third, with occasional appearances at first and second. In 45 games with 78 at bats, Lazzeri collected only 15 hits, including 4 doubles, 2 triples and 1 home run, for a .192 average. He also got a chance to pitch in one game, returning to what had been his primary position as a schoolboy when playing for the Daniel Webster team. On July 21, in a 22–5 drubbing at the hands of the Portland Beavers, Lazzeri started the game at second, but with the game out of reach he was sent to the mound in a mop-up role. In one-plus inning he gave up five runs, walked four, and struck out one. The game, which featured a total of 27 runs and 33 hits, lasted two hours and sixteen minutes.

Given his limited playing time and sub-par performance, Lazzeri understandably received little publicity, and what he did receive was not flattering. On July 23, two days after Lazzeri's mound appearance, Steve Moloney of the *Salt Lake Telegram* lamented the sorry state of the Bees' bench players: "With all of the improvements that Duffy Lewis has put into the Bee lineup, the Salt Lake baseball club continues its rather weak policy of failing to provide the team with proper reserve strength. Lazzeri is such a poor batter that he should have been a pitcher."[2]

Following his disappointing 1922 season, Lazzeri returned home and played for the police department team, one of twelve squads in the San Francisco Midwinter League, many of whose players were professionals. The following March, when he was once again at the Bees' spring training camp, the *San Francisco Examiner* noted that in 1922 "Tony wasn't the worst infielder in the league by any means" but predicted that if two new infielders acquired by the Bees lived up to expectations, he "will again play in emergencies only."[3]

But the following week Moloney reported that "it looks like Tony Lazzeri is scheduled to take the utility position in the infield. During the winter Tony has been under the tutorship of Tim Harrington [the same friend who had recommended him to Duffy Lewis] and his stance at the plate, his grip on the bat and his cut at the ball have all been changed so that he puts up the appearance of having improved 50 to 100 per cent. He is in perfect condition already and should have a great year."[4]

However, as the *Examiner* had predicted, Lazzeri appeared sparingly in the Bees' spring training games, playing at second and short, and then appeared in a handful of regular-season games. His final appearance with the Bees came on April 15; in a 15–7 loss to the Portland Beavers he was inserted as a pitcher late in the game, allowing one earned run with three walks and two strikeouts. Salt Lake City, which had control over Lazzeri's contract, optioned him to the Peoria Tractors of the eight-team Class B Three-I (Indiana-Illinois-Iowa) League, hoping that he would improve with the chance to play regularly.

Lazzeri would not be making the trip to Peoria alone. While playing for the Golden Gate Natives, he had been introduced to Maye Daisy Janes by Paul Pettingill, her brother-in-law and one of Lazzeri's teammates. "A couple of days later I was invited to her house for dinner," Lazzeri recalled in 1930, "and that was that."[5]

The sixth of eight children of George and Grace (Hardress) Janes, Maye was born on May 4, 1906. Her father, a streetcar conductor in San Francisco, was a native of Missouri, while her mother was born in Australia. In 2012 Jayn Pettingill, the granddaughter of the man who introduced Maye to Tony, wrote the following about her great aunt:

> She read tea leaves, had a serious talk radio habit and believed that the dearly departed were watching over us. Maye was one of the toughest ladies, and yet one of the most elegant, I have ever met. For me, she epitomized the ideal San Francisco woman.
>
> My love of baseball came through my great aunt and my grandfather. He regularly wore the tools of ignorance for a semi-pro baseball club in San Francisco—the Golden Gate Natives. He had married my great aunt's sister and eventually introduced Maye to

her future husband, a young infielder on his team named Tony Lazzeri.

The Irish and the Italians in San Francisco have a long history of sharing neighborhoods side by side. Sometimes things were not as friendly as one would think: in reality there was some friction. Maye explained that Tony's mother did not like her at first. She wasn't Italian to begin with and, just as importantly, she couldn't cook. It took learning how to cook from Tony's mother that earned her a degree of respect. Out on the field, Tony was having to prove himself as an Italian that could play baseball.

Maye told me the things she missed most about San Francisco were its sunsets and the sourdough. In the off season, they would return to the west, gathering many of the Yankee ball players at their house in the Marina. Tony would stuff as many Murderer's [sic] Row guys as he could into their new Cadillac, put it in a low gear and off they would go, trying to see how many hills they could get up, or not.

In 1946, Maye was widowed. Maye never remarried and always spoke of Tony with great love and affection. Visiting her when I was in college, she would tell me that she had seen Tony in a part of her house, telling her that he was waiting for her. She died not too long after, a long life lived in extraordinary times.[6]

Before leaving for his new assignment, Lazzeri asked Maye to marry him, saying he would not go to Peoria without her. In a 1989 interview Maye recalled her surprise when Tony proposed. "I thought he was just teasing me when he said he wanted to marry me and take me with him to Peoria," she said. "But when he said he wouldn't go unless I went with him, I knew he was serious. I wasn't sure he loved me, but I knew Tony loved baseball. I couldn't believe he was ready to give up baseball for me."[7] On April 23, 1923, Tony, nineteen, and Maye, two weeks shy of seventeen, were married in San Francisco, then headed east to Peoria.

The Tractors, who moved into brand new Woodruff Field in 1923, were led by newly appointed player-manager Dick Breen, a thirty-seven-year-old catcher entering the sixteenth year of his nineteen-year career, all in the Minors. Within three weeks of his transfer to Peoria, Lazzeri and his teammate, pitcher "Duke" Duchalsky, were excoriated by the *Salt Lake Telegram* for "still playing the brand of ball they displayed while with the Bees this spring." According to the story, Lazzeri's batting average after he had appeared in ten games was .220. Then the *Telegram* reported that "Tony Lazzeri and Duke Duchalsky, two ex-Bees who were farmed out to the Three-I league [*sic*], have not hit their stride as yet. Lazzeri's average for the last two weeks with the stick is .187."[8]

By midseason Lazzeri's performance had improved noticeably. In a July story in his column, "The Sport Trail," Peoria sportswriter Robert Poisall wrote that after "falling into a slump which on several different occasions very nearly called for his release, this strong hearted player from the Golden shores of Italy outran all opposition and today is playing great ball for the local club. Today Tony ranks as one of the most popular players that ever performed in this city. When a ball player is performing in a bad way and then comes to life and plays wonderful ball for his club the whole world is for him, to the finish." In extolling Lazzeri's work ethic and noting his popularity with fans, Poisall prefigured what would be written about Lazzeri throughout his career. Furthermore, Poisall opened his column with a line that is emblematic of Tony Lazzeri's entire career in baseball: "Pushing barriers to one side is a specialty of Tony Lazzeri."[9]

Eddie Jacquin, sports editor of the *Peoria Journal Transcript*, also took note of Lazzeri's comeback from his early-season struggles at the plate. Following an 8–7 win over Rockford on July 15, in which Lazzeri hit two home runs, Jacquin wrote: "Tony Lazzeri put up another brilliant game at second. This lad from the west, who at one time almost lost a position, has now struck what seems to be his true stride and he looks like a great comer."[10]

The seasoning Tony got in Peoria was paying off. A sidebar that appeared on September 5 noted Lazzeri's improvement since

the spring when "he was erratic both in his fielding and throwing." His greatest improvement was at the plate: "Whereas he
was a wild swinger, often missing the ball by feet, he now takes
an even swing at the ball and times it nicely." Following a game-
winning homer, an undated story took further note of Lazzeri's
improved hitting: "From being one of the poorest hitters on the
club, Lazzeri is developing into one of the most dangerous. The
shouting that followed Lazzeri's mighty clout shook the stadium
to its foundation."[11]

Lazzeri appeared in 135 of Peoria's 136 games, playing mainly
at second base. While his long slump kept his batting average at
a modest .248, his slugging average of .427 was an early indication of his ability to hit with power. In addition to 22 doubles and
7 triples, he hit 14 home runs, the most on the team and tied for
third best in the league. On August 9 in a home game against the
Evansville Evas, he hit what the *Decatur Herald* described as "one
of the longest home runs ever made at the local field."[12] Then in
the second game of a season-ending doubleheader on September
9 against the Moline Plow Boys, Lazzeri finished on a high note.
Hitting in the seventh spot, as he did for much of the season,
in the fifth inning he clouted a three-run homer that one journalist described as "the longest drive ever seen in the new Peoria field, the ball clearing the left field wall, which is more than
400 feet from the home plate."[13] On August 17 it was announced
that Lazzeri would be recalled to the Bees following the end of
the Three-I League season on September 9. After Peoria finished
in sixth place with a 71–65 record, Lazzeri was on his way back
to Salt Lake City.

By September 15 Tony was back in the Bees lineup, taking over
the shortstop position for the remainder of the season. Appearing
in 39 games with the Bees, he hit .354, with 7 home runs and 21
RBIs. But in spite of a powerful lineup that led the PCL in average, home runs, and runs scored, the Bees finished in fifth place
with a record of 94–105.

The outlook was promising as Lazzeri headed to spring training in 1924. During the off-season both Bees owner Bill Lane and manager Duffy Lewis expressed confidence in Lazzeri for the coming season. Lewis was quoted as saying that he was counting on Lazzeri for the shortstop job in 1924 as much as he was counting on Clarke "Pinky" Pittenger, the former Boston Red Sox shortstop acquired by the Bees in a trade, feeling that Lazzeri "is about right for Coast League company and will give Pittinger [sic] a hard fight."[14]

Lazzeri got off to a good start in spring training. The *Salt Lake Telegram* reported that "the work of Lazzeri has been the talk of the camp since the boys settled down to work. Lazzeri, shortstop, who has been hitting the ball at a terrific clip, stepped into the limelight yesterday as a fielder. Tony proved he could handle the ball on either side and his powerful throwing arm is a wonder."[15] Just prior to the start of the regular season, the *Oakland Tribune* reported that Lazzeri "has landed the shortstop job for the present, but he may have a fight on his hands if Pittinger [sic] decides to go after it when Vitt gets into the lineup."[16] Vitt had come to the Bees in 1922 after a ten-year Major League career with the Tigers and Red Sox, mainly as a third baseman. He had been the Bees starting third baseman in both 1922 and 1923 but was a 1924 holdout until the end of March and didn't appear in the Bees lineup until April 18.

Lazzeri did indeed have a fight on his hands as he struggled early in the season. Moloney attributed the problem to Lazzeri's Latin blood: "The failure of Tony LaZerre [sic], shortstop, to live up to advance notices is another disappointment to the Bees. It is possible 'Our Tone' is in a slump. Possessed of Latin blood, the youth is emotional and excitable. Having youth makes it doubly hard for him. Little things are inclined to throw him off his stride. Undoubtedly Tony has ability. He needs encouragement and a few favorable breaks."[17]

Neither was forthcoming. By the end of June Lazzeri was edged out of his starting role by the two former Major Leaguers when Duffy Lewis decided to go with the hot-hitting Pittenger at short and start Vitt at third. At a time when Lazzeri was hitting .276 with thirteen homers, the *Salt Lake Telegram* printed this announcement: "Tony LaZerre [sic], one of the brightest young prospects that the Bees have picked up in years, has been given to the New Haven club of the Eastern league [sic] under an optioned agreement. He leaves for the East today."[18]

Lazzeri, in fact, did not leave for the East that day. Nor did he leave at all. Frustrated by the thought of being optioned by the Bees twice in two years, he refused the assignment, a move that essentially threatened to end his career. But it didn't take long for him to reconsider. On July 10 it was announced that the Lincoln Links of the Class A Western League had closed a deal to acquire Lazzeri from Salt Lake City.

When Lazzeri was signed by Lincoln, Josh Clarke, manager of the Links, predicted that "Lazzeri will hit in this league. We need another spanking good hitter and Lazzeri should fill the bill. They play fast, smart baseball on the Coast and Lazzeri should go great in the Western."[19] On July 15 Lazzeri was in the Links lineup at third base, hitting in the seventh spot. He made the most of his debut, hitting a single, triple, and home run. Two days later he was hitting cleanup.

In advance of a doubleheader against the St. Joseph (MO) Saints on Sunday, July 20, the *Lincoln Star* ran a photo and a brief introduction of the "Links' New Third-Sacker." In a classic example of the exuberant sportswriting style of the era, it reads as follows: "Prior to coming to the Links Tony did his stuff with the Salt Lake club in the Pacific Coast loop. In nearly 40 games last season Tony slapped the apple for an average of .354. His first day out with the Josh Clarke clan [on July 15], he malleted a single, a triple and a home run in four times at bat. Tony brings something else to make him a valuable acquisition—a shotgun arm which shoots the ball across to Chili McDaniel with bullet speed."[20]

In spite of his three-hit barrage in his first game with the Links, by July 26, after appearing in eight games, Lazzeri was hitting a modest .242 (8 for 33). But he then went on a hitting spree. On

July 28 he went 3 for 5 with a three-run homer to lead the Links to a 10–8 win over the Tulsa Oilers, earning him his first headline in a Lincoln paper. The next day he hit two homers in a 9–6 loss at Tulsa, then two days later he duplicated that feat with two more round trippers in a 14–7 loss to Tulsa, giving him five home runs in four days and another headline. In the August 12 game against St. Joseph, Lazzeri hit a two-run homer that was described as "one of his famous home runs, which in all travel about two miles, a mile up and a mile down." On the same page was a photo of Lazzeri, with the caption "Lazzeri is a brilliant fielder as well as a terrific hitter. His clouts will win many a game for Josh Clarke's tribe."[21] At this point, however, the Links were languishing in seventh place with a record of 40–69.

The accolades for Lazzeri continued in a rather curious fashion in the *Lincoln State Journal*, on the editorial page no less, under the heading of "The Melting Pot." The column referred to the game on August 12:

> It was a rather dreary afternoon Tuesday at Landis Field [home of the Links, with the team trailing in the eighth and] little in the record to charm the local breast. Then a chap came to bat and lifted a fly across the milky way into the city dump grounds a mile or so northeast of the ballpark. It wasn't enough to win the game, but it betokened the unquenched fire in the Lincoln breast and fanned many a tear from many a Lincoln eye.
>
> What great name was that written on the local scroll of fame? You'll have to spell it out! Lazzeri, Tony Lazzeri was the chap that did it. Without looking up the record we venture to say that Tony did not come to Lincoln by way of the Mayflower. We would bet something that he isn't so much as a son of the American revolution. Yet here he is pulling America out of the hole in the eighth inning of the great American game.[22]

The writer then points out that after "this same non-Nordic Lazzeri" had reached base in the second inning, he was driven in by "none but that dark complexioned streak of greased lightning surnamed Chavez. Now that's so alien you don't dare try to pronounce it. To see and hear the Lincoln fans at that time, you wouldn't have known there was an Americanization problem in the world. A two-bagger from Chavez and we acclaim the hero as if he were Eddie Moore or Pid Purdy or any other pedigreed early arrival on these shores."[23]

In order to understand the environment in which Tony Lazzeri entered professional baseball and that fostered the kind of response illustrated in this editorial, some historical perspective may be useful. Early in the twentieth century many Americans perceived the large influx of certain immigrants as a national crisis and a threat to American values. Scientists posited theories alleging that people of Mediterranean origin were inherently inferior to people of northern European heritage.[24] In 1911 the report of the Dillingham Commission, formed by Congress in 1907, concluded that the large influx of South and East European immigrants posed a serious danger to American society because those people were dramatically different from old stock European Americans. The commission also declared that "certain kinds of criminality are inherent in the Italian race. In the popular mind, crimes of personal violence, robbery, blackmail and extortion are peculiar to the people of Italy."[25]

Fueled by widespread negative media depictions, stereotypes of Italian immigrants as shiftless, argumentative people prone to violence had become deeply imbedded in the public consciousness by the end of the nineteenth century. The largest mass lynching in U.S. history occurred in New Orleans on March 14, 1891, when an armed mob stormed the jail and killed eleven Italians, some of whom had been suspected of killing police chief David Hennessy but had been acquitted by a jury. Two days later a *New York Times* editorial, while stating that the actions of the mob, whose leaders were "all well-known citizens of New Orleans," were neither justifiable nor proper, assumed that the mob's victims were "ruffians and murderers," in spite of their acquittal. "These sneaking and cowardly Sicilians, the descendants of bandits and assassins, who have transported to this country the lawless passions, the cutthroat practices, and the oath-bound societies of their native country, are to us a pest without mitigations. Our own rattle-snakes are as good citizens as they."[26]

Prejudice is fueled by the fear of differences. The writer of the *Lincoln State Journal* editorial cited above singles out Lazzeri and Chavez because of their "alien" names. And while the sense of the editorial appears to be that the "great American game" welcomes such people regardless of their origins, there is great irony in the statement that "you wouldn't have known there was an Ameri-canization problem in the world." In late May of that year Con-gress passed the 1924 Immigration Act, legislation that turned into law the rampant xenophobia of the time. By creating a per-manent quota system based on national origins, the act effec-tively closed the doors of America to immigrants from southern and eastern Europe.

Within that context, by focusing on the oddness of their names and their non-Nordic origins, the *Lincoln State Journal* writer helps perpetuate the notion that people like Lazzeri and Chavez are dif-ferent from "pedigreed" Americans. To identify someone's name as "alien" is to stamp the same label on the person who bears that name, thereby marginalizing him or her as being "other." This type of commentary on what was perceived as the difficulty of Lazzeri's name (and by implication, on his newcomer status rel-ative to old-stock Americans) would continue to be a matter of discussion through much of his career.

The issue of bias may also account for a curious change that occurred during the Bees' spring training in 1924. As had happened for much of Lazzeri's life, his name once again became a source of confusion. Throughout his first two seasons, in both Salt Lake and Peoria, with the exception of an occasional misspelling, his name had appeared as "Lazzeri." Suddenly, beginning at the end of March 1924, Utah newspapers were identifying him as "Lazerre," "LaZerre," and "La Zerre." The first example of "Lazerre" I found appeared in a brief game summary in the March 20 edition of the

Ogden Standard Examiner. Throughout spring training the *Salt Lake Telegram* had spelled his name as "Lazzeri." Then, on April 6, Moloney, who had been covering Lazzeri since 1922, identified "Tony Lazerre" as one of the Bees' infielders. A report on a Bees practice game in the April 7 edition of the *Telegram* mentioned "a homer by Tony Lazerre," and the next day his name appeared in the *Telegram* as "LaZerre." A search of Utah newspapers revealed no explanation for the sudden change in spelling.

The pattern would continue throughout the remainder of the 1924 season and the entire 1925 season, and not only in Utah newspapers. In both the *San Francisco Examiner* and the *Los Angeles Times* Lazzeri was identified as "Lazerre." It is curious, however, that the change in spelling never occurred during his stay with the Lincoln Links. From the time he signed with them on July 10 through the end of 1924, I found no spelling of his name in either the *Lincoln Star* or the *Lincoln State Journal* other than "Lazzeri."

In October 1925, following the purchase of Lazzeri by the Yankees, a story by Copeland C. Burg of the International News Service appeared claiming that "the Yankees' prize beauty changed his name to Lazerre because he preferred the French nomenclature" and quoted Lazzeri as saying, "I've got a right to change my name if I want to. Some fans think it is clever to kid an Italian about liking spaghetti and garlic. Sure, I like 'em both, but I'm not crazy about the fans yelling at me all the time about being an Italian. That's why I took the French spelling for my name. So, in the majors I'll be known as Lazerre." (Earlier in the story Burg noted that his subject's real name was Antonio Lazzerri.)[27]

While this explanation for the name change echoes the reasons other ballplayers chose to conceal their Italian heritage, the comments attributed to Lazzeri by Burg raise several questions. Did Lazzeri ask newspaper editors to make the change? If the change was made at Lazzeri's request, why did he wait until 1924? Was he never heckled in 1922 or 1923? And if he made the request in March, why did the change appear in Utah newspapers but not in the Nebraska media, where his name appeared as

"Lazzeri" throughout his stay in Lincoln beginning in July 1924? It seems unlikely that if, in fact, fans were yelling at him "all the time about being Italian," Lincoln, Nebraska, would have been the one exception.

Given the anti-immigrant attitude common in Salt Lake City at the time, Lazzeri's alleged remark that fans were heckling him about being Italian is not shocking, though it's not clear if he was referring to Bees fans, those on the road, or both. Moreover, there is no indication in 1924 or 1925 newspaper reports that he was subject to ridicule or heckling. On the contrary, the Utah press emphasized how popular, even beloved, he was by Bees fans in his history-making season. And if the spelling was changed to conceal Lazzeri's Italian heritage, how curious that Moloney, in his May 4 article regarding Lazzeri's early-season struggles (cited above), spelled the name "Lazerre" but attributed the young player's excitability to his "Latin blood."

Other publications sought to clarify the confusion over the various spellings of Lazzeri's name, as well as his ethnic heritage. In an "Editor's Note" the *Lincoln Star* cited a New York story that listed various spellings of Lazzeri's name that had appeared in print: "Lazarre, Lizerrie, Lizerre." The paper's advice?

Spell it "Lazzeri." Tony pursued the national pastime during the 1924 season in Lincoln club duds and assured this department it was "Lazzeri" and nothing but. Tony is of Italian descent, born in San Francisco. The effort in New York to make out that Tony is of French origin—that he spells it LaZerre—seems like poor business. There are Italians by the tens of thousands for every Frenchman in New York and Tony, correctly heralded as a son of sunny Italy, would right soon be a favorite with a large [word missing] of Gotham's population. . . . [Lincoln fans] hold in high esteem the sworthy [*sic*] San Francisco athlete, whose throwing arm is second to none in the national game and whose ability to sock the old apple for frequent home runs made him ace high with baseball bugs in Nebraska's capital city.[28]

In January 1926 *The Sporting News* also attempted to set the record straight: "Ever since the big bronze Italian boy from the Pacific Coast began hitting home runs and his exploits became more prominent in the sports pages there has been a wide difference in the spelling of his name. *The Sporting News* thought that Tony himself should be given a chance. A letter was dispatched to his San Francisco home and the youngster came back with this: ANTHONY LAZZERI. So let's take Tony's word for it."[29]

Lazzeri was certainly not the first Italian surname to baffle sportswriters and typesetters. When Ed Abbaticchio—in all likelihood the first Major Leaguer of Italian descent—made his debut with the Philadelphia Phillies in 1897, a time when baseball was dominated by players of Irish descent, his was the only name on the squad that contained more than two syllables. Sportswriters routinely abbreviated his name to "Abby" and "Batty." Ping Bodie, the slugging outfielder who was the first in what would be a long line of Italian Major Leaguers from San Francisco, spent nine seasons in the big leagues between 1911 and 1921. Born Francesco Pezzolo, he chose to play under an assumed name so as to appear less "foreign." A 1918 story by Wood Ballard in the *New York Tribune* makes it clear why Bodie felt compelled to take on a new identity: "Ping needs a stage name. Pezzolo wouldn't look well in a box score."[30]

Even Joe DiMaggio's name was problematic at first, as this exchange among sportswriters at spring training in his rookie season of 1936 demonstrates:

"He says you pronounce it Dee-Mah-gee-o," one of the sports writers said gloomily.

Another added, "That's a very tough name to pronounce and also tough to spell."

One writer said in disgust, "DiMaggio sounds like something you put on a steak."[31]

Whatever the reasons for the various spellings of his name, Lazzeri continued to dominate, both on the field and in the news reports.

He continued his power surge in August. After he hit two homers on August 15, a sidebar in the *Lincoln State Journal* noted that Lazzeri had hit four home runs in the last three days, adding, "At that rate he'll be up among the leaders irrespective of his late start in the Western league [*sic*]. The way he 'cuts' something has to give when he connects."[32] Lazzeri was hitting homers with such regularity that on August 22, the day after he had hit a grand slam, the *Lincoln Star*, in its "Here and There in Baseball" column, paid him the ultimate compliment: "In 34 games Tony has clouted 13 circuit trips. Davis of Tulsa leads the league in walloping homers with a total of 35, but Davis has participated in a total of 112 games. The comparison, therefore, proves that the Links have the league's most consistent home run hitter; that Tony is the Babe Ruth of the Western loop."[33]

The home runs kept coming as the season moved into September, and Lazzeri finished with a total of 28, sixth best in the league. To put that number in perspective, he hit them in 82 games, with 316 at bats. The next lowest number of at bats for the top ten home run hitters in the Western League was 558. Finishing ahead of him in fifth place was his childhood hero and fellow San Franciscan Ping Bodie. Playing for Des Moines, the thirty-six-year-old former Major Leaguer clouted 32 home runs in 624 at bats. Lazzeri hit .316 with a .671 slugging average, second highest in the Western League. The Links, however, finished last in the league with a 57–108 record.

Following the end of the Western League season, Lazzeri returned to Salt Lake City in early October, primarily playing at third in place of Vitt, who missed several weeks at the end of the season when a spike wound to his leg became infected. The Utah newspapers again identified him as "Lazerre" or "LaZerre." For the season he appeared in 88 games with the Bees and hit .283 with 16 home runs and 61 RBIs. Fielding was more of a challenge for the young infielder; he made 44 errors.

As it turned out, Lazzeri's 1924 power surge was only a sneak preview of a remarkable main feature to follow in 1925, when the young slugger would do something that had never been accomplished in Organized Baseball.

3

"The Greatest Thing I've Ever Seen"

When Lazzeri returned to Salt Lake City in the spring of 1925, he was part of a team that was well established as the offensive powerhouse of the PCL. Even though the Bees finished fifth in 1923 and 1924, in both seasons they led the league in average, runs scored, and home runs. In 1924 the Bees slugged 194 home runs and player-manager Duffy Lewis led the league with a .392 average, just edging out newly signed San Francisco native Frank "Lefty" O'Doul, who would go on to become a two-time National League (NL) batting champion, a successful PCL manager, and a major promoter of the development and popularity of baseball in Japan.

It was their home run prowess that set the Bees apart; they led the league in home runs in nine of the eleven seasons (1915–25) they played in Salt Lake City, and in that span seven Bees hitters won home run titles. A significant factor in the large home run production was the small size of Bonneville Park, the smallest venue in the PCL. Add in the high altitude of Salt Lake City—an average of 4,327 feet—and the park was a veritable launching pad. Clearly the most hitter-friendly ballpark in the league, Bonneville was the PCL's precursor to Denver's Coors Field.

Contrary to the common notion that fans love the long ball, Salt Lake City patrons didn't find the Bees' home run barrage compelling enough to draw them to the ballpark, and attendance was lackluster. Perhaps they were aficionados of the dead-ball-era game, or perhaps they stayed away because the team's record was consistently mediocre, or perhaps they were simply showing animosity toward Bill Lane, the acerbic majority owner who was unwilling to spend money. After the owners had acquired the San Francisco Missions franchise, they had moved the team to Salt Lake City in 1915, but rumors had been circulating for some time that Lane was looking to sell or move the team. According to a 1924 story by Steve Moloney, Lane "just feels that it isn't right for him to face a loss of between $25,000 and $50,000 annually in the Coast league [sic], when the fans and no one else in fact seems to give a whoop whether the team is here or not."[1]

Lane did make one major change during the off-season, firing Duffy Lewis, who had managed the Bees since 1922, and replacing him with Ossie Vitt. Vitt's lineup promised to again provide plenty of power, with six of the seven players who hit fifteen or more homers in 1924 returning, the lone exception being Lewis. But it would be twenty-one-year-old shortstop Tony Lazzeri who would stun the baseball world in 1925. Lane claimed that Vitt knew how to handle Lazzeri better than did Lewis. In a story in July 1926, Jack Gallagher wrote: "Where Lewis had been harsh with Tony, Oscar gave him a pat on the back with the result [that] Lazzeri became the outstanding star of the Pacific Coast League in 1925."[2]

The 1925 season was crucial for Lazzeri. An article in the *Deseret News* on February 14 with the foreboding title "It's the Last Big Chance for Tony" noted that since Lazzeri was out of options with the Bees, this was the season he had to prove that he belonged in Double A baseball. The article cited manager Vitt's promise that Lazzeri would be given every chance to prove himself and ended on a hopeful note: "La Zerre [sic] is a long distance hitter of great promise and possesses a wonderful throwing whip."[3] The Bees got off to a torrid start, winning eight of their first nine games, all at home, against Vernon and Portland. Lazzeri, playing short and batting seventh, was hitting consistently but had no home runs to that point. Then on April 16 he made his first big splash, clouting two homers—one a grand slam—and driving in six runs in a 4 for 5 performance as the Bees routed Portland 18–9 and took sole possession of first place. He followed that the next day with another homer and a double in a 16–12 win that gave the first-place Bees a 10–1 record. When the Bees arrived in Los Angeles on April 21 to take on the second-place Angels, Lazzeri's average stood at .478, second in the league to his teammate Lefty O'Doul's .510 mark. That afternoon Lazzeri homered again as the Angels took the first game of the series, 7–6. After splitting the first two games of the series, the Bees won the third, 4–3, with Lazzeri driving in three of the Bees' runs on a homer and a single. By now the press was taking note of Lazzeri's hitting. In its game story the *Los Angeles Times* wrote that "Tony Lazerre [*sic*], the Bee's young shortstop, continued to slug the agate with reckless abandon."[4] On that same day the *Ogden Standard-Examiner* ran a photo of "Salt Lake's Own Tony" with the caption "His work this season with the willow is nothing short of phenomenal."[5]

Lazzeri, who was hitting in the fifth spot in the lineup by mid-May, cooled off somewhat following his hot start, but by May 25, with the Bees in second place behind the San Francisco Seals, he was tied for the league lead in homers, triples, and stolen bases, with a .373 batting average.[6] He then picked up the pace in mid-June. In a doubleheader sweep against Sacramento on June 14, he hit three homers. Two days later he hit two more in a 16–5 win over Oakland. But Lazzeri was also proving to be an excellent all-around player whose contributions were not limited to hitting the ball over the fence. In a 6–5 win over Oakland on June 18, he stole two bases and scored four of the Bees' six runs.

The stage was now set for the biggest series of the season when San Francisco came to Salt Lake City on June 23. The Bees were 10½ games behind the surging Seals, who had yet to lose a series. Going into the series, Lazzeri was leading the league in homers and steals and was ninth in average at .364. The Seals maintained their pace by taking the opener before the Bees bounced back to win the next two, both times coming from behind. They repeated the feat in the fourth game, with Lazzeri leading the way. Going into the bottom of the eighth, the Seals held what seemed to be a comfortable 5–2 lead. However, "the San Francisco crew forgot to reckon with 'Our Tony.' Instead of passing out peacefully in the eighth, he let out a dying kick. The ball sailed high and far and dropped over the center field score board."[7] With the score now 5–4, the Bees tied the score at 5–5 in the ninth, and Lazzeri drove in the winner with a base hit to left. The Bees now led the crucial series three games to one, but the best was yet to come.

On Saturday, June 27, before the first overflow crowd at Bonneville since the season opener, Lazzeri had his single best game of the season; he hit three homers and a triple to drive in eight runs in an 11–7 win to clinch the series. His performance inspired what was to become a common occurrence at Bonneville Park following a Lazzeri homer.

> Tony got a silver shower with each homer and his mates were kept busy most all afternoon picking dollars, quarters and halves out of the dirt. It was the first coin throwing that had been done in historic old Bonneville in many moons. An admiring throng of fans was parked outside the park gate after the game to catch a glimpse of the "Wonder Boy" who single handed batted in enough runs to beat the league leaders and hand them their first series defeat of the season.
>
> Lazerre's [sic] miraculous feats with the bat today were none the less amazing than his great work in the field. Indeed, the oldest observer here cannot recall when a shortstop ever had such a week as "Our Tone."[8]

But Lazzeri had more heroics in store. The next day, in the first game of the series-ending doubleheader, in what was described as "undoubtedly the most spectacular game ever played in [Salt Lake City]," Lazzeri hit two more home runs to lead the Bees to their fourth straight win over the Seals, and he did it in dramatic fashion.[9] With the Seals leading 9–3 in the bottom of the eighth,

Lazzeri hit a three-run blast to bring the Bees within three runs. In the ninth cleanup hitter Lefty O'Doul, who had the PCL's highest batting average, tied the score with a three-run homer.

That brought up Lazzeri, "the greatest ball player that ever performed in this city," who promptly "wafted another prodigious home run to win the game and send the frenzied fans into pandemonium."[10] Lazzeri's game-winning blow "touched off the greatest demonstration of a ball player that has ever been seen in Salt Lake. Tony was lifted to the shoulders of wild-eyed fans and paraded before the multitude. . . . In many respects the series which closed yesterday was the most remarkable in the history of the Coast league."[11] The Seals won the second game, but the Bees had taken five of the seven games in the series. Lazzeri now led the league with twenty-three homers, six ahead of the runner-up, and was seventh in average at .371.

By midseason Lazzeri's performance was attracting the attention of major league scouts. In July he was one of six PCL players tabbed by the *Los Angeles Times* as destined for the big leagues; the paper noted that "the hard-hitting Salt Lake shortstop has been hitting the apple viciously all year and is leading the loop in home runs. Also, he has improved wonderfully in his fielding."[12] The *New York Daily News* reported that Yankees scout Ed Holly was following several PCL players, including Lazzeri.[13] Other reports were indicating that the Yankees were considering spending as much as $250,000 to sign PCL players in an attempt to rebuild their team.

Even before the end of July it was clear that Lazzeri was an outstanding all-around player. He was at or near the top of the PCL in home runs, triples, batting average, and stolen bases, and he was acknowledged as a solid fielder with the strongest arm in the league, if not all of baseball. Yet while many teams showed interest in Lazzeri, they were reluctant to sign him. Why the hesitation to acquire a twenty-one-year-old phenom who was called "PCL's Mr. Everything in 1925" by historian R. Scott Mackey and who was tearing up the league, which was tabbed by some as the "third major league" because of the quality of its players?[14] What were the barriers that Lazzeri faced this time?

Some writers expressed skepticism regarding Lazzeri's home run production, given both the hitter-friendly dimensions of Bonneville Park and the thin air of Salt Lake City. (Thirty-nine of his sixty homers were hit at home.) And there was the failure of Paul Strand, the Bees' star slugger who hit .394 and set a PCL record with forty-three homers when he won the Triple Crown in 1923. That performance had convinced Philadelphia Athletics owner and manager Connie Mack to pay $32,500 and send three players to Salt Lake City for Strand. But when Strand hit a paltry .228 in 167 at bats with no home runs in 1924, Mr. Mack quickly traded him back to the Minors, where he would spend the final four years of his career. Since the specter of Strand's colossal failure loomed large in the minds of scouts, the question for any Major League team was: Would Lazzeri prove to be just another "high-altitude hitter"?

Among those who were hesitant to sign Lazzeri was Yankees GM Ed Barrow, even though he was anxious to strengthen his roster since the Yankees were struggling through a disastrous 1925 season and headed for a seventh-place finish. There were other factors beyond the skepticism regarding the high altitude and small ballpark that gave him pause. He balked when Paul Krichell, his most trusted scout, told him about the youngster's tendency to strike out. But Krichell, having seen how far Lazzeri hit the ball when he swung at good pitches, was convinced that he would do well in the Majors and assured Barrow that all Lazzeri had to do was learn the strike zone.[15] But Barrow was even more concerned when he heard reports that Lazzeri suffered from epilepsy. In his autobiography he wrote that if Lazzeri had not had that affliction, he may never have played for the Yankees. The Cubs, who had a working agreement with Salt Lake City, were "scared off by the knowledge that Lazzeri took fits" and passed him up. The Cincinnati Reds also passed him up, and "Garry Herrmann, owner of the Reds, wrote to [Yankees owner] Colonel [Jacob] Ruppert, telling him why his club had not bought Lazzeri."[16]

In spite of those reports Barrow sent Ed Holly to scout Lazzeri. "Holly reported he was sensational," wrote Barrow. "Tony was tearing the cover off the ball." He also sent Krichell and Bob Connery, a former Yankees scout who was then president of the St. Paul club in the American Association, to check out Lazzeri, and he sent Holly to San Francisco "to look into Lazzeri's family history." Holly reported that no other member of the family was affected by epilepsy and that the insurance company that covered Lazzeri was willing to increase the policy. When Krichell confirmed the reports about Lazzeri's epilepsy, Barrow said, "As long as he doesn't take fits between three and six in the afternoon, that's good enough for me." Meanwhile, Connery reported, "I don't care what he's got. Buy him. He's the greatest thing I've ever seen."[17]

An alternative explanation for the reluctance of several teams to sign Lazzeri was offered by Glenn Stout and Richard A. Johnson: "At the time only a handful of Italians had played major league baseball, and baseball wasn't particularly eager to increase that number. Italians were among the least desirable immigrants. Accepted only slightly more than American blacks, they were subject to all kinds of vicious stereotyping and prejudice. Sportswriters, even in New York, would refer to Italians in unflattering terms until after World War II, often calling them 'Fascists,' 'Wops,' and 'Dagos.'"[18] Leigh Montville, in his biography of Babe Ruth, concurred: "Other teams stayed away because [Lazzeri] was Italian, a minority not in favor with white, old-line managers of the game."[19]

Baseball historian Charles Alexander also addressed the impact that anti-immigrant sentiment had on baseball:

> Baseball players altered their names for the same reason as did immigrants and their offspring in other areas of American life: the United States was a country in which not only racial but ethnic and religious prejudices and stereotypes had always been and

continued to be basic to the way people looked at and understood one another. And while the National Pastime was supposed to exemplify the expansive, democratic way of life, inherited attitudes died very slowly—if they ever did die. . . . Ethnic stereotyping was particularly pronounced where Italian-American players were concerned.[20]

In all likelihood the ethnic issue played a part in Barrow's willingness to sign Lazzeri. While others may have shied away because of Lazzeri's heritage, Barrow knew that if the young slugger were to fulfill his potential at the Major League level, his success in New York could attract the largely untapped audience of the city's Italian population, which at that time was close to one million, or roughly one in seven New Yorkers.

Speculation about the sale ended on August 1, when the Yankees confirmed that they had purchased Lazzeri from Salt Lake City but refused to divulge the price: "Tony, an Italian, and said to be the greatest throwing shortstop ever seen doing his stuff along the Pacific slopes, no doubt cost the Rupperts a whole sockful of cash."[21] The agreement between the Yankees and Bees, dated August 3 and signed by Lane and Ruppert, states that the Yankees "shall pay said Salt Lake club the sum of Fifty Thousand ($50,000.) Dollars" and shall transfer five players, three of whom are named (Alex Ferguson, Mack D. Hillis, and Martin Autry) and two to be named later. To further add to the confusion over Lazzeri's name, it appears in the agreement as "Antone Lazzere."[22]

Lazzeri did not slow down following the purchase of his contract as he continued to prove he was more than a home run hitter. On August 30 he was leading the PCL in home runs, triples, and stolen bases, and his .378 batting average was fourth best in the circuit. On September 12, in the second inning of a loss to the Vernon Tigers, Lazzeri hit his forty-fourth home run, breaking the previous PCL record of forty-three set by Strand in 1923. When, on the following day, he hit three homers in a doubleheader split with Vernon, one headline story read "Bee Bambino Runs Mark to Forty-Seven Clouts."[23] Papers were now beginning to note the possibility that he could reach Babe Ruth's record of fifty-nine homers in 1921.

Lazzeri hit number fifty-five in Portland on October 1 to tie the Minor League record set the previous season by Clarence Kraft of Fort Worth in the Texas League, then hit another the next day to set a new mark. With two weeks left in the season he was three shy of Ruth's record. Two more homers in a doubleheader in Seattle on October 11 raised the total to fifty-eight. It would be six more days before Lazzeri tied Ruth's record in Sacramento on Saturday, October 17, one day before the season finale double-header. Vitt placed Lazzeri in the lead-off spot on the final day to give him more at bats as he attempted to set the record. In the opener Lazzeri went 1 for 5 with a double, then was hitless in his first two at bats in the second game. He came up in the seventh with a runner on first and, according to the Associated Press (AP) wire report, "slammed one into deep center-field that eluded the Sacramento middle gardener and rolled to the extreme center-field corner as Lazerre [sic] raced to the plate close on the heels of the first base runner. He made it, and with time to spare, and tonight is the possessor of a new world's home-run record."[24]

In a 1956 story the *Los Angeles Times* wrote that by setting a new home run record in 1925, "Lazzeri had become a baseball immortal."[25] However, surprisingly little was made of the record-setting homer in Salt Lake papers at the time. It was mentioned in headlines but not widely discussed in game stories. Later there appeared revisionist commentary on the nature of Lazzeri's record-setting blow that perhaps explains the lack of fanfare in the local press. In 1969 *Salt Lake Tribune* columnist John Mooney wrote that Lazzeri's inside-the-park homer was tainted by lackadaisical play in the outfield. He cited author Pete Raymond, who contended that the "Sacramento outfielder, brimming with league loyalty, ran away from the ball," then casually fielded it, but not before Lazzeri had time to circle the bases.[26]

In addition, Bill Conlin, writing in *The Sporting News* in 1974, confirmed Raymond's description of the play, claiming that the Sacramento center fielder "deliberately misplayed Lazzeri's line drive single over second base." He also noted that traditionally, unless the pennant were at stake, the final game in the PCL was a "high jinx occasion," an observation that accords with a comment made in the *Sacramento Bee*, which called the contest "a typical closing game [with] no serious play predominating."[27]

Even if the allegations about that climactic home run were true, Lazzeri obviously bore no responsibility for the outcome of the play; his job was to hit the ball, then run until someone threw him out. Nor does that one play in any way diminish his extraordinary all-around performance that season. Regardless of the "legality" of his sixtieth homer or the friendly confines of PCL ballparks or the high altitude in Salt Lake City or the length of the PCL season, the undeniable truth is that no one in Organized Baseball had ever hit more home runs. And even in the PCL the closest anyone had ever come to that number was Strand's forty-three in 1923. Nor has any succeeding hitter matched Lazzeri in the history of the PCL, which had been in existence since 1903.[28]

Nor should it be forgotten that in 1925 Lazzeri, who played in 197 games, excelled in many aspects of the game. His 60 home runs, 222 RBIs, and 202 runs scored remain to this day the all-time PCL records. In addition, he led the league in runs scored (202) and total bases (512), and he batted .355. Particularly overlooked in the shadow of Lazzeri's home run extravaganza was his speed and base-running skills. He stole 39 bases and led the league for much of the season until, for some reason, he stopped running in September and finished second, three behind Bill Hunnfield of Portland.

In his game story of the August 8 game between the Bees and Angels, Robert E. Ray described an unusual base-running play by Lazzeri that illustrated his skill on the base paths. In the second inning Lazzeri walked, then stole second. With the hit and run on for the next batter, Lazzeri, "the loop's leading base-stealer," took off with the crack of the bat. The batter hit a slow bouncer in front of the plate, which the Angels pitcher picked up and threw to first for the out. But Lazzeri never stopped running; he rounded third and scored before the Angels knew what had happened, "pulling the unusual feat of scoring from second on an infield out."[29]

Lazzeri's superb performance was a major reason the Bees compiled a record of 116–84 and finished second to the San Francisco Seals, their best finish since 1915, the franchise's first season in Salt Lake City. The following year Lane moved the team to Los Angeles, where it shared Wrigley Field with the Los Angeles Angels and played as the Hollywood Stars.

Newspaper accounts often pointed out how popular Lazzeri was with Salt Lake City fans, who got into the habit of tossing coins on the field when he hit a home run and even carrying him off the field after a particularly outstanding performance. Apparently no one was a bigger fan than a local restaurateur named Cesare Rinetti, co-owner of the Rotisserie Inn. An avid baseball fan, he had taken a liking to his fellow Italian American and his wife, who were frequent visitors to Rinetti's restaurant. In his summary of Lazzeri's time in Salt Lake City, John Sillito wrote: "According to local sports legend, Rinetti became a kind of stepfather to Tony, and later his wife Maye, providing a sense of home, and feeding them good Italian food."[30] It was during a game on Saturday, May 23, when, with Lazzeri at the plate, Rinetti reportedly shouted, "Poosh Um Up, Tony," and the fans picked up the chant. Lazzeri then obliged by hitting a home run in a 12–2 win over the Seattle Indians. At least that's the way sports editor John C. Derks reported it in the *Salt Lake Tribune* the following day under an eight-column banner that read "Poosh Um Up, Tone, Yella Da Fan, an' Tone She Poosh."[31]

According to Hal Schindler's 1993 retrospective of Derks's coverage of Lazzeri, "From that day forward Lazerre [sic] was known as 'Poosh 'Em Up' to the fans and 'our Tone' to John C. Derks."[32]

The following day, in a doubleheader sweep by the Bees, Lazzeri hit two triples in the second game after going 1 for 4 in the opener, inspiring Derks to run another eight-column headline: "Tone She Poosh Um Down, an' Den She Poosh Um Up."[33] It should come as no surprise that even Lazzeri's nickname was subject to variable spellings. When or why the standard spelling became established as "Poosh 'Em Up," rather than Derks's initial "Poosh Um Up," is not clear. In any case the nickname would stick with Lazzeri for the rest of his career.

Derks continued to write about Lazzeri as the season progressed but dropped the "dialect" headlines until the Bees slugger closed in on Babe Ruth's home run record set in 1921. Then Derks was at it again with this headline: "Our Tone She Poosh Um Oop for da Feefty-seex." Then, following a two-homer game: "Our Tone, She Poosh Um Oop Two Time, Maka da Feefty-eight." Finally, when Lazzeri surpassed Ruth, the headline shouted: "Gooda da Tone, She Poosh Um Up for Beat Bambino."[34]

Derks's affection for "Our Tone" was obvious, even if expressed in a somewhat patronizing manner, and it mirrored that of Salt Lake City fans. Given Lazzeri's historic performance in 1925 and his role in leading the Bees to a second-place finish, it should not be surprising that he became a fan favorite, and not just among the small Italian American community of Salt Lake City. But within the context of the prevailing attitude of many citizens at that time, and especially the presence of the resurgent Ku Klux Klan, his popularity was anything but inevitable.

The widespread animosity across the nation toward South and East Europeans, especially those who were Roman Catholic, was particularly virulent in Salt Lake City. Precisely when Lazzeri was setting his home run record, "Klan activity reached a high point in Salt Lake City in 1925," such that "many immigrants lived in a state of uncertainty."[35] That Tony Lazzeri could achieve such a level of admiration and even affection in that city at that time was remarkable. Nevertheless, Derks's stereotypical portrayal of Lazzeri through his "dialect" headlines provided a subtle reminder that in spite of his greatness on the diamond, the vowel at the end of his name set "Our Tone" apart, even in America's national game.

Lazzeri maintained fond feelings for Salt Lake City long after 1925. Sillito noted that the former Bee star "visited occasionally in later years as he crossed the country between his San Francisco home and New York." In 1932, when he and Yankees teammate Frank Crosetti made a stop as they drove home after the season, they "visited many of Tony's friends from the time he had played in Salt Lake, and dined at Rinetti's restaurant."[36] Proof that the relationship with Rinetti remained intact throughout the years is a telegram found in the Lazzeri Scrapbooks in which Rinetti expressed his condolences to Maye following Tony's sudden death in 1946. Sillito also cites an interview with Maye, who had fond remembrances of Salt Lake, which she called "a beautiful and clean city" where the fans, and not just those of Italian heritage, took an interest in the players and their families. She also recalled how Tony liked to unwind after a game. "Someone would lend us a car and we would often drive up to a place in the canyons just to enjoy scenery and have dinner," she said. "Tony didn't bring his problems home from the ball park, he left them there."[37]

According to Sillito, Lazzeri's success had an impact on the small Italian American community in Salt Lake, which numbered about one thousand: "No doubt they viewed Lazzeri's exploits as a useful corrective to the nativist sentiments of the Klan and its support- ers. At the same time, the obvious talent of an Italian-American like Lazzeri, competing so successfully in the national pastime, must have been a source of pride for the children of immigrant parents seeking to make their way in the larger society."[38] The fact that the local Italian American community not only recognized Lazzeri as one of their own but also considered him an inspiration further calls into question the notion that Lazzeri had sought to identify himself as being of French origin while in Salt Lake City.

One young Italian American who enjoyed Lazzeri's exploits in Salt Lake City was Herman Franks, who would grow up to become a Major League player, manager, and general manager. (The original family name was Franch, but his father, an immigrant from northern Italy, anglicized it to Franks when he settled in Utah.) Franks, who was born in 1914, said in a 2001 interview, "When I was a kid I used to watch Tony Lazzeri in Salt Lake. He was very popular." He also recalled that even as a four-sport athlete he himself was subject to some prejudice in high school. "In the twenties and early thirties," he said, "when you were Italian, you didn't talk about eating spaghetti and garlic."[39]

Another person who witnessed Lazzeri's record-setting performance was the Bees' bat boy in 1925, whose recollections appeared in a 1956 story by Don Snyder of the *Los Angeles Times*. In setting the scene, Snyder wrote: "Through the wide eyes of a 15-year-old boy, Harry Guss saw 'Poosh 'Em Up' approach the plate. There was always that serious, but pleasant expression on the raw-boned face of the lean, young man with the bat." Snyder continues:

> "When I see a bag of peanuts, I always think of Tony Lazzeri," recalled Guss. "Pop corn, hot dogs, beer, no. But peanuts, yes. Lazzeri ate peanuts all the time in his Salt Lake City days. I remember him as about 5–10 tall and 145 or 150 pounds. He was very skinny. He had tremendously long arms. He could throw a baseball farther than anyone I've ever seen throw. He was a deer on the base paths. That is why he had so many inside-the-park homers in 1925. Most of Tony's hits were line drives. He had great wrist power, took a solid crack at every pitch.
>
> "Salt Lake fans were crazy about Lazzeri. He made them love him by his modest ways. They'd empty coins from their pockets and throw them onto the field when Tony came crossing home after hitting a homer. Tony had a lot of change in those days.
>
> "He had a lot of Italian followers. One day, an Italian fan wanted to shout, 'Hit it up over the fence, Tony!' What came out though was, 'Poosh 'em up, Tony!' Lazzeri was Poosh 'em Up Tony ever after."[40]

Looking ahead to the 1926 season, when Lazzeri and Ruth would be in the same lineup, Les Goates of the *Deseret News* in Salt Lake City wrote in *The Sporting News* that "Coast League fans who have seen the tall Italian boy knock 'em miles and miles believe that he will give the king of swat a real battle for the throne. It will be a case of the King and Crown Prince of Biff competing on the same club for the home run crown."[41]

A Consolidated Press story dated November 23 compared the two home run kings that would appear in the Yankees lineup. The prediction about Ruth (who had not played up to his standards in 1925) was that "old baseball men believe he is losing his punch." The article went on to make an interesting comparison between the hitting styles of the Sultan of Swat and the soon-to-be Yankees rookie: "This boy Lazerre [*sic*] gets hold of the ball, not as Ruth does, with a long, swinging, golfing punch, but with a straight arm motion typical of the manner in which batters of the past landed on the ball."[42] In a few months the two sluggers with contrasting styles and personalities—the bombastic "Bambino" who was already a baseball icon and the reticent rookie who had almost walked away from the game in 1924—would meet face to face in spring training.

4

New Challenges

One can only wonder what was going through Tony Lazzeri's mind in early February 1926 as he made the cross-country trip from San Francisco to St. Petersburg, Florida, site of the Yankees' spring training camp. Sure, he had set records and been wildly popular in Salt Lake City, but now he was heading to the Majors and not just any big league city but *the* city, New York. He had never even seen a Major League game, and here he was, about to step onto the biggest stage in the nation's favorite sport, a crucible unlike anything he had yet encountered in his brief career as a professional ballplayer. As one writer put it, Lazzeri "comes to New York under the severe handicap of too much publicity and the burden of a home run record never before equaled."[1]

Whatever confidence his record-setting season in the PCL may have given him—not to mention the large amount in cash and players that Ed Barrow had been willing to risk to bring him to New York—the newcomer must have felt a fair amount of anxiety as he made his way east. The burden was now on him to prove that he was worth the gamble Barrow had made by signing him. What if he failed? He was familiar with the bitter taste of failure from his demotion to the Minors in 1923 and 1924, which had led to his short-lived decision to quit the game and go back to the iron mill.

As if the task of succeeding in the big leagues was not enough of a mental burden for a young rookie, Lazzeri faced additional challenges. He was aware that, to many, his record-setting home run barrage in the thin air of Salt Lake City was a sham and that many expected big league pitching to reveal his weaknesses. What could he do as a followup to that extraordinary season? How would he, a shy twenty-two-year-old who was never comfortable talking to reporters, deal with the New York writers? At that time newspaper coverage of sports was rapidly increasing, with greater competition among the city's numerous dailies. He was a highly touted rookie who had been labeled the "Little Bambino" during his home run chase in 1925, but at the same time he was also highly doubted, given the skepticism about home run totals in the PCL. In any case he was certain to be a prime target of writers eager for a scoop.

And how would he fit in with his teammates, especially with Babe Ruth, the exuberant Sultan of Swat, the greatest and most famous player in the game? Given the competitiveness among ballplayers whose careers depended on one-year contracts, would the veterans resent this hotshot Italian kid from the West Coast? There were only sixteen teams in the Major Leagues at the time, which meant that each year there were only sixteen starting jobs available at any position other than pitcher, and every player knew there was always someone ready to take his job if he faltered or went out with an injury. Dick Bartell, an infielder who broke into the Majors in 1928, described the situation this way: "It was deadly serious. An older player who'd lost a step in the field fighting off a speedy young threat to his livelihood. Most of them never had much money, had little or no savings and no other jobs or skills to fall back on."[2]

It wasn't just the sportswriters who were waiting to see what Lazzeri could do in New York. He had become the darling of the small Italian community in Salt Lake City, but could he meet the expectations of New York's one million Italians? Though not of his own choosing, he represented an entire ethnic group, and he did so in the media capital of America. If he failed, it would not be just another promising rookie who flamed out but the most publicized and anticipated player of Italian descent ever to make it to the Major Leagues.

And how would he be received by Yankees fans in general? Lazzeri was entering a world that was new to him, and not just in terms of baseball. It is impossible to appreciate the magnitude of Lazzeri's sudden success and popularity in New York without some understanding of the historical context. Certainly as the son of Italian immigrants, he had encountered some discrimination in his hometown, but San Francisco was generally a more cosmopolitan city than New York. There had been a steady influx of Italian immigrants in California, primarily from northern Italy, since the days of the gold rush in the 1850s, and many of them had settled in San Francisco when the promise of the gold rush went unfulfilled. According to historian Deanna Paoli Gumina, "California offered immigrants a share in the process of building, molding, developing, and institutionalizing a new state that bore the stamp of Italianism. . . . Italians felt they were competing on a par with their American counterparts, with an equal chance for advancement."[3] As a result, before the turn of the century the Italian community of San Francisco was prosperous enough to support opera and theater companies as well as several Italian-language newspapers.

When Lazzeri arrived in New York in 1926, the city had a much larger Italian American population than did San Francisco, and that was part of the problem. The influx of so many immigrants caused earlier arrivals to fear that their jobs would be taken away by these foreigners, who were willing to work for lower wages. And old-stock nativists saw these newcomers, with their different language and customs and their Catholic religion, as a threat to the American way of life. As noted in chapter 2, it was not the best time to be of Italian ancestry in America. Lazzeri was making his debut only two years after Congress had passed the Immigration Act, which reflected and legalized the widespread hostility toward immigrants from southern and eastern Europe. Since the late nineteenth century anti-Italian sentiment in particular had been fueled by the press, including the *New York Times*,

which depicted Italian immigrants as inherently prone to criminality and violence. It didn't help that in Lazzeri's rookie season
the public figures of Italian descent best known by most Americans were Al Capone, the most famous of the Prohibition-era
gangsters, and Nicola Sacco and Bartolomeo Vanzetti, the two
Italian-born anarchists who, in one of the most publicized and
controversial trials in American history, had been convicted in
1921 of murdering two men during a robbery and were in prison
awaiting execution.[4]

And on top of all of this uncertainty there was the unspoken
fear that was perhaps Lazzeri's greatest concern: What if the public were to find out that he was an epileptic? What if he were to
have a seizure during a game?

Frank Graham described the new arrival in camp, who stood 5
feet 10 inches and weighed about 165 pounds, with black hair and
brown eyes: "He was tall, lean, square-shouldered, and, for all
his comparatively slight build, exceedingly strong and durable.
He had a face like those of the Italian masters—olive-skinned,
oval, with high cheekbones and smoldering eyes. He spoke seldom, and when he did his voice had an angry quality, although
he was seldom angry."[5] Will Wedge of the *New York Sun* wrote:
"Lazzeri is swarthy, with black hair that grows low on his forehead. He has high cheek bones and rugged features. His eyes are
brown and smoldering, the kind that flash readily into angry glints.
Umpires may find him no complacent citizen to deal with. He
has color, and the fans around the circuit will soon discover it."
(Wedge's prediction about the new rookie's clashes with umpires
proved to be unfounded; Lazzeri was ejected from games only
three times in his career.)[6] Referring to Lazzeri as "the Babe Ruth
of the coast," Damon Runyon provided a more terse description:
"Tony is long, lanky, swarthy"; then he added that "Tony is fond
of his red wine and spaghetti."[7]

Lazzeri joined the Yankees at an interesting time in their evo-
lution. After struggling for much of their first twenty years in

the American League (AL), they had won three consecutive pennants beginning in 1921; they won their first World Series title in 1923—the year they moved into the brand new Yankee Stadium—and finished a close second in 1924. All of this came on the heels of acquiring Ruth from the Red Sox on December 26, 1919, in one of the most famous—or infamous if one is a Red Sox fan—transactions in baseball history.

But in 1925, at the same time that Lazzeri was like a comet blazing across the western skies of the PCL, the Yankees were more like a burnt-out meteor plunging into the ocean. They plummeted to seventh place with a record of 69–85, 28½ games out of first, the result of sub-par performances by some veterans and a disastrous season by Ruth. The thirty-year-old Bambino suffered a serious illness at the start of the season—brought on by excessive eating and drinking—played in only ninety-eight games, and was fined and suspended by manager Miller Huggins for his off-field escapades and insubordinate behavior.[8]

In spite of Ruth's failure in 1925, management was confident that the contrite slugger, who had promised to behave and take better care of himself, would bounce back in 1926. The other two outfield spots were set; in left was veteran slugger Bob Meusel, who had led the AL in home runs and RBIs in 1925, and in center was Earle Combs, the "Kentucky Colonel" who had hit .342 in his rookie season of 1925. The pitching staff was solid, with Waite Hoyt, Herb Pennock, "Sad Sam" Jones, and Urban Shocker. Catching was in the reliable hands of Pat Collins and Benny Bengough.

The biggest question marks were in the infield. The one proven veteran was twenty-nine-year-old third baseman "Jumping Joe" Dugan, generally considered the best in the league. However, he had been limited to 102 games in 1925 due to knee surgery. At first base was twenty-three-year-old Lou Gehrig, the shy young star signed out of Columbia University who had shown great promise in 1925, his first full season, hitting .295 with twenty home runs, but who was unsteady on defense. Mark Koenig, a twenty-one-year-old native of San Francisco, had made his big league debut on September 8, 1925, and had appeared in twenty-eight games at short, hitting .209 with no home runs and four RBIs. The twenty-two-year-old Lazzeri, who had been moved to second base after playing primarily at short in the Minors, was the only one of the four with no Major League experience.

Whatever concerns may have been weighing on Lazzeri as he entered spring training, others expressed their doubts openly, not only about him, but also about the prospects for the team as a whole. The preseason prognosticators were not optimistic. A main target of the criticism was Huggins's decision to start Koenig and Lazzeri, two novices, at the key middle infield positions. In his history of the Yankees, Graham wrote: "This seemed so glaring a weakness that none of the critics could overlook it, and all but one of them thought it would be fatal."[9]

Ford Frick resorted to sarcasm in his report from spring training: "Despite reports to the contrary, the Yankees are not the worst ball club in the world. Over a long schedule they probably would finish ahead of Saskatoon and Medicine Hat. But finishing ahead of Philadelphia, St. Louis, Detroit and other AL clubs is quite another question."[10]

The most blistering assault came from Westbrook Pegler, whose prognostications infuriated Barrow: "If Miller Huggins knew how to manage a ball team, he might manage a pretty good club this year if he had a ball team to manage." While conceding that "there are still some pretty able players," including "the abundant Babe Ruth, who has trained down to the aggregate weight of the average infield," he came to this conclusion: "They aren't a ball team, they're just a lot of ball players who think their manager is a sap."[11]

The widespread skepticism about the team's prospects could have only enhanced whatever concerns lingered in Lazzeri's mind. However, none other than Babe Ruth came to his new teammate's defense during spring training. One headline in a front-page *Sporting News* story read, "Even George Herman Ruth Puts His Okeh on Mr. Tony Lazzeri." After noting that "the best news from St. Petersburg seems to be the splendid impression already made by Tony Lazzeri," the story goes on to say that "Babe Ruth has stamped the Westerner with his seal of approval, and so has Joe Dugan, who believes Tony will be a howling success."[12]

The writers' dire predictions of the Yankees' fate seemed right on target when the team was battered by the Boston Braves in their first three exhibition games, but by the time the Yankees headed north while playing a series of exhibition games with Brooklyn—then known as the Robins in honor of their manager, Wilbert Robinson—things were coming together for the revamped squad. After winning four straight in Florida, they swept all twelve games against the Robins.

It wasn't long before at least some of the skeptics were reconsidering their view of Huggins's decision to start Lazzeri and Koenig. In a story with the headline "Lazzeri Looks Like Prize Recruit of 1926 Season," Joe Vila wrote: "Doubt as to the quality of the young players now wearing Yankee uniforms no longer prevails," with Lazzeri "a fixture at second base" and Koenig "a howling success at shortstop." He further described Lazzeri as "rather awkward in style, but he is a real ball player—a fast, snappy fielder and a powerful hitter." In the series against the Robins, "Tony knocked out three home runs and otherwise maltreated the old apple in a way that indicated real skill." Acknowledging that much of the Yankees' success would depend on these two youngsters, Vila concluded that "just at present each looks like a million dollars."[13]

Early evidence that Lazzeri's ethnicity would be a focus of his media coverage came in a *Sporting News* article following his first home run of the spring on March 29 in a 10–2 win over Brooklyn. The subhead read "Walloping Wop Comes Through," a tag that would be adopted by several others.[14] Two months later a story in the *Los Angeles Times* began: "Tony Lazzeri, the Walloping Wop from the West, evidently has hit his home run stride for the Yankees."[15] With all thoughts of Lazzeri being of French heritage long forgotten, among other ethnic identifiers that appeared in his rookie year were "the bronze Italian," "the noble Roman," "the solemn visaged Italian," "the popular Italian," "the hard-hitting Italian," and the "favorite son of Italy."

When Lazzeri hit a grand slam on April 1 as the Yankees won their fourth straight over the Robins, Harry Cross wrote: "Tony Lazzeri lived up to his noble Roman ancestry here today. . . . It seems that back in sunny Italy the house of Lazzeri has been famed for centuries for striking while the iron is hot." After Lazzeri had three hits and a walk the next day, Cross followed up with this bit of creative journalism: "Signor Tony Lazzeri, the famed spaghetti-farmer, showed his fine Italian hand again today when the Yanks made it five straight against the Robins. . . . Not a ting the mat wit Tony."[16]

Early in the season it appeared that Lazzeri had acquired a new nickname. A story in the *Brooklyn Daily Eagle* referred to Lazzeri as "Tony 'the silent,' more familiarly known as 'Bananas,'" and another story reported that the plea that greeted Lazzeri when he went to the plate was, "Come on, Bananas. Give us a homer!"[17] Marshall Hunt of the *Daily News* identified him as "Bananas Lazzeri, for indeed he is known as Bananas among the trade."[18] ("Bananas" was presumably inspired by the stereotypical image of Italians as push-cart vendors. Babe Ruth, who had trouble remembering his teammates' names, called Frank Crosetti "Dago Bananas.") But the new title didn't stick; Lazzeri would forever be known as "Poosh 'Em Up." Years later he admitted to a reporter that he was not fond of the nickname: "Some times the sports writers refer to him as 'Poosh 'Em Up' Tony, to which Tony scowls, for the idol of Millbrae youngsters does not particularly relish the moniker."[19]

The Yankees continued to play well once the regular season got under way. Lazzeri was in the opening day lineup on Tuesday, April 13, a cold and breezy day in Boston. Hitting in the sixth spot (as he would most of the season) behind Koenig, Combs, Gehrig, Ruth, and Meusel, he walked in the first as the Yankees jumped out to a 4–0 lead, was hit by a pitch in the third and later scored, and grounded into a force play in the fifth. In the seventh he got his first hit and RBI, driving in Ruth with a single to give the Yanks a 12–8 lead before making an out in the ninth. The final score was 12–11, meaning that Lazzeri's first Major League RBI in the seventh proved to be the winning run.

Lazzeri's first home run came on Tuesday, April 27, at Yankee Stadium. With two outs in the fourth, he hit a solo shot off knuckleballer Eddie Rommel in an 8–2 win over the Philadelphia Athletics. Two days later he hit his second round tripper, another solo shot, off Joe Bush in an 8–5 win over the Washington Senators. After going 5–3 in their first eight games, the Yankees won eight in a row, and by May 1 they were in first place with a 13–3 record.

A front-page story in *The Sporting News*, which boldly proclaimed that the "reorganized Hugmen are playing pennant ball," noted that "Tony Lazzeri has mastered the intricacies of second base play, although the position is new to him." Moreover, "Koenig and Lazzeri not only have 'made' the Yankees in defense, but have won unstinted praise from thousands of fans with whom they stand ace-high."[20] Four days after that story appeared, the surprising Yankees began a sixteen-game winning streak that catapulted them to an 8½ game lead over Cleveland. At that point Lazzeri had only two homers but was hitting .306 with an impressive 37 RBIS in 39 games, 11 coming in the final seven games of the winning streak. On May 18, in the middle of the streak, with the Yankees trailing the White Sox, 3–1, he hit an eighth-inning grand slam—the first of his career—to provide the winning margin in a 5–3 win.

James Harrison provided this colorful account of Lazzeri's game-winning blow: "The Yankees were drowning yesterday and Mr. Tony Lazzeri tossed them a rope. They were thirsty and he gave them water." Lazzeri's blast "was no mere synthetic homer into a friendly bleacher" but "a saucy clout that winged tremendously over Johnny Mostil's head in deep centre [*sic*] field, struck near the cinder track and rolled out to the flagpole while Yankees pounded over the plate and 15,000 blasé New Yorkers succumbed to the advanced stages of violent delirium" as Lazzeri crossed the plate behind Combs, Gehrig, and Ruth. It was "one of the longest smashes ever seen at Colonel Ruppert's stadium." (At that time the distance to the wall in straightaway center field was 490 feet.) Harrison then described the unlikely nature of the crowd's response to Lazzeri's heroic feat: "In real life a rookie from the West, great home run hitter in Salt Lake City but only a rookie in New York, doesn't hit a homer with the bases full and make thousands of fans stand up and welcome him with a hysterical ovation."[21]

Lazzeri's grand slam inspired the *Daily News* to run this banner headline on the back page of its May 19 issue: VIVA LAZZERI! WHAT A HOMER! Hunt, a talented writer who personified the sensationalist style that was the newspaper's trademark, would, throughout the years, routinely call attention to Lazzeri's ethnic origins, calling him "Signor Lazzeri" and "Antonio." His story of Lazzeri's game-winning homer was a classic example of stereotypical depiction, introduced by the headline "Spaghet! Tony Wins For Da Yanks" and followed by this subhead: "Lazzeri Hits Homer Wit Da Bases Drunk." Then, as if channeling the inventive "dialect" adopted by John Derks of the *Salt Lake Tribune* in 1925, Hunt added:

> Signor Lazzeri, he do what?
> How come Tony, he beega da push, da bigga, da guy?
> Macaroni, raviola [sic], spaghet!
> Tony he slappa da baseball for beeg home run with bases full . . . and winna da game for hees Yankees, 5 to 3.
> O, Tony he bigga da push![22]

Hunt even attributed to Lazzeri the standard image of the hotheaded Italian ballplayer. In one story he wrote that when an umpire called Lazzeri "the home run champ of the bushes" during a spring training game, "[t]he latent Latin fire in the bosom of

Signor Lazzeri burst into a belligerent flame."[23] Hunt's depiction of Lazzeri as a fiery Latin runs counter to the prevalent media portrayal of the rookie throughout the season as reticent and possessing uncommon maturity for a twenty-two-year-old.

Ford Frick had expressed little hope for the Yankees' prospects in a preseason report (cited above). Later, in an otherwise undated story from 1926 with the headline "Lazzeri Most Valuable Newcomer in AL," the future commissioner of baseball wrote: "Tony Lazzeri is at his best in a pinch. He makes his hits when hits mean runs." But like Derks and Hunt, he too could not resist resorting to Italian "dialect," opening his article with verse that read in part:

> Dese Tony Lazzeri he mucha big man,
> He maka dose home-a run clout.
> He socka dose ball like it nuttings at all
> And they can't get dese Tony boy out.
> He's a much-a big man is dese feller 'Banan'—
> Dese Tony—dese Tony da Wop![24]

The 1926 Yankees were by no means as dominant as they would be in 1927, but they were good enough to win consistently in the first four months of the season, then hold on in spite of a less impressive performance in the final two months. Nevertheless, they led the league at the end of each month from April through September. At the end of June they led the second-place White Sox by 9½ games and were nine games ahead of Cleveland at the end of July. But their lead over the Indians had slipped to 5½ games by the end of August. The real test came in September, when they played their last seventeen games on the road. On September 15 they began a six-game series against Cleveland holding a 6½ game lead. But after winning the opener, they lost four straight, narrowing their lead to 3½ games, before bouncing back to win the final game. In their final eight games, at Detroit and St. Louis, they limped home with a 3–5 record, but Cleveland, which played its final seventeen games at home, could not take advantage, going 3–4 against Boston and Philadelphia, enabling the Yankees to win the pennant by three games.

As noted, the Yankees' pitching staff was led by Pennock (23–11), Shocker (19–11), and Hoyt (16–12), while a significant part of their offensive success was due to the powerful quartet of Gehrig, Ruth, Meusel, and Lazzeri. The Yankees hit 121 home runs, 49 more than their nearest rival. Just as the Yankees' brass had hoped, Ruth did bounce back; he led the league in home runs (47) and RBIs (139) and hit for a .372 average. Gehrig added 16 home runs, drove in 109, and led the league with 20 triples. After leading the league with 33 homers in 1925, Meusel hit only 12 but drove in 78 runs while hitting .317.

As for Lazzeri, whatever concerns he may have had when he began spring training, they apparently had no effect on his debut performance. It would have been understandable if the young rookie had crumbled under the pressure of living up to the expectations. Instead, not only was he not rattled by the moment, but he also excelled on the field, played in all 155 games, and displayed maturity beyond his age. He set a rookie record by driving in 117 runs (second in the league to Ruth) and hit 18 homers (third behind Ruth and Al Simmons). He had a respectable .275 batting average, hit 14 triples (surpassed by only four other American Leaguers), stole 16 bases (tying for fifth place in the AL), and was ninth in the AL with 272 total bases. Still something of a free swinger—as Paul Krichell had warned Barrow the previous year—he led the league with 96 strikeouts, finishing 20 ahead of Ruth, the runner-up. In addition to starting at second base in 149 games, he also started at short 6 times in early July, filling in for the jittery Koenig.[25]

Lazzeri's home run total of 18 obviously pales in comparison to his record-setting 60 the previous season, seemingly justifying the prediction made by many that his numbers were inflated in the PCL. However, if Lazzeri's home run record was downplayed in 1925 because of the small dimensions of Bonneville Park, his smaller production in 1926 should also be put into perspective. First, only four players hit more homers than Lazzeri did in his rookie season, placing him among the elite sluggers in the Major Leagues. And all four—Ruth and Simmons in the AL and Hack Wilson (21) and Jim Bottomley (19) in the NL—played in the outfield or at third base, the typical power-hitting positions. At that time slugging middle infielders were about as common as left-handed catchers. People were amazed that someone weighing 165 pounds could hit the ball so far. (By comparison, Ruth weighed 215 pounds; Gehrig, 200; and Meusel, 190.) Finally, right-handed hitters like Lazzeri were at a disadvantage in Yankee Stadium, which was more favorable to left-handed power hitters like Ruth and Gehrig. Between 1924 and 1936 the average outfield distance in left field was 401 feet, compared to an average of 346 feet in right field.

Even though Lazzeri's batting average was modest, in that debut season he established a reputation as a player who made his hits count. Huggins called him "the most dangerous hitter in the clutch we have on our club."[26] In assessing Lazzeri's performance in his rookie year, Graham wrote: "His batting average wasn't high, but he hit a long ball and made most of his hits in the clutch. He was good all the time, but he was at his best under pressure."[27] In fact ten of his eighteen home runs came with men in scoring position, and his batting average with runners in scoring position was .348, seventy-three points higher than his overall average of .275.

In one of a series of columns called "Doping the World Series," Frederick G. Lieb examined a possible matchup between the Yankees and Cardinals. After noting that, should such a series come to pass, the great Rogers Hornsby, the second baseman and manager of St. Louis who had hit .424 in 1924 but dropped to .317 in 1926, was still "the boy the Yankees will have to keep an eye on," Lieb turned his attention to Hornsby's Yankee counterpart. While giving the edge to Hornsby, he warned that "the Cardinals had better not gauge Tony Lazzeri's batting prowess by his .278 [sic] average either. That is one of the most deceptive set of figures in this year's record. 'Push 'em up Tony' saved his hits for moments when they were needed most. No member of the Yanks, not even Ruth, has broken up as many close games this year as the California Italian and former Pacific Coast home-run leader."[28]

The once skeptical sportswriters (who liked Lazzeri in spite of his reluctance to speak with them) were praising his performance throughout the season. He was even lauded by umpires. Graham quoted Tommy Connolly, "dean of American League umpires," as saying in 1926: "I shouldn't be saying this, being an umpire, but I can't help it: This Italian is one of the greatest ballplayers I ever saw. Next to Huggins he's mainly responsible for the Yankees' success. He's all baseball. That's all he thinks about and all he talks about and when he opens his mouth everybody on the club pays attention, including the big guy in right field."[29] (Connolly was the sole umpire in the first AL game in 1901, was appointed as the AL's first supervisor of umpires in 1931, and in 1953 became, along with Bill Klem, one of the first two umpires inducted into the Hall of Fame.)

Umpire Billy Evans wrote: "Without a doubt, Lazzeri is one of the best looking young infielders to break into the American League in years. He is destined to be a star. Tony, however, is not strong on oratory. He is a tough guy to interview."[30] So tough, in fact, that Graham, like many others, quoted an unnamed writer as saying that "trying to interview Tony Lazzeri is like trying to mine coal with a comb and a nail file."[31]

A front-page story in *The Sporting News* reported that Lazzeri "has been a consistent winning factor from the moment Huggins assigned him to second base. The hard-hitting Italian has played great baseball all season. When older members of the Yankees looked like bush league players in Cleveland, Lazzeri stood out in bold relief." The story quotes an unidentified New York writer as saying that Lazzeri "has become one of the important cogs in the Huggins machine. Although he is finishing his first year in major league company, Tony acts like a veteran star." Also gone was the widespread skepticism about Huggins's decision to start two rookies in the infield. "[Lazzeri] and Koenig have developed into a fine double play combination, one of the smartest in the American League. The 'experts' who declared last Spring that Huggins couldn't win the pennant with a 'kid infield,' have gone into the woods to eat crow."[32]

Given his record-setting power surge in 1925, Lazzeri's offensive production as a rookie was not shocking, though it may have surprised the skeptics. What could not have been predicted, however, was the youngster's emergence as the de facto captain of the Yankees. Doubted by so many, the rookie proved to be supremely poised. What makes the twenty-two-year-old Lazzeri's emergence as the team leader even more remarkable was the prevailing attitude toward rookies. At a time when guaranteed long-term contracts were not even a pipe dream and even established players had little security, a rookie was perceived as someone who was out to take a veteran's job. Phil Rizzuto, a rookie in 1941, would later recall how the Yankee veterans resented him because he was slated to replace Frank Crosetti, the popular longtime shortstop. They wouldn't let him get into the batting cage to hit until Joe DiMaggio intervened on his behalf. "I had a rough time," Rizzuto said. "Crosetti was one of their big favorites and a great guy, and here I was a fresh rookie trying to take his job."[33]

More tolerated than welcomed, rookies were to be seen but not heard and speak only when spoken to. The reserved Lazzeri was not one to make himself heard very often in any case, but he was the one—not Ruth or other veterans like the moody Meusel or the dignified Combs—who, with his surprising maturity, quickly won the respect of his teammates. Lazzeri had the innate ability to steady the nerves of both Gehrig and Koenig. He was the one who would go the mound when a pitcher was struggling to either comfort or cajole, depending on the individual.

Both writers and management praised Lazzeri for his maturity, calm demeanor, and innate leadership ability. Barrow, who had taken the risk of signing the PCL star when others had backed away, had this to say about the novice who played alongside Ruth, the most dominant player in the history of baseball: "In our comeback from a calamitous seventh-place finish in 1925 to a championship in 1926 there is one man who stands out above all others—Tony Lazzeri. He was the making of that ball club, holding it together, guiding it, and inspiring it. He was one of the greatest ballplayers I have ever known."[34] And in a *Los Angeles Times* column signed by Huggins, the Yankees manager said of his rookie: "He's the coolest youngster I've ever seen come up to the big leagues."[35]

"From the day he walked into camp he was a major league player," wrote Graham, who covered the Yankees as a beat writer for the *New York Sun*. "Gehrig at times was uncertain on defense— although never at the bat—and Koenig, a high-strung kid, was inclined to be jittery. Between them, Lazzeri had the poise of an old stager and a wisdom that must have been born in him, since he had so little time in which to acquire it. . . . The other players, who for so long had looked to Ruth to lead them, now were looking to this amazing busher. And when, as it frequently did, the team faltered, he was the one who pulled it together and sent it on its way again."[36]

In his 1946 obituary of Lazzeri, Pulitzer Prize–winning columnist Arthur Daley wrote: "Although he was only a rookie, his was the voice of authority. The Yankees had no captain in a formal sense, but the kid from Frisco, not yet 22 years old, was the captain in fact, if not in name. He encouraged and he berated. He spurred them on by word and by example."[37]

Whatever doubts Lazzeri may have had about his reception in New York were quickly erased. His sudden success as a rookie soon captured the imagination of the fans, and several observers began comparing his popularity to that of Ruth. According to Yankees historian Marty Appel, "He was, almost overnight, the second-most popular player on the team."[38] Though not a fan of Lazzeri's defense ("he owns a pair of capacious hands and has a strong throwing arm, but is given to fumbling"), Jack Gallagher wrote that "Lazzeri already seems to be the recipient of more applause from the Yankee partisans than the Sultan of Swat."[39] In order to fully comprehend the extraordinary nature of these comments on Lazzeri's popularity, it is necessary to keep in mind the widespread negative portrayal and perception of Italian Americans at that time.

If Lazzeri's maturity and leadership ability were a surprise, so too perhaps was his quiet, unassuming personality, which contradicted the stereotypical image of Italians as hot-blooded and temperamental. According to Paul Gallico, "There was a gentleness about Tony Lazzeri and a warmth that was appealing and endearing."[40] F. C. Lane characterized Lazzeri's personality as follows: "Italians are noted for their volatile nature and excitability. In the main they are a joyous race. Lazzeri, however, moves in an atmosphere of settled calm, verging upon melancholy. He is quiet, even reticent in his ways."[41] Graham described him as "sensitive, thoughtful, shy and, even among his friends, had little to say."[42]

By the time Lazzeri joined the Yankees, the home run revolution led by Ruth was challenging the old-school norm of inside baseball in which runs were manufactured one base at a time rather than with one swing of the bat. Nevertheless, the take-no-prisoners, win-at-all-costs approach to the game characterized by such legendary figures as John McGraw and Ty Cobb remained largely intact. Brawls broke out, runners slid into second base with spikes high, intent on doing anything necessary to break up a double play, or crashed headlong into catchers attempting to block the plate. Babe Ruth even threw a punch at an umpire in 1917. When Hornsby became player-manager of the Cardinals in 1925, he told his pitchers that any time they got ahead with an 0–2 count they were to knock down the batter with the next pitch. Brushback pitches and beanballs were a common but risky practice at a time when balls, which were not replaced regularly, became scuffed and darker as the game wore on. The result in one case was fatal. On August 16, 1920, Yankees pitcher Carl Mays, a notorious "headhunter," threw a pitch that hit Indians shortstop Ray Chapman in the temple. Chapman was helped to his feet but soon collapsed. He never regained consciousness and died the next day. In other words, baseball was not a game for the faint of heart.

As for Lazzeri, lest one think that the gentleness and warmth attributed to him by Gallico suggest a player who shied away from the hardscrabble nature of the game, keep in mind that he was a product of his time who, as a youngster in San Francisco, was a street fighter who "never got licked" and an amateur boxer. He was quoted years later advising a promising young second base- man: "Don't worry about getting hurt when a runner is sliding into you. Forget personal safety or you'll never make a good dou- ble play man."[43] According to Harrison, "Lazzeri, of the warm Italian blood, is also what is known in baseball as a tough cus- tomer. Tony doesn't say much, but when he makes up his mind all the king's horses and all the king's men cannot budge him."[44]

Frank Graham recounted one example of Lazzeri's competi- tive fire. During the 1927 World Series George Grantham of the Pirates was on first base when a grounder was hit to Lazzeri. As he passed Lazzeri, who tagged him before throwing to first to complete the double play, Grantham tried to knock the ball out of Lazzeri's hand. Lazzeri then approached him and said, "You try that again and I'll stick the ball down your throat." At that point the first base umpire said, "I don't think he meant to do it, Tony." To which Lazzeri replied: "Back off. This isn't your busi- ness."[45] If Lazzeri didn't get into fights on the ballfield, it may have been because others knew how tough he was. His obituary in *The Sporting News* went so far as to say that he "was the real fighter of the swashbuckling Yankee crew of two decades ago. He was a quiet man, but his language was pungent and to the point. He had half the league afraid of him."[46]

The public perception of Lazzeri that was generated and fos- tered by the press was that of a taciturn young man little inclined to open up to sportswriters. But as reserved as he was, Lazzeri was neither reclusive nor aloof with his fellow ballplayers. By all accounts he was not only respected, but was also well liked by his Yankees teammates. Lieb, whose sixty-nine-year career began in 1911, was friendly with such stars as Cobb and Ruth and was a close friend of Gehrig. In his 1977 memoir, he wrote that when Gehrig was still living with his mother and father, "Ruth was often at the Gehrig home, along with Bob Meusel, Tony Lazzeri, and Joe Dugan, all of whom came to be known as Mom's boys."[47]

For all their obvious differences Lazzeri and Ruth established a long-lasting bond. In her biography of Ruth, Jane Leavy wrote that the Babe "didn't have a lot of friends. Perhaps a half a dozen or a dozen people he really liked." Among those she listed were Maye and Tony Lazzeri.[48] One thing the two ballplayers had in common was their love of boxing. On August 3, 1927, Lazzeri, Ruth, and Gehrig were in ringside seats at Ebbets Field for a heavyweight match between Roberto Roberti, a young Italian fighter, and Emanuel Jonidis, the Greek heavyweight champion. According to one writer, "Tony and the Babe are red hot fight fans. They never miss an opportunity to be at the ringside."[49] Lazzeri's interest in boxing is not surprising given his one-time aspiration to box professionally, as well as the growing number of Italian American fighters who were reaching the highest ranks of the sport in the 1920s, when they won no fewer than fourteen world titles. However, for the same reason that Francesco Pezzolo played Major League baseball as Ping Bodie, many Italian Americans fought under assumed names. For example, Peter Gulotta, the bantamweight champion from 1917 to 1920 and again in 1921, fought as Pete Herman. And Fireman Jim Flynn, the only fighter to knock out Jack Dempsey—in a 1917 bout in Utah—was born Andrew Chiariglione. But while boxing enjoyed widespread popularity, particularly when it came to heavyweight title fights, its association in the public's mind with the ethnic ghetto and organized crime prevented it from becoming as universally popular as baseball. Consequently no fighter of Italian descent in the twenties and thirties reached Lazzeri's level of acclaim.

Finishing near the top of the league in several offensive categories; showing uncommon maturity and calm in pressure-packed
situations on the diamond; serving as a team leader—any one of
these accomplishments would be remarkable for a twenty-two-
year-old rookie in Major League Baseball. But what truly dis-
tinguishes Tony Lazzeri's performance in 1926 is that he did all
of this while dealing with his secret illness. As sports columnist
Robert Poisall had written in 1923, when Lazzeri was struggling
to succeed in Peoria, "Pushing barriers to one side is a specialty of
Tony Lazzeri."[50] No barrier he faced was greater than his affliction with epilepsy, which meant that every day he faced the possibility of a seizure. If Lazzeri demonstrated extraordinary poise
for a rookie, perhaps it was because to someone facing the daily
challenge of living with epilepsy, the challenge of playing big
league baseball paled by comparison.

Lazzeri also faced the disturbing possibility that someone would
disclose his illness to the public. Whereas today an athlete such
as Lazzeri might be celebrated for his courage in overcoming the
effects of his affliction, for a good part of the twentieth century
epilepsy was such a stigmatized illness that, if known of by others, it threatened to bring humiliation or worse to those afflicted.

Dr. Chad Carlson, a professor of neurology at the Medical College of Wisconsin who specializes in epilepsy, spoke of the continuing stigma attached to the illness:

> If you go back far enough in time, it wasn't uncommon to put peo-
> ple with epilepsy into asylums and lock them away from society.
> That is going to lead to people wanting to keep it secret. Even today
> there is a stigma associated with epilepsy that people can't escape.
> Most people assume that it is associated with some sort of cogni-
> tive disability or physical disability or both. They assume you're
> not going to be smart, that you're maybe not able to walk nor-
> mally. With epilepsy affecting 1 percent of the population, that's
> a huge number. You can talk about a number of well-known peo-
> ple with depression and anxiety, but the number of famous peo-

ple who talk about their epilepsy is much, much smaller. It still, despite a lot of effort, carries a lot more stigma.[51]

After signing Lazzeri, Barrow continued to be concerned about his condition and the possibility of seizures: "There was never a time thereafter that I didn't watch Lazzeri with the greatest apprehension, fearful always that he would have a seizure on the ball field. He never did. He had one attack on the train coming north from the South that first spring; and he had another that I knew about in the clubhouse before a game in St. Louis. I heard of a couple of others at second hand." Barrow was also aware of the sensitive nature of Lazzeri's affliction. "I don't believe the public ever knew this about him. Certainly we took every precaution we could to see that the public never did, and in this the sports writers traveling with the club were likewise as considerate of Tony's feelings and welfare."[52]

Interviewed years later, Koenig spoke of his roommate's seizures. "He'd be standing in front of the mirror, combing his hair. Suddenly, the comb would fly out of his hand and hit the wall. One morning in Chicago, he had a fit. He fell on the floor and started foaming. I didn't know what to do, so I ran out of the room without a stitch of clothing on to get [Waite] Hoyt, who was a mortician in the off-season."[53]

Even though, from all indications, Lazzeri's seizures occurred in the morning, there was no way he could be certain that they would not occur at other times. Any rookie will admit that he feels the jitters in his first Major League game. How secure did Lazzeri feel on Tuesday, April 13, opening day of the season, in Fenway Park in front of eleven thousand fans? Or on April 21, the home opener at Yankee Stadium, in front of forty thousand fans? Did he wonder if the excitement of the moment, the inevitable anxiety, might trigger an episode? His anxiety may have diminished as time went on, but did it ever go away entirely? As with other aspects of Lazzeri's life, there is no way to provide a definitive answer.

When asked if epileptics are likely to be consistently anxious about the possibility of having a seizure, Dr. Carlson replied: "Most people are. It's kind of a sword of Damocles; you never know when it's going to happen; you're always worried about it. There's always the possibility that you'll have a seizure at a bad time. There is going to be stress and anxiety about the loss of control and the unpredictability."

If, as an epileptic, Lazzeri was prone to even a moderate level of anxiety, second base was a challenging position for him to play. As the pivot man on double plays, the second baseman, who often has his back turned to the approaching runner, is vulnerable to being wiped out by the runner, who is intent on breaking up the double play. Being at bat was also not for the squeamish at a time when batters were routinely hit by pitchers, sometimes with serious—and, in the case of Ray Chapman, deadly—consequences.

Dr. Carlson also discussed the treatment available to Lazzeri: "We're talking about 1920s, 1930s, so our pharmacology was much more limited than what we have now. Phenobarbital . . . came about in 1903 or thereabouts; that would've been the drug of choice then." (Based on what Maye Lazzeri had told her, Lazzeri's daughter-in-law, Marilyn, confirmed that Tony did take phenobarbital.)[54] As to the drug's possible effects on Lazzeri, Dr. Carlson said: "Phenobarbital is a barbiturate, so it slows you down. Reaction times can be affected by that. It could definitely have an impact on [Lazzeri's] game. So the kind of cognitive decision making he has to make to be a good hitter is potentially vulnerable to the kind of slowing down of a medicine like phenobarbital." It is impossible to know to what extent, if any, the phenobarbital affected the split-second timing Lazzeri needed to hit Major League pitching, but if the medication did indeed slow down his reflexes, his hitting prowess is all the more impressive.

At the same time, the calming effect of phenobarbital might account, at least in part, for Lazzeri's calm under pressure. "Does phenobarbital potentially calm you down?" asked Dr. Carlson.

"I think for most people the answer is yes. Phenobarbital has a very similar effect on the brain as alcohol. If you have that small drink, it gets you to that sweet spot where you are just a little bit more calm, but you very quickly go to the point where you're not worth anything because your reaction time is down and you can't accomplish what you need to accomplish."

The issue of Lazzeri's epilepsy was discussed by Pulitzer Prize–winning columnist Ira Berkow. Reflecting on Lazzeri's quiet nature, Berkow wrote: "Perhaps Lazzeri spoke little because he was naturally reserved. . . . Or perhaps Lazzeri was quiet because he hid a secret: he suffered with an illness, epilepsy, and in those days particularly epilepsy was considered a taboo subject." Berkow then cited Reina Berner, director of the Epilepsy Institute of New York, who indicated that epileptics could be anxious and terrified that they could have a seizure at any moment. "And the epileptic worries: 'When will it happen? What will they think of me? Will I be able to keep my job?' And epileptics were often considered dangerous, or incompetent, and were unable to handle stress. It's not true, though stress can sometimes trigger a seizure, but much less so today because of modern medicine. But, my God, think of a ballplayer in front of all those people, and in those times. I can't believe he played."[55]

Although the Yankees stumbled late in the season before wrapping up the pennant and won only two more games than St. Louis, they entered the World Series heavily favored to beat the Cardinals, who had edged the Reds by two games in the NL. Among non-Yankees fans, however, there was widespread sentiment favoring the Cardinals, who had never appeared in a World Series under that name. (The franchise had last appeared in a World Series in 1888, when the team was known as the Browns and played in the American Association.) Also two of the Cardinals veteran stars were fan favorites. Grover Cleveland "Pete" Alexander, the thirty-nine-year-old right-hander who was nearing the end of his illustrious twenty-year career and had been picked up midsesason after being let go by the Cubs, had played a major role by winning nine games down the stretch. Rogers Hornsby, then in his twelfth year with St. Louis and his first full year as manager, was one of the game's all-time great hitters, hitting over .400 in three of the previous five seasons. Neither had ever been on a World Series winner.

The Yankees won the opener at home, 2–1, behind the pitching of twenty-three-game winner Pennock, but the Cardinals evened the Series the next day when Alexander pitched a complete game, struck out ten, and allowed one earned run in a 6–2 win. At Sportsman's Park in St. Louis the Cardinals gained the advantage when knuckleballer Jesse Haines pitched a 4–0 shutout and hit a two-run homer. The next day Ruth took charge, hitting three home runs in a 10–5 win that evened the Series. Game Five was tied at 2–2 after nine innings when Lazzeri came up in the top of the tenth with one out and the bases loaded. His sacrifice fly to left scored Koening with the lead run, and the Cardinals went quietly in the bottom of the inning. The Yankees headed home needing only one more win. Facing elimination, the Cardinals again called on Alexander, who pitched another complete game, holding the Yanks to two runs while the Cards hammered three New York pitchers for ten runs. The stage was now set for one of the most dramatic seventh games in World Series history.

More than sixty thousand fans had attended each of the first two contests at Yankee Stadium, but the crowd dropped to 48,615 for Game Six, apparently due to chilly temperatures better suited for football. The weather was even worse for the finale, dropping the attendance to 38,093. The Series was being broadcast nationwide on a network hookup originating at WEAF in New York with thirty-eight-year-old Graham McNamee as the play-by-play announcer. Prior to the start of the game, he set the scene for Game Seven: "It is cold; it is dreary; it is dark; it is dripping; it is damp and thick. The infield had been covered all night and all morning."[56]

On the mound were two future Hall of Famers: Hoyt, the Game Two winner, for the Yankees, and for the Cardinals, Haines, who had pitched a shutout in Game Three. Ruth opened the scoring with a two-out solo homer in the third, his fourth of the Series, but the Cardinals came right back in the next inning, with considerable help from the Yankees. After a one-out single by Jim Bottomley, Les Bell hit a tailor-made double play grounder to short, but Koenig bobbled it, and both runners were safe. A short fly by Chick Hafey fell between Koenig and Meusel for a single to load the bases.

McNamee: "This is a ball game, I want to tell you, some excitement."

When Bob O'Farrell, the St. Louis catcher named the NL MVP that season, lofted a routine fly ball to left-center, Meusel, with the stronger arm, waved off Combs and settled under the ball, ready to make a throw to home. Instead the ball popped out of his mitt, allowing Bottomley to score the tying run.

McNamee: "Oh-Meusel, he feels mighty bad about it."

Tommy Thevenow, the hitting star of the Series for the Cards, then rubbed salt into the wound by dumping a Texas League single over the head of Lazzeri, sending two runs home for a 3–1 lead.

McNamee: "You have got to feel kind of sorry for Waite Hoyt out there, pitching a peach of a game and his team simply going blah on him."

The Yankees cut the margin to one in the bottom of the sixth when, with two outs and nobody on, Dugan singled and scored on a double by catcher Hank Severeid. With the top of the Yankees order up in the bottom of the seventh, Combs led off with a single, then advanced to second on a sacrifice bunt by Koenig. Ruth was walked on four pitches but was forced out at second on a grounder by Meusel. Gehrig then walked to load the bases, bringing Lazzeri to the plate with the tying run on third with two outs. Haines, who had recently injured the index finger on his pitching hand, was obviously struggling; the finger had split and was bleeding. Hornsby approached the mound, determined that Haines could go no further, and signaled for a reliever.

In from the left-field bullpen casually strolled the unmistakable figure of Alexander, tall and burly, wearing a scarlet Cardinals sweater and with his cap typically tilting to one side.

McNamee: "The crowd gave the veteran pitcher a great hand as he came in the box."

Alexander's condition when he was summoned has long been debated. He was a habitual drinker, and some reported, or assumed, that he was sleeping off a hangover in the bullpen after celebrating his complete-game win a day earlier. Famed columnist Damon Runyon went so far as to write: "They say Grover had been heating himself up under the bleachers. Others claim he was found in his favorite chair down at the tavern," and the Cardinals had to send a taxi to retrieve him.[57] But still others made the case that after Game Six Hornsby had urged "Pete" to stay in his room that night so as to be ready the next day in case he was needed, and the veteran had complied with his manager's request. Whatever condition "Alex" was in, Hornsby handed his reliever the ball and headed back to his position at second.

So there on the mound stood the crafty veteran of sixteen Major League seasons with 333 regular-season wins to his credit and on his way to 373, tying him with Christy Mathewson for the most wins in NL history. In 1938 he would become one of the first nine players voted into the Hall of Fame. Alexander was blessed with extraordinary skill on the mound but cursed off the field. He was a veteran of seven weeks on the front lines in World War I that had left him shell-shocked and deaf in one ear. He had been a drinker before entering the service, but his experience in the war led him to become addicted to alcohol.

Standing in the batter's box was the twenty-two-year-old rookie with only 155 games under his belt. As Bob Broeg put it years later: "[Lazzeri] was a World Series green pea facing one of the greatest pitchers ever."[58] The Nebraska farm boy versus the San Francisco city kid. Veteran versus rookie. But they did have one thing in common: like Lazzeri, Alexander was an epileptic.[59] When Alexander completed his warm-up tosses, Lazzeri stepped into the box.

McNamee: "Lazzeri is up," and the crowd is again shouting, "Poosh-em-up-Tony, Poosh-em-up-Tony."

Lazzeri took the first pitch for ball one; then Alexander evened the count with a called strike. On the next pitch, a fastball on the inside part of the plate, Lazzeri took a hard cut, driving the ball deep down the left-field line. The ball was clearly heading for the seats; the only question was whether it would stay fair. To the disappointment of the Yankees players who had jumped to their feet in the dugout, the ball hooked foul. Depending on which description is read, it was either foul by inches or by several feet.

Then, with the count 1–2, Lazzeri succumbed to the siren call that snares so many hitters: a breaking ball that looks like a strike, then falls off the outside corner. Obviously fooled by the pitch, he took a feeble off-balance cut and missed badly. The momentum of his awkward swing turned his body 45 degrees so that when he finished, he was directly facing Alexander. Frustrated, Lazzeri took a couple of steps forward, then flung his bat toward the Yankee dugout and trotted out to his position at second base. Alexander, meanwhile, strolled toward the dugout as his teammates crowded around to congratulate him.

McNamee: "The crowd gave Alexander a great ovation as he walked to the dugout."

The crisis had been averted, but the Yankees still had two innings to overcome the one-run deficit. Instead Alexander retired the next five batters before issuing a walk to Ruth—the Babe's fourth in the game—with two out in the bottom of the ninth. That brought Meusel to the plate with a chance for redemption. But when Alexander delivered the first pitch, Ruth surprised everyone by taking off for second. O'Farrell made a perfect throw, Hornsby dropped the glove on the sliding would-be thief, umpire Bill Dineen flashed the out sign, and the Cardinals won their first World Series.

Lazzeri's strikeout was a disappointing ending to what was otherwise a dazzling rookie season. But neither he nor anyone else could have imagined that his strikeout, that one swing and miss, would haunt him for the rest of his life. The strikeout is even immortalized on Alexander's Hall of Fame plaque, which has been on display since 1939 (and today hangs only a few feet from Lazzeri's plaque). It reads in part: "Won 1926 world championship for Cardinals by striking out Lazzeri with bases full in final crisis at Yankee Stadium."

The phrase that pops up again and again when people write about Lazzeri is: "He is best remembered for . . . ," followed by the inevitable reference to the strikeout. The term "best" is particularly ironic in a reference to what would prove to be the worst moment of Lazzeri's career and the one that would forever taint his legacy. It is also ironic in that no one at that time would have predicted that outcome since Lazzeri was not blamed for the Yankees' loss in Game Seven. While his strikeout was obviously disappointing to the Yankees and their fans, it was not particularly shocking, given the disparity in experience between the protagonists. Then, too, that season Lazzeri had led the league in strikeouts by a wide margin and had already struck out twice against Haines in Game Seven before he faced Alexander.

Rightly so, "Alexander the Great" was hailed in newspapers across the country as the hero of the deciding game, elevated to quasi-mythic status as the old man who saved the Cardinals from potential disaster by getting them out of the bases-loaded jam. The headlines read, "Alexander Fans Lazzeri to Save Series"—or some variation thereof—but the focus of press reports was on the veteran's nonchalant attitude and masterful command of his pitches, not on the rookie's failure.

With one exception, I found no criticism of Lazzeri's strikeout or suggestion that he was the goat of the Series. In the opening line of his *Daily News* story, Will Murphy wrote: "It is a game for grown men, this world series, and no sport for youths. . . . [E]ach of the goats was a lad who had not been around the majors for long." Singling out Koenig's error and Lazzeri's strikeout, he wrote: "When Tony Lazzeri stuck out, . . . Hug must have repeated sadly the ancient saw: 'Never send a boy on a man's errand.'"[60] In fact Huggins downplayed the significance of the strikeout. "Any one can strike out," he said, "but ballplayers like Lazzeri come along once in a generation."[61]

In all the other game stories and columns I reviewed, the goat label was pinned not on Lazzeri but on Koenig, Meusel, or both; they made the errors that allowed all three unearned runs to score in the 3–2 loss. In his front-page story for the *Times*, Harrison summed up the game, and the Series, succinctly: "After millions of words had been scribbled and tons of white paper covered with calculations, the world's series worked itself down to four short words: Koenig's fumble, Meusel's muff. . . . Everything was incidental to those two errors." Even Lazzeri's strikeout "was incidental, though highly dramatic. . . . If Meusel and Koenig had held on to the ball Alex would have been merely a gallant old pitcher on a losing ball club."[62] Paul Gallico's story in the *Daily News* began: "The play is done. The actors have trailed into the wings. . . . The goat, the butt, the poor fellow in pantaloons hit soundly on his trousers with the two-bladed slapstick, was Robert Meusel of California."[63] And in a syndicated column under his byline published the day after the game, Meusel wrote: "If there is any world series goat, I am it."[64]

As for Koenig, even a year later he was still identified as the goat of the 1926 Series. A story by Daniel M. Daniel on October 10, 1927, about Koenig's starring role in the Yankees' World Series win over the Pirates, appeared under the headline: "Mark Koenig, Goat in 1926, Proves Hero of 1927 Series."[65]

The inimitable Grantland Rice placed the onus on both players: "For it was through an open breach in the left wing of the Yankee defense, where Mark Koenig and Bob Meusel crashed together, that Hornsby's galloping Western tribe rushed on to win the most dramatic battle of the year on any field."[66]

Nevertheless, as much as they were emphasized at the time, those errors have long been forgotten, replaced by a single strikeout as the defining moment in the World Series and, for many, as the defining moment of Lazzeri's career. But why? The lingering magnitude of that one at bat raises some interesting questions. Would the strikeout have become so iconic had the pitcher been someone other than "Alexander the Great"? He was already regarded as one of the all-time best and had shut out the Yankees the day before, all of which enhanced the drama of the moment. Given the contemporary focus on the errors that cost the Yankees the game, would the strikeout still be considered an iconic World Series moment had a run-of-the-mill reliever come in to face Lazzeri?

Perhaps most important, would the moment have been magnified and immortalized had the strikeout not been mentioned on Alexander's plaque, there to be seen by everyone who has visited the Hall of Fame since it opened in 1939? In the words of Shirley Povich, "[Lazzeri] gained admission to Cooperstown in the role of a stooge, as it were."[67] With the exception of Dennis Eckersley, the Oakland A's pitcher who gave up Kirk Gibson's two-out, game-winning homer in the first game of the 1988 World Series, Tony Lazzeri may well be the only Hall of Famer who has had his entire legacy tarnished by a single at bat.

Following the World Series Tony and Maye boarded a train for the trip back to California. On October 15 Lazzeri arrived in Los Angeles to take part in some exhibition games pitting a squad of Major Leaguers against Minor Leaguers for the benefit of the Association of Professional Ball Players of America, which provided funds to aged, sick, and injured players. Then in late November he headed to Hollywood to make his film debut. A *Los Angeles Times* story announced that "a group of baseball celebrities has arrived at the Metro-Goldwyn-Mayer Studios to appear in the training-camp sequences" for a new film entitled *Slide, Kelly Slide*. A number of Major Leaguers "headed by Bob and 'Irish' Meusel and Tony Lazzeri, world series celebrities," would be playing the roles of players hoping to make the New York team.[68] The film, which was a hit when it came out in 1927, stars William Haines as Jim Kelly, the wise-cracking, abrasive ace pitcher for the Yankees who alienates his teammates and his girlfriend but then redeems himself in time for a happy ending.

Notwithstanding his strikeout in Game Seven, Tony Lazzeri had proven that he not only belonged in the big leagues, but that he could also be one of the game's elite players, by both putting up impressive statistics and establishing his credentials as a team leader. In his column umpire Billy Evans proclaimed that "Tony Lazzeri of the New York Americans was probably the most valuable first-year player in either league last season. Lazzeri, by his general all-around play did as much for the Yankees as did Ruth with his batting or Pennock with his pitching."[69] Nevertheless, in spite of all the positive results and accolades, Lazzeri went into the off-season knowing that his rookie year had ended with a major letdown; the clutch hitter had failed to come through in his biggest clutch moment, missing the opportunity to put his team in position to win the World Series. So once again he would face questions going into a new season. For all the poise and maturity he had shown as a rookie, did he have the mental toughness to get past the stinging memory of his final at bat? Or would the aftereffects of that moment carry over into 1927 and make him vulnerable to the so-called "sophomore jinx" that victimizes so many young players?

5

The Reign of Terror

Having rewarded the trust placed in him by both Ed Barrow and Miller Huggins with his outstanding rookie season performance, Tony Lazzeri was in turn rewarded by the Yankees with a 60 percent increase in salary for the 1927 season. On April 8 he signed a contract for $8,000, plus travel expenses for Maye to join him in New York, as well as expenses for both to return to San Francisco at the end of the season. His new salary was the same as Gehrig's but less than that of several of the veteran players. Ruth of course eclipsed everyone with a record-setting three-year contract at $70,000 a year.

Along with his salary, Lazzeri's performance in 1926 also raised expectations for 1927. The new challenge was to prove that he was a bona fide Major League star, not a one-year wonder. As he had done in 1926, Lazzeri more than lived up to the expectations. Obviously past whatever impact his strikeout against Grover Cleveland Alexander in Game Seven of the 1926 World Series may have had, he not only did not succumb to the sophomore jinx, but he also performed even better in 1927. He again hit 18 home runs; drove in 102 runs; and raised his batting average, on-base percentage, and slugging average. He continued to be popular with the fans, and his standing in the Italian American community was such that he was honored at banquets in three AL cities.

But then it was an extraordinary year for the entire team. The Yankees reached unprecedented heights, leading the AL almost the entire season, winning the pennant by nineteen games, then sweeping the Pirates in the World Series. After almost a century the 1927 Yankees continue to loom large in baseball lore. They remain prominent in any discussion of the game's greatest teams, and many continue to rank them the all-time number one team. Six of their players (Ruth, Gehrig, Lazzeri, Combs, Hoyt, and Pennock) are in the Hall of Fame, as well as manager Miller Huggins, GM Ed Barrow, and owner Jacob Ruppert. In the early years of the live-ball era, the Yankees were the first big league squad to field power hitters—Ruth, Gehrig, Meusel, and Lazzeri in 1927— in the third, fourth, fifth, and sixth spots in the order. Although the label "Murderers' Row" had been attached to the Yankees as early as 1918, this 1927 quartet of sluggers achieved such epic stature that they made it stick to this day. It was the birth of long-ball baseball, and the game has never been quite the same. Ruth was the creator; Gehrig, Meusel, and Lazzeri were his progeny.

But even though the 1926 team had confounded its critics by winning the pennant and coming within two runs of winning the World Series, like spring flowers popping up out of the soil, the doubters resurfaced in 1927. They pointed to the team's second-half slump in 1926, the relative youth of its position players, and the relative old age of its veteran pitching staff. Even Fred Lieb, who had boldly predicted that the Yanks would win the 1926 pennant, concluded that "it is doubtful if their pitching strength is sufficient to send the club into another World Series."[1] The majority of the pundits favored Connie Mack's powerful Philadelphia Athletics lineup, which included seven future Hall of Famers: Eddie Collins, Ty Cobb, Zach Wheat, Al Simmons, Lefty Grove, Gordon "Mickey" Cochrane, and Jimmie Foxx. Mack, who was in his twenty-seventh year as manager and co-owner of the A's in 1927, had built a previous dynasty, winning four pennants and three World Series titles between 1910 and 1914. Known as the "Tall Tactician," he managed the A's for fifty years before retiring at the age of eighty-four. The all-time leader in wins (3,731), in 1937 he became part of the second group to be elected to the Hall of Fame.

The Yankees kept their roster mainly intact, adding only catcher Johnny Grabowski, infielder Ray Morehart, and outfielder Cedric Durst as backup players. They also signed Wilcy Moore, a thirty-year-old Oklahoma farmer and career Minor League pitcher who had posted a remarkable 30–4 record in the Class B South Atlantic League in 1926. The folksy rookie would prove to be a most unlikely hero in New York's historic run.

Huggins did make one major change in the batting order. In 1926 Ruth had primarily hit fourth, behind Gehrig and ahead of Meusel. Now he placed Gehrig, who drove in 109 runs in 1926, in the cleanup spot to ensure that opposing teams would pitch to Ruth, who had led the league with 144 walks in 1926. Huggins may have had a hunch that his young first baseman was about to come into his own as a power hitter. In fact Gehrig's quantum leap in home runs and RBIs was a major reason for the legendary status of the 1927 lineup now known as "Murderers' Row."

With the starting lineup the same as in 1926, there was little drama in spring training. But in a story in the *Daily News*, Marshall Hunt wrote of a batting tip that Babe Ruth claimed to have given to Lazzeri. According to Hunt, "Ruth recently explained to the signor that his method of swinging his bat was wrong, that he swung from his knees rather than 'leveling out' his swing." He then quoted Ruth as saying: "I guess I got that skinny wop fixed now. That Eyetallyun is going to be one of the greatest batters in the league this year and a helluva fielder. You mark my word."[2] What impact, if any, Ruth's tip had on Lazzeri's hitting remains unknown.

In an apparent effort to inject some excitement into the spring training routine, the press hyped the nine-game series between the Yankees and Cardinals (who also trained in St. Petersburg) as the "Little World Series," and some writers even envisioned the series as an opportunity for Lazzeri to gain revenge against Alexander. Richards Vidmer of the *Times* elevated the encounter to high melodrama by writing that "revenge began to seep into the heart of a tall, lithe, dark browed Italian lad" the previous October, to the point that when the series was announced, "Lazzeri raised clenched fists in the air and shouted, 'Vendetta! I shall have revenge.'"[3]

As for Vidmer's claim that revenge had begun to seep into Lazzeri's heart in October, I have found no indication that Lazzeri publicly expressed a desire for vendetta against Alexander at any time during the offseason. Moreover, it seems out of character for someone as reserved as Lazzeri, for whom silence was a way of life, to raise his fists and shout his desire for vendetta, especially with a sportswriter as a witness. Vidmer does not indicate whether he witnessed this scene or heard of it second hand, and I have found no reference to it in any other news source. Given the lack of drama at the Yankees' spring camp, such an uncharacteristic act by Lazzeri would seem to have merited mention by other writers. It is also notable that G. H. Fleming, who includes other stories by Vidmer in *Murderers' Row*, his day-by-day recreation of the 1927 Yankees by means of contemporary news stories, did not include this article.

But let's give Vidmer the benefit of the doubt and accept that Lazzeri did in fact shout his desire for revenge, perhaps in the privacy of the clubhouse. Perhaps the most overlooked aspect of Lazzeri's personality is his mischievous sense of humor. Beneath his outwardly laconic demeanor lay the impish soul of a notorious prankster. If a teammate would suddenly hop around due to a hotfoot or find that the corner of the newspaper he was reading was on fire, the most likely suspect was always Lazzeri. He had been honing his skills at least as early as his Minor League days.

Lefty O'Doul told the story of the time in 1924 when he and Lazzeri, then teammates with the Salt Lake City Bees, were playing a prank on their teammate Les Cook, who was in a room below and across from theirs. "We started peppering him with cherry pits," said O'Doul. "When he got mad and stuck his head out the window, we let him have it with a laundry bag full of water. We ducked for cover, because in those days Cookie carried a pistol he used for shooting rabbits when we traveled from Salt Lake across the desert."[4]

If Lazzeri did shout what Vidmer describes, it seems more plausible that he was acting in jest for the amusement of his teammates rather than expressing a genuine desire for revenge. Vidmer may have heard that from a source who witnessed the event but chose to go with his more dramatic version. It was not uncommon at that time for writers to "massage" quotes attributed to Major Leaguers, if not create them out of whole cloth, or to pass off anecdotes as fact. Certainly it was not uncommon for writers to embellish their stories.[5] And even if Lazzeri privately hoped for a chance to redeem himself in another encounter with Alexander, it seems unlikely that he would have thought that a base hit, or even a home run, in a meaningless spring training game could make up for his World Series strikeout.

Whatever the truth, the issue proved to be moot when a knee infection kept Lazzeri out of the first games with the Cardinals. In fact when the Yanks broke camp on March 30 to begin their annual barnstorming tour as they made their way north, Lazzeri was left behind in St. Petersburg. Lazzeri rejoined the team on April 7 in Nashville, going 0 for 3 in a 10–6 loss to the Cardinals in the finale of their nine-game matchup. Alexander did not pitch in that game.

The Yankees opened the season at home against the Athletics on April 12 in front of more than seventy-two thousand fans. Prior to the start of the game Mayor Jimmy Walker threw out the first pitch, and the AL pennant was raised on the center-field flag pole. New York won easily, 8–3, as Lefty Grove gave up all eight runs (only three earned) in six innings, while his teammates committed five errors. Westbrook Pegler wrote what would prove to be an accurate forecast of the Athletics' weakness: "There was a good deal of muffing and fumbling by Mr. Mack's elderly people, and the creak of ancient knee joints and elbows was heard plainly above the rumbling comments of the crowd. 'That,' remarked one of the New York customers with ghoulish pleasure, 'is how Mr. Mack is going to lose the pennant with his old people.'"[6] (Cobb and Collins were forty years old; Wheat was thirty-nine.)

The Yankees took all three games from their primary rivals, but by the end of April they had a 9–5 record, tied for first with the Athletics. Then, on May 1, before more than sixty thousand spectators at Yankee Stadium, a 7–3 win over the Athletics gave the Yankees sole possession of first place, a position they held for the remainder of the season. In his account of that game, Rud Rennie wrote of Lazzeri: "Tony the Wop handled four chances cleanly yesterday, and in so doing he brought his total to 79 chances without an error."[7] Lazzeri's errorless streak stretched to twenty-two games before it ended in Chicago on May 9.

After going 19–9 in May, the Yanks held a two-game lead over the White Sox, with the Athletics behind by six. A 21–6 record in June put them 10½ games ahead of the White Sox and Senators, and their lead only increased in each succeeding month. While their AL rivals went limp like so many strands of overcooked pasta, the Yankees coasted to the pennant with a record of 110–44, finishing nineteen games ahead of the preseason favorite Athletics. Essentially the 1927 Yankees became merciless bullies who intimidated and dominated their helpless opponents. Already by early May, Dan Howley, manager of the St. Louis Browns team that would lose twenty-one straight games to New York, was begging for mercy. "Those fellows hit too hard," he said. "They pack too much of a punch for the rest of us. They ought to penalize them one strike before they step up to the plate, so as to give us a chance."[8] No wonder Paul Gallico dubbed the Yankees' 1927 onslaught the "reign of terror."[9]

While the Yankees' relentless drive to the title sucked all of the drama out of the pennant race, Ruth and Gehrig created their own two-man drama of dueling homers. Suddenly the twenty-three-year-old first baseman in his third season as a regular had come into his own as a slugger who could, for the first time, challenge the thirty-two-year-old Bambino's status as the greatest slugger in history. Their epic gladiatorial contest, which Gallico called "the most astonishing thing that has ever happened in baseball," became the dominant baseball story of the year.[10] For the first five months it was a seesaw battle as they hit home runs at a pace never before set, except by Ruth himself. Entering September, Ruth led by two, 43–41. But Gehrig managed to hit only 6 round trippers the rest of the way, while the Babe went on a record-setting rampage by clouting 17 more, topping it off by hitting number 60 on September 30, breaking his previous record of 59 in 1921.

Gehrig's 47 homers were the most ever hit by anyone other than the Bambino. Their combined total of 107 was more than the total for any other Major League team and almost twice the number hit by the A's (56). Gehrig, who led the league in RBIs and total bases while hitting .373, won the AL MVP Award. Ruth, who led the league in runs, on-base percentage, and walks in addition to home runs, was not eligible for the award since he had won it in 1923, and at that time a player could win it only once. Gehrig received seven of the eight first-place votes in the balloting; the other first-place vote went to Lazzeri, who finished eleventh in the overall voting.

As a whole, the Murderers' Row lineup led the Major Leagues in home runs, batting average, runs scored, slugging average, and total bases. Four players—Gehrig, Ruth, Meusel, and Lazzeri—drove in more than one hundred runs. "It was," wrote Gallico, "a miracle team . . . one of those accidents or freaks of sports."[11] Given such a dominating and intimidating power surge, it is easy to overlook how balanced a team it was. The pitching staff, which was considered suspect before the season, led the league in ERA and shutouts, with Moore, Hoyt, and Shocker compiling the top three ERAs in the AL. Moore, who had never pitched in the Majors, was the surprise of the year; appearing in 50 games, only 12 as a starter, he posted a 19–7 record with 13 saves. In addition, the Yankees stole 90 bases, fourth best in the AL.

In spite of their relatively easy road to the pennant and their power-laden lineup, the Yankees went into the World Series only slightly favored over the Pirates, whose 94–60 record had edged out the Cardinals by 1½ games. Featuring speed and pitching, they had no home run hitters to match Ruth and Gehrig. Pittsburgh did, however, have two outstanding young hitters in the Waner brothers, Paul and Lloyd, both future Hall of Famers, who had batted .380 and .355 respectively during the regular season but hit a total of only eleven home runs. The infield featured another future Hall of Famer: third baseman Pie Traynor.

Perhaps only the oddsmakers and Pirates fans were surprised when the Yankees won four straight, but what was really surprising was the manner in which they swept the Series. The mighty Murderers' Row crew produced only two homers—both by Ruth in the final two games—but the Yankees pitching staff gave up only ten runs. Only the third game was a rout at 8–1. Game Two was a 6–2 win, while the first and final matches were decided by a single run, 5–4 and 4–3. And fittingly the Series ended not with a bang but a whimper.

With the fourth game tied 3–3, the Yankees loaded the bases in the bottom of the ninth before Johnny Miljus, the reliever who had entered the game in the seventh inning, struck out Gehrig and Meusel. Then, just as he had in the seventh game of the World Series one year earlier, Lazzeri stepped to the plate with another chance to be the hero. In a scene eerily reminiscent of his 1926 duel with Alexander, he lashed at the first pitch from Miljus and hit a long drive to left that landed in the seats, once again in foul territory. After missing the plate to even the count, Miljus uncorked a pitch that was high and wide, clipped the top of catcher Johnny Gooch's glove, and then rolled to the stands as Earle Combs crossed the plate with the run that gave the Yanks a four-game sweep.[12]

One of the enduring stories about that relatively ho-hum Series is that the Yankees intimidated and demoralized the Pirates by putting on an awesome display of power in batting practice at

Forbes Field before the opening game. As the Pirates watched, one hitter after another drove balls over the fence, leaving their opponents convinced that they had no chance to win. While the story has been dismissed by many as apocryphal, years later Gallico provided an eyewitness account: "Though it has the ring of legend, it was fact because I was there and saw it, and it was even more impressive to witness than to hear tell about it. . . . So there I was, hanging out back of the batter's cage right up against one of the most furious bombardments of hits ever seen anywhere."[13] Dick Bartell, a nineteen-year-old rookie infielder called up by the Pirates late in the season, was also an eye witness to the batting practice onslaught. "We all turned out early," he wrote in his 1987 autobiography. "It was like watching the field artillery in action. Boom. Boom. Boom. . . . It was enough to scare, not just the pitchers, but all of us to death."[14] Also years later Pirates pitcher Carmen Hill provided his account of the scene, with a particular twist. "Before the 1927 World Series opener, the Yankees were hitting balls out of the park all over in batting practice to intimidate us," he said. "They had special balls made just for that. When one of those balls came over to our dugout and we tried to get it, one of their men ran over and picked it up before we could get to it."[15]

Playing in 153 games, Lazzeri improved as a hitter in virtually every category, and he again was among the league leaders in several. He became a more selective hitter, with 14 fewer strikeouts and 15 more walks, and he raised his batting average by 34 points, to .309. He again hit 18 homers, good for a distant third place in the AL behind his record-setting teammates. His 102 RBIs were eighth best in the league, and his slugging average of .482 put him in a tenth-place tie with Cobb. He was third in stolen bases (22), only 5 fewer than league leader George Sisler and 2 fewer than Meusel.

Part of the Murderers' Row mystique stemmed from the team's ability to come from behind and win in the late innings. With games beginning at 3:30 p.m., their late-inning rallies occurred around five o'clock, giving birth to the term "five o'clock lightning." A classic example was the game on June 8 against the red hot White Sox, who came in trailing the Yankees by only two games. Lazzeri's two-run homer in the second gave the Yanks a 2–1 lead, but going into the bottom of the eighth Chicago had gone ahead, 9–5. In the eighth Lazzeri narrowed the margin to three by hitting an inside-the-park home run to the deepest part of Yankee Stadium. Chicago came right back with two in the ninth to stretch its lead to five. But in the bottom of the inning, after three singles and a double had given the New Yorkers three runs, Lazzeri came to the plate with Durst on first. "Poosh 'Em Up Tony" promptly greeted reliever "Sarge" Donnally with his third homer to tie the game. In the eleventh Durst tripled, Lazzeri was walked intentionally, and Morehart singled to drive in the winning run.

Lazzeri became the first Yankee, and only the sixth player in AL history, to hit three homers in a regular-season game. Not even Babe Ruth had accomplished the feat, though he would do so in the 1928 World Series. So extraordinary was the story at that time that it made sports-page headlines all across the North American continent, from Miami to Montreal to Saskatoon.

Already in his rookie season Lazzeri had established a reputation as the leader of the team, someone who could remain calm in the midst of a storm. But his calm demeanor belied the intense competitive fire that burned inside him. Here is how Gallico described what it was like for pitchers to face the twenty-three-year-old slugger who, he suggests, would have batted in the cleanup position on any other ball club: "Unlike the other players you have faced in this string, Lazzeri comes to the plate to fight *you* personally. His black eyes blaze from his olive brown face, his chin sticks out and he waves the old bludgeon in an unmistakable gesture that means *you*. . . . Tony is all temperament, fire, fight and push, a natural competitor and a natural born ballplayer. In his own way, he'll take it out of your hide and sap your energy and resistance as much as Ruth and Gehrig will. Against Lazzeri, you are suddenly embroiled in a deeply emotional personal conflict."[16]

In his sophomore season, Lazzeri got almost as much attention for his defense as he did for his hitting. He made early headlines by opening the season with his twenty-one-game errorless streak. After the streak ended on May 9, he was quoted as saying: "That run of perfect fielding was beginning to get on my nerves. It isn't human to play errorless baseball, and I'm a human being."[17] What particularly impressed writers in 1927 was Lazzeri's Swiss-knife versatility as an infielder, which had already been noted when he was in the Minors. In 1926, other than playing 6 games at short, he was at second for the other 149 games. In 1927, however, for much of June and into the middle of July, Lazzeri was missing from his regular position. Filling in for the injured Koenig and Dugan, he appeared in 38 games at shortstop and 9 at third base, reducing his time at second to 113 games.

In June the "Pickups and Putouts" column of the *Times* called Lazzeri "the best second baseman–shortstop–third baseman the Yanks have ever had, a cracking good ball player, a fighter and a good fellow as well as a star."[18] That same month Bill Slocum of the *New York American* wrote: "Leave out the eight circuit drives which has Tony in third place among American League clouters, excelled only by Babe Ruth and Lou Gehrig. Even without these spectacular socks, this former Coast Leaguer stands out today as one of the great players in the major leagues. Besides rating as the best second baseman in his league today, he can perform at third base and shortstop as if he had always specialized in these positions. And what an arm!"[19]

No less an authority than Art Fletcher, a Yankees coach in 1927 who had been a defensive whiz at shortstop for John McGraw's Giants, considered Lazzeri to be as good an infielder as he ever saw. Frank Graham quoted him as saying: "You look at him at shortstop and you are sure that's where he belongs. Then you look at him at second base, and you're sure he belongs there. The long and short of it is that he is great on either side of the bag."[20]

In his syndicated column umpire Billy Evans nominated Lazzeri as "the most versatile ball player in the major leagues. Within one week I have seen Lazzeri shift from second to third, then short, and play all three positions with remarkable brilliancy." Above the column was a sketch of a ball field with Lazzeri's portrait pasted in all nine positions on the diamond.[21] In December 1927 F. C. Lane quoted Miller Huggins as saying, "Tony Lazzeri is a great ballplayer. I've seen a few better second basemen, but not many. He has a phenomenal pair of hands, a great throwing arm and he covers acres of ground."[22]

As in 1926, media references to Lazzeri's Italian heritage were once again common. In the April issue of *Baseball Magazine* Lane reported that when he asked Lazzeri the secret of his ability to hit so hard, Ty Cobb walked by and provided this answer: "It comes from eating spaghetti and drinking wop wine." In the December issue of that same magazine Lane recalled a recent conversation with Lazzeri in the dugout that was interrupted by Ruth, who, in attempting to get the attention of his Italian teammate, called him "you Spaghetti eating Dago Wop!"[23]

Lazzeri's three-homer performance on June 8 prompted numerous references to the young slugger's ethnic identity. A sidebar in *The Sporting News* proclaimed that "there was great excitement in the spaghetti belts of New York and San Francisco." The stereotypical Italian dish also figured in a UPI dispatch: "Spaghetti grew cold on the dinner tables of 'Little Italy' while the admirers of 'Poosh-em-up' Tony Lazzeri saw the husky Italian infielder hit three tremendous home runs."[24]

Not even Gallico, a fellow Italian American, could restrain himself when he described the scene as Lazzeri came to the plate with the winning run on third in the ninth inning of Game Four of the World Series: "Sure enough, fate has stored up this moment for the Wonderful Wop. He shall be decorated by Mussolini. He shall have as much spaghet [*sic*] as he can eat."[25]

Following the Yankees' World Series sweep of the Pirates, the *Literary Digest* included Lazzeri among the Yankee players it congratulated but didn't feel the need to mention his name, writing: "So hats off to Combs, Koenig, Ruth, Gehrig, Meusel, Push'm-Up-Wop, and all the rest of the celebrated batting order."[26]

While other writers were not hesitant to refer to Lazzeri as a "wop," the most persistent purveyor of ethnic descriptors was Marshall Hunt of the *Daily News*, which by then was the largest selling newspaper in America with a circulation of just under one million. On the occasion of Lazzeri's three-homer game on June 8, Hunt opened his story with these lines: "Spaghetti, spumoni, a garlic or two / Pastries with whipped cream atop / A garland, a cheer—for nothing, my lads / Is anything too good for the Wop! . . . Hence your agent sings the praises of the fiery Italian."[27] On July 5 the Senators scored five runs in the top of the first, but by the end of the seventh the Yanks had tied the score at 6–6. In the bottom of the ninth, with two out and none on, Lazzeri hit the game-winning homer off Hod Lisenbee. "The walloping wop, the spaghetti mangler, or whatever one chooses to call this magnificent infielder," Hunt wrote, "hoisted a magnificent home run into the left field stands and won the game. Whatta wop! Whatta team!"[28]

Granted, at that time terms such as "wop" and "dago," like epithets directed at other ethnic groups, were part of the common vernacular and not yet widely regarded as socially unacceptable slurs. They even appeared in such prestigious publications as the *New York Times* and *The Sporting News*. And it was common for ballplayers to hear those and other slurs hurled at them by opposing players and fans. Babe Pinelli (born Rinaldo Paolinelli), a Major League infielder who was involved in more than one fight, wrote in his autobiography: "From 1922 to 1925 I was the only Italian in the National League. I'd taken a riding from the bench jockeys and I'd had to keep my fist cocked."[29] Angelo

"Tony" Giuliani, a catcher who played against Lazzeri, told me: "The fans would holler out, 'dago,' 'wop,' 'guinea.' You got a little bit sizzled at that."[30] In 1927 Lane noted that "opposing catchers and coaches try to get Lazzeri's goat by calling him Dago and Wop."[31]

In the late nineteenth and early twentieth centuries baseball was declared by many as the embodiment of the American ideals of democracy and equal opportunity. In a 1923 article Fred Lieb concluded that "next to the little red school house, there has been no greater agency in bringing our races together than our national game, baseball." That same year *The Sporting News* asserted that with the exception of "a player of Ethiopian descent," baseball, "a democratic, catholic, real, American game," excluded no one. A player's nationality "is never a matter of moment if he can pitch, hit, or field."[32] In other words, with the exception of African Americans, all were welcome to step into the melting pot of baseball and assimilate.

However, there was a duality inherent in this description of baseball's open-arms policy. On the one hand, if all were welcome to take part in baseball, a player's ability to play the game should be the only criterion, and his ethnicity should have no relevance. Yet it was common for sportswriters to adopt common stereotypes in describing those early ballplayers. According to historian G. Edward White, "the ethnic origins of two groups of players [Italians and Jews] were treated as highly relevant and even as a basis for exclusion, for the first three decades of the twentieth century."[33] And, as noted in previous chapters, there was evidence of anti-Italian bias in baseball at the time Lazzeri began his career. By the time he became a Yankee, only fifteen men clearly identifiable as of Italian descent had ever played in the big leagues, and some of those changed their names to mask their ethnic identity.[34]

Lazzeri was not the first Major Leaguer to be identified in print as a "wop" or "dago," and he would not be the last. However, as the first major star of Italian descent and as one of the most prominent players on baseball's best and most widely publicized team, he received far more coverage than any previous Italian player. Especially at a time when anti-immigrant bigotry was still widespread and Italians were linked in the public consciousness with bootlegging mobsters, the ongoing references to Lazzeri's ethnicity, whether intentional or not, were a reminder that the "walloping wop spaghetti mangler" was somehow different from his teammates.

For some, one subtle marker of Lazzeri's difference was the color of his skin. Hunt, in the opening line of his story on the final game of the World Series, referred to Lazzeri as "a swarthy skinned boiler maker from San Francisco."[35] It was not the first or last time that his complexion was described as "swarthy," an adjective that bore negative connotations at a time when social scientists argued that the dark skin commonly associated with southern Italians raised questions about their racial makeup, thereby suggesting their inherent inferiority. (Keep in mind that although Lazzeri's parents were from northern Italy, Hunt routinely referred to him as a Neapolitan.) In 1912 Prescott Hall, one of the founders of the Immigration Restriction League and an advocate of eugenics, warned that "the south Italian . . . is one of the most mixed races in Europe, and is partly African, owing to the Negroid migration from Carthage to Italy."[36]

Of all the Yankees Lazzeri alone was routinely singled out because of his heritage. Gehrig, for example, who was about the same age as Lazzeri, was the son of German immigrants, but since Germans had been largely assimilated by then, his ethnicity was not a matter of discussion. On occasion Hunt would refer to him as "Herr Gehrig," but he did not use indelicate epithets equivalent to "wop" as he so frequently did with Lazzeri. In mingling praise with the subtle condescension implicit in his ethnic references, it's as if Hunt were simultaneously lauding "Signor Lazzeri" for his skill on the diamond and reminding readers that he was not quite one of us. In other words, Lazzeri may not have been Al Capone, but neither was he Lou Gehrig, Babe Ruth, or any other fully assimilated Yankee. He may have been a star in America's national pastime, but he remained, essentially, equal but separate, somewhere on the fringes of mainstream American culture.

Considering the virility and scope of nativist bigotry Italians faced at the time, it is not hard to understand the excitement caused by the sudden emergence of Lazzeri as a role model and source of ethnic pride for people who had long felt marginalized. Here was this son of immigrants who was not just playing at the highest level of the national pastime but was also being recognized as a superior player and a leader of the best team in baseball. And thanks to the increased newspaper coverage of baseball, as well as the rapid expansion of the media in the 1920s—radio, movie newsreels, magazines—Lazzeri benefitted from the newly created celebrity culture by becoming more widely known to a national audience than any other Italian player before him. That exposure and recognition in turn created greater public awareness of, and gave credibility to, the presence of Italians in the American game. In Lazzeri, Italians found a nationally recognized public figure who could counter the negative images that had been promulgated for decades.

Lazzeri of course was not the first celebrity with an Italian name to capture the attention of the American public. Neapolitan opera star Enrico Caruso, considered the greatest singer of his era, thrilled American audiences from 1903 to 1920, when he was the primary attraction at the Metropolitan Opera in New York and performed in theaters across the country. Rudolph Valentino, who had emigrated from Italy in 1913, achieved stardom in 1921 with his starring role in *The Sheik*, which established the standard for cinematic Latin lovers. He starred in several other movies before his untimely death at the age of thirty-one on August 23, 1926. As popular as both figures were, their public impact, while historic in their relative genres, was not nearly as widespread at that time as that of a star in baseball, the undisputed national pastime. Neither was as regularly in the public spotlight as a ballplayer like Lazzeri, who was in the news almost daily for at least six months a year. Nor did opera or films have the same widespread appeal as did baseball in the 1920s. For example, the caption of a photo of Caruso in the *New York Times* identified the singer as "the Babe Ruth of operatic tenors."[37]

Tony Lazzeri proved to be a game changer in more than one way. It is fair to say that it was Lazzeri and not, as many assume, Joe DiMaggio who first drew large numbers of Italian fans to the ballpark. Lieb, one of baseball's greatest chroniclers, wrote: "Many New York fans of Italian ancestry had hardly heard of baseball until Tony Lazzeri joined the Yankees."[38] At the end of Lazzeri's career with the Yankees, Slocum was more expansive: "Tony is the fellow who first brought the banana peels, the lunch baskets, the salami sandwiches and the bottles of homemade red wine to the towering three deck stadium on the right bank. That is to say, he's the guy who first made the Italian population of greater New York City big league baseball and Yankee conscious."[39]

This is not to say that no Italian Americans had been fans of the game before the arrival of Lazzeri. Fellow San Francisco native Ping Bodie (Francesco Pezzolo) had been popular with fans in his nine-year career with the White Sox and Yankees between 1911 and 1921, as much for his colorful personality as for his on-field performance. And Babe Pinelli, the Cincinnati Reds second baseman from 1922 to 1927, was cheered by local Italians who formed the Pinelli Rooters Club.

However, prior to Lazzeri's sudden fame in 1926, the great majority of immigrant Italians, who had little if any tradition of sports in the old country, considered baseball to be a waste of time and discouraged their sons from playing. Now suddenly they had someone in the national spotlight they could be proud of. One of their own was even rivaling the incomparable Bambino as the most popular player in the game. Not content to just read about the young star from California, for the first time thousands of first- and second-generation Italian Americans were heading to ballparks throughout the AL, cheering Lazzeri to "Poosh 'Em Up" and waving the Italian flag. A folk hero, Lazzeri made baseball acceptable to the immigrant generation. As early as June 1926, the *Brooklyn Daily Eagle* reported: "His countrymen flock to the stadium to watch him play. When Tony errs or fails to hit, they are his staunch defenders. When he pulls off a great fielding stunt or cracks out a hit, they are his loudest boosters."[40] As *Time* magazine would report years later, "Thousands of New York's Italians, who up to that time had been content with boxing and boccie [*sic*], began to stream into Yankee Stadium."[41]

Because of Lazzeri, Italians who had shunned baseball began to embrace the national pastime, one of the nation's most fundamental social institutions. And as time passed, their passion for the game was passed on to following generations of Italian Americans until the game became part of their DNA. While Major League Baseball was tapping into a whole new market, fans of Italian descent were moving a little closer to the American mainstream. Such was their pride in their newfound hero that Italian communities in three AL cities—Boston, Detroit, and New York—chose to honor the twenty-three-year-old star with banquets in 1927. The first was held on the evening of June 21, following "Tony Lazzeri Day" at Fenway Park. Between games of a doubleheader players of both teams and local dignitaries gathered near home plate as Lazzeri was presented a diamond ring. The banquet, which was sandwiched between back-to-back doubleheaders, drew more than five hundred people to the Elks Hotel. (Bad weather forced the Yankees to play four doubleheaders between June 21 and June 26.) The *Boston Globe* reported that "the walls of the hall literally rocked as young Tony Lazzeri, blushing and hesitant, acknowledged the greetings and the gifts," which included a check for $1,000. Among the dignitaries were the mayor of Boston, the governor of Massachusetts, and Fiorello La Guardia, then a U.S. Congressman and later mayor of New York City from 1934 to 1945.[42]

The speakers included Miller Huggins and Babe Ruth. Huggins praised his infielder for "being full of desire and ambition to get better in his profession, very modest in his accomplish-

ments," and concluded by saying that "there is no better example for the Italian youngsters of Boston to follow." Ruth followed
by saying that "everybody on our ball club loves Tony. There's
not a fellow who would say there's a wrong hair on his head."
Lazzeri, "in a voice which stern efforts could hardly keep from
trembling," expressed his gratitude and "promised that he would
try to prove himself worthy of the praise which was showered
upon him." Two days later at the Boston City Hall, Mayor Nichols presented Lazzeri with a key to the city.[43]

James Harrison noted that at the banquet Lazzeri "heard himself being compared to Columbus, Marconi, and Mussolini." Then,
describing a play Lazzeri (who had played short that day) had
made in the second game of the June 22 doubleheader, Harrison
added: "Tony didn't discover America, but, on the other hand,
Columbus never went back of third for an overthrow and killed
off the tying run at the plate in the ninth inning."[44]

On August 24 Lazzeri made sports-page headlines across the
country when his ninth-inning, two-out grand slam broke a tie
that gave the Yanks a 9–5 win, snapping the Tigers' thirteen-
game winning streak, the longest in the AL that season. Prior
to the next day's game "Tony Lazzeri Day" was celebrated at
Detroit's Navin Field, where the honoree was presented with a
large floral horseshoe and an elegant silver set that had the letter "L" engraved on each of its seven pieces. That evening the
local Italian community honored the young hero with a banquet
at the Book Cadillac Hotel. Noting the earlier banquet in Boston
as well as the current one in Detroit, Frank Graham wrote that
"all this is a trifle embarrassing to Tony, as modest a young man
as one could wish to know."[45] It is not surprising that Lazzeri's
remarks were brief. "I can't make a speech," he said. "I'm only a
ball player. But I promise you that out at that ball park I'll give
you the best I've got every day."[46]

In anticipation of the third "Tony Lazzeri Day," scheduled
for September 8 at Yankee Stadium, *United America*, a weekly
English-language newspaper for Italian Americans, encouraged

all its readers to attend the event. "Tell your friends about this day," wrote sports editor A. J. Palange. "You'll never forget Tony Lazzeri once you see him in action. He's a sensational ball player. MODEST. Just the kind of feller we've been waiting to see come into the big leagues."[47]

On "Lazzeri Day" the honoree fell victim to the jinx associated with such an occasion when he struck out his first two times up. But he redeemed himself in the fifth when he drove in what proved to be the winning run with a sacrifice fly, giving the Yankees a 2–1 win, their nineteenth in a row over the Browns. Hunt, with a curious allusion to Mussolini's regime in Italy, described the scene: "It was this same Fascist who drove in the winning run for the Yanks." And, for good measure, he added: "Before the game a band blasted woppy arias."[48] That evening more than one thousand guests paid tribute to Lazzeri at the Commodore Hotel in Manhattan. Players from both the Yankees and Browns attended, as well as representatives of Italian organizations from Boston, Providence, and Jersey City. The *Times* reported that "speeches lauding the brilliant work of the popular infielder and his exemplary conduct off and on the field rang through the grand ballroom," and when Lazzeri was presented a chest of silver worth $1,000, "there was a deafening roar."[49]

In 1931 Joe Vila looked back on that season of banquets honoring Lazzeri. "'Poosh 'em up, Tony!' which began as a supplication by his Italian admirers in this city, became a battle cry and resounded through the AL towns. And Tony captured the admiration and affections of the Italian quarters in those towns as the Yanks swept around the circuit." Regarding Lazzeri's response to the banquets, Vila wrote: "The emotions they aroused in him were those of wonderment and gratitude that at times threatened to overwhelm him. But never did he become even mildly obsessed with a sense of his own importance."[50]

Representing an entire ethnic group was not a mantle someone as reserved and private as Lazzeri would have sought or welcomed. He was not one to speak out about social injustice or much of anything else, for that matter. But whatever his attitude may have been—and here too there appears to be no public record of it—his unprecedented success as a Major League star of Italian descent at that particular moment in time made his status as a heroic figure inevitable.

Tony Lazzeri's big league career began in the midst of the Roaring Twenties. It was, as we have seen in previous chapters, a time when prejudice against immigrants from southern and eastern Europe was widespread among those who feared that their way of life was being threatened by unwelcome newcomers. But it was also a time of broad social and cultural change. The unprecedented prosperity of the post–World War I era generated a new sense of freedom and exuberance, as well as an unprecedented appetite for entertainment, including sports. The stock market was booming, booze was illegal but readily available, automobiles were providing newfound mobility, jazz was the new rage, and young people were challenging and often ignoring long-established social norms.

The year 1927 was marked by momentous events, with the story of Charles Lindbergh's solo flight from New York to Paris in May topping the list. On his return to New York "Lucky Lindy" was celebrated with a ticker-tape parade up Broadway on June 13 that drew a crowd estimated at four million. On August 23, after six years in prison, Sacco and Vanzetti were executed, bringing to an end one of the most controversial court cases in American history. In October millions of moviegoers were astonished when they saw, and heard, Al Jolson in *The Jazz Singer*, the first "talkie." In the world of sports 145,000 fans flocked to Soldier Field in Chicago from all over the country on September 22 and paid an estimated $2.8 million to watch the historic "long count" heavyweight championship fight between Jack Dempsey and Gene Tunney.

The other major sports story of course was the record-setting season by the Yankees, highlighted by Ruth's sixty home runs. The 1927 Murderers' Row Yankees were the right team in the right place at the right time. Situated in the financial, commercial, and media capital of the world, they dominated America's national pastime and embodied what became known as the golden age of sport, as well as the sophisticated urban aura of the Jazz Age. Newspapers responded to, and fostered, the growing appetite for entertainment by greatly expanding their coverage of sports, especially baseball. Noted sportswriter Dan Daniel said that "in those days baseball writing was the number-one assignment on any paper." Writers such as Grantland Rice, Damon Runyon, Heywood Broun, Ring Lardner, and Gallico were, in effect, inventing the profession of sportswriting. According to Gallico, "We had an overwhelming innocence in those days. Not only we sportswriters but the whole country. Everybody was happy. There was a big boom. You could let yourself go on sports."[51]

The kind of hero worship that sportswriters created then is unimaginable today. We simply know too much about athletes to maintain a simplistic image in our minds. The age of innocence, when we knew little about heroes other than what we read in the papers or magazines, is long gone. The pedestals have crumbled under the weight of 24/7 media coverage. But in the 1920s the so-called "Gee Whiz" school of sportswriting made legends of such stars as Dempsey, Red Grange, Bobby Jones, and Bill Tilden, glorifying them in florid prose. Dwarfing them all was Ruth, the single greatest celebrity in the history of American sports. The irrepressible man-child of insatiable appetites and boundless energy was the embodiment of the flash and fury of the Roaring Twenties, the poster boy of the Jazz Age.

Compared to Ruth—a large hot fudge sundae smothered in whipped cream and topped by a cherry—Lazzeri was a single scoop of plain vanilla. No egotism, no showboating. But that didn't prevent him from winning the hearts of baseball fans, and not just those of Italian descent. He was, according to Graham, "almost as big a drawing card as Babe Ruth."[52] He may not have been as colorful as the incomparable Bambino, but he was a leader who possessed dignity and humility. Having inherited from his parents the immigrant work ethic, he was a blue-collar infielder who went about his business efficiently and quietly, just as he had when working at the Main Street Iron Works. His low-key demeanor, the polar opposite of Ruth's and a contradiction of the stereotypical image of Italians as hot-blooded Latins, may well have enhanced his standing with the fans. And by replicating and in some ways surpassing his outstanding rookie-year performance, he established himself even more firmly as one of the best and most respected players in the Majors.

6

Playing through the Pain

T ony Lazzeri did not stay away from the baseball diamond for long following the 1927 World Series sweep over the Pirates. On October 12, one day after Babe Ruth and Lou Gehrig began their three-week nationwide barnstorming tour with a game in Trenton, New Jersey, he began his own barnstorming tour with a team that featured "other Italian ball players from the metropolitan district," as well as Yankees teammate Ray Morehart.[1] The tour began in Long Island City, where Lazzeri's team lost to the semi-pro Springfield Club, 3–2. On October 17, the *New York Times* reported that the Tuckahoe baseball team, "Lazzeri's nine," defeated the Yonkers Knights of Columbus team before a crowd of seven thousand in Yonkers, New York. The only other mention of the tour I found was a sidebar noting that "Tony Lazzeri and his bunch of barnstorming 'Wops' were insulted in a Newark Hotel. They were served a dinner without spaghetti on the menu."[2]

Once back home in San Francisco, Lazzeri continued to appear in exhibition and benefit games. The Ruth-Gehrig tour was met with great fanfare when the two sluggers arrived in San Francisco on October 21. In every stop on the tour the Yankees sluggers would each lead a team usually consisting of local amateur and semi-pro ballplayers, with Ruth's Bustin' Babes in black uniforms and Gehrig's Larrupin' Lous in white. In San Francisco, however, several current and former Minor and Major Leaguers from the Bay Area were enlisted. A game was scheduled for October 22 at San Francisco's Recreation Park, followed the next day by a morning game in Oakland and an afternoon game in San Francisco, all to benefit the *San Francisco Examiner*'s Christmas Fund.

On October 19 the *Oakland Tribune* reported that Lazzeri would play short for the Bustin' Babes on Sunday, but on October 22, the eve of the Oakland game, it listed either Lazzeri or Loris Baker of the San Francisco Seals at shortstop for the Larrupin' Lous.[3] The circumstances are unclear, but there is no mention of Lazzeri in game reports of any of the three games in San Francisco and Oakland. In any case it is unlikely that Lazzeri played in either of the games on October 23 since that same day he was in Los Angeles, where he was being honored by the local Italian American community at White Sox Park. Built in 1924 by Joe and John Pirrone, Italian American owners of a wholesale fruit business, White Sox Park was the home of the California Winter League, which Joe had organized to attract Negro League teams to play against local semi-pro teams at a time when black teams were not allowed to play in PCL ballparks.[4]

The game on "Lazzeri Day" pitted the Pirrone All Stars, featuring Lazzeri and Bob Meusel, against the Philadelphia Hilldale Giants, which the *Los Angeles Times* described as "a club composed of colored diamond stars." In fact the Giants, a member of the Eastern Colored League, had won the 1925 Negro League World Series, defeating the Kansas City Monarchs. Two of its biggest stars were in the lineup in Los Angeles that day: center fielder Clint Thomas and catcher Biz Mackey. (Acknowledged as one of the elite catchers of his era, Mackey was elected to the Baseball Hall of Fame in 2006.) The game drew a capacity crowd of seven thousand fans, including "a large delegation of local Italian admirers of Lazzeri," who saw the Pirrone team win, 5–1. Prior to the game the Italian consul presented a gift to Lazzeri.[5]

A week later Lazzeri played in a benefit game at Recreation Park (home field of the San Francisco Seals) pitting a squad of Major League stars against a team of PCL stars. The purpose was to raise funds for the Professional Baseball Players of America, which provided support for ailing and indigent ballplayers. Lazzeri drove in two of the Major Leaguers' runs with a homer and single in a 5–3 loss to the Minor League squad.[6]

In January 1928 it was announced that Lazzeri had agreed to coach the baseball team at St. Ignatius College. A Jesuit school founded in 1844 that would be renamed the University of San Francisco in 1930, St. Ignatius began fielding a baseball team in 1907. The plan was for Lazzeri to work with the team from early February until he left for spring training. Regarding Lazzeri's role as coach, *The Ignatian*, which served as the school's yearbook, alumni magazine, and literary journal, wrote: "The St. Ignatius ballyard took on a big league glow this spring, with Tony Lazzeri, San Francisco's gift to the New York Yankees, acting as mentor of the Gray Fog nine." The article included photos of Lazzeri, as well as the fifteen players on the team. Lazzeri's time as coach was relatively brief as bad weather interrupted practice. According to *The Ignatian*, "after about two weeks of intermittent workouts, he was forced to pack up and hie himself to the training camp of the world's champions. At his departure, the club was taken over by Mr. L. M. Malone, S. J., moderator of athletics, who remained as pilot throughout the season."

In one of the biggest stories of the offseason it was announced in early January that Colonel Ruppert startled Yankees opponents by paying what John Kieran of the *New York Times* called a "price only mentioned in whispers," but was rumored to be at least $140,000, to the Oakland Oaks of the PCL for the contracts of their highly touted double play combo of shortstop Lyn Lary and second baseman Jimmie Reese.[7] Why, others wondered, would the Yankees pay so much for two prospects when Mark Koenig and Lazzeri, their own well-established middle infielders now being dubbed by some writers as the "keystone kids," were only twenty-three and twenty-four years old? Ruppert pointed out that Lary and Reese would not be delivered to the Yankees until 1929 and were simply insurance should something happen to Lazzeri or Koenig. Regardless, news of the acquisition disturbed the management of other teams that were also interested in signing the two prospects. They argued that there was little hope for them to overtake a franchise that could afford to spend so much money to buy young prospects merely as insurance for the future rather than to meet an immediate need. In effect they were accusing the Yankees of establishing a monopoly.

In early February newspapers were identifying Lazzeri as one of the Yankees who had yet to sign a contract, along with Hoyt, Combs, and Koenig. One report claimed that since Lazzeri had established himself as one of the best infielders in the AL, he was looking for more than the two-year contract at $11,000 a year he had reportedly been offered.[8] Urban Shocker had announced that he was retiring to become a radio broadcaster, but Miller Huggins was hoping he was bluffing and would return.

By the time the team held its first workout on February 27, only Lazzeri, Hoyt, and Shocker remained unsigned. (What few knew at the time was that a heart ailment had caused Shocker to lose a lot of weight, which he was trying to regain in order to return to baseball.)[9] By March 1, the deadline for players to report, Lazzeri and Hoyt had still not appeared in St. Petersburg. Will Murphy outlined Huggins's approach to his forthcoming negotiations with his lone remaining holdouts: "He will reason with the recalcitrants," wrote Murphy, noting that the Yankees manager was a licensed attorney. "Though he may lack the courtroom presence of a Clarence Darrow, [Huggins] can, when put to it, plead a case with the best of them."[10]

Soon after reaching the Yankees' camp, Lazzeri met with Huggins, after which Murphy wrote: "Ten minutes today under the persuasive influence of Mr. Huggins' reasoning sufficed to bring Tony to the point of signing a two-year contract for more money than he ever earned."[11] The terms of the agreement were not made public, but it would later be confirmed that Lazzeri signed for $12,500 a year. After several meetings with Huggins, Hoyt signed a two-year contract on March 15 for $16,000 a year. Shocker finally signed on April 24, thirteen days after the start of the season, but with the proviso that his salary would not begin until he was in shape to pitch. Sadly the veteran spitballer made only one appearance for the Yankees—two innings in relief against Washington on May 30—as the long-term effects of his heart ailment caught up to him. His condition worsened, and on July 4 he was given his unconditional release.

After being an iron man in his first two seasons, playing in all but one of the Yankees' 309 games, Lazzeri faced a new challenge in 1928. For the first time he had to deal with a serious injury, one that not only forced him to miss a number of games, but even threatened to end his career at the age of twenty-four. Injuries, it seems, were contagious within the Yankees clubhouse in 1928, keeping key position players (Meusel, Dugan, and Koenig) as well as pitchers (Pennock and Moore) out of the lineup for extended periods. Ed Barrow wrote that by the time they won the pennant, the Yankees "were held together by wires, pins, string, and sticking plaster."[12]

Only ten days after Lazzeri arrived in camp, he and Koenig were confined to the hospital with blistered feet. Then on March 27 Lazzeri sprained his back while swinging at a pitch in batting practice. The injury was serious enough for the Yankees to send him directly to New York to rest rather than make the annual spring tour as the team headed north. Unable to play in the first seven games of the regular season, Lazzeri was replaced at second by Leo Durocher, a brash rookie from West Springfield, Massachusetts, who acquired the well-earned nickname of "Leo the Lip" for his incessant chatter and biting bench jockeying.[13] In his three seasons in the Minors he had established a reputation as a "great field, no hit" shortstop. However, hitting in the seventh spot in the order, he surprised everyone by going 12 for 27 with 6 RBIs in those first seven games. Appearing in 102 games over the season, Durocher would compile a .270 average, well above his career average of .247. Babe Ruth, never a fan of the cocky infielder, dubbed his weak-hitting teammate "the All-American Out."

Lazzeri had not appeared in a game for twenty-six days when he finally made his debut on April 21 at Yankee Stadium against Connie Mack's Philadelphia A's, once again considered the Yankees' most serious challengers. The Yankees had spoiled the A's season-opening series in Philadelphia by winning both games. The A's returned the favor when they beat the Yankees 2–1 in their home opener on April 20, with Lefty Grove pitching a complete game. Prior to the game the Yankees' World Series pennant was raised, and Lou Gehrig was given a $1,000 check as the 1927 AL MVP.

After his long layoff Lazzeri got his season off to a hot start the next day. Back in his usual sixth spot in the order, he hit two doubles, but the team managed only six hits off Rube Walberg in a 10–0 loss. After two days off due to rain, on April 24 Lazzeri again went 2 for 3 and drove in two runs in a 4–0 win over Washington. He followed that up the next day by driving in three runs with a single and triple as the Yanks beat the Senators, 12–4. In a sidebar adjacent to that day's game story, Murphy described the construction work on the new left-field stands at Yankee Stadium as the "staccato music of riveting machines and carpenters' hammers." Such noise "may bother some players, but not Tony Lazzeri. 'Push 'Em Up' used to work for his father in a San Francisco bay shipyard. [Actually, as noted above, he worked *with* his father in a boilermaker factory.] He says the racket makes him think of home."[14] At the end of April Lazzeri was batting .474 with seven RBIs and a .565 on-base percentage in his first five games.

Postponements forced the Yankees to play four doubleheaders between May 21 and 25, including back-to-back twin bills against the A's on May 24 and 25, followed by single games on May 26 and 28. Going into that series the A's had won five in a row and trailed the Yanks by 3½ games. In the first game on May 24, with Grove (6–1) on the mound, Lazzeri drove in six runs on two singles and a bases-clearing triple that provided the winning runs in a 9–5 win. In the nightcap homers by Lazzeri and Ruth provided the only New York runs in a 5–2 loss. The next day three

RBIs by Gehrig and a complete game by Pennock led New York to a 4–2 win in the opener. Then Ruth and Dugan each hit two home runs and drove in all nine runs as the Yanks routed the A's, 9–2, in the nightcap.

The fifth game matched two veteran spitballers: thirty-eight-year-old Stan Coveleski, who had won all three of his previous starts for the Hugmen, and forty-two-year-old John Quinn, who had won his previous five starts. And just as the A's top two starters, Grove and Walberg, had been, in the words of James C. Isaminger, "cannon fodder for the heavy Yank artillery" earlier in the series, so too was Quinn, who gave up six hits and five runs in two innings. Lazzeri hit a solo homer in the fifth as the Yanks coasted to a 7–4 win. In his "Shibe Park Shorts" column, Isaminger noted: "Cops were posted in the upper pavillion to curb offensive remarks of some patrons with ingrown faces who think that the purchase of a ticket gives them license to say anything. Decent spectators have complained."[15] In the sixth and final match New York beat Grove for the second time in the series, 11–4. Lazzeri hit his third homer in as many days, drove in two runs, and scored twice. For the series he was 12 for 27 with ten RBIs, and his batting average stood at .368. By winning five of six, the Yankees stretched their lead to eight games.

In July the *Los Angeles Times* offered high praise for the Yankees infielder: "Tony Lazzeri is rapidly winning recognition as one of the greatest second basemen the game has ever known. The young gentleman from Telegraph Hill is pounding the ball harder now than he ever pounded iron and steel in his days as a boilermaker."[16] That same day the Yankees met the second-place A's in a doubleheader at Yankee Stadium before sixty thousand fans. In the opener, a 12–6 win for the Yanks, Gehrig hit two homers and Lazzeri, who entered the game with a .344 batting average, fourth-best in the AL, went 4 for 4 with two doubles and scored twice. He topped that in the nightcap by hitting two homers (his seventh and eighth) and driving in four runs in an 8–4 win. The sweep gave the New Yorkers a 13½ game lead, their largest of the season.

After going 2 for 2 in the July 2 game against the Senators, Lazzeri was hitting .368, trailing only Goose Goslin in the AL. He also led the league in stolen bases and was third in RBIs, slugging average, and triples. With his name appearing regularly near the top of the AL's batting leaders list, Lazzeri was getting increasing press coverage nationwide.

A major sign of Lazzeri's national celebrity status was his selection to appear in ads for Lucky Strike cigarettes in 1928. While occasional examples of baseball players endorsing products can be found as early as the 1870s, it was the unprecedented fame of Babe Ruth and clever marketing by his agent, Christy Walsh, in the 1920s that triggered a burgeoning source of income for athletes. Thanks to the precedent set by Ruth, others were able to cash in on their celebrity by lending their names to a variety of brands. One of the products for which athletes were most commonly enlisted as pitchmen was cigarettes. In 1928 Lucky Strike launched the most aggressive tobacco advertising campaign ever seen, part of which was a series of five full-color trolley car and bus ads. Measuring 10 inches x 20 inches, these metal ads were like mini billboards that appeared along the upper walls above the windows of the vehicles. It is significant to note that Lazzeri was one of only five ballplayers—along with Lloyd and Paul Waner, Harry Heilmann, and Lefty Grove, all future Hall of Famers—to appear in Lucky Strike's "Cream of the Crop" ads. In the ad Lazzeri, identified as "New York Yankees Star Infielder," is seen to the right of the red Lucky Strike logo, reaching out with the ball to tag an unseen base runner. He is quoted as saying, "I like Luckies. They are mild and mellow."

Lazzeri also appeared in other promotions for Lucky Strike, including a print ad that resembles an autographed baseball card, with a smiling portrait of Lazzeri tucked behind a pack of Luckies. As in the trolley ad, Lazzeri asserts that he likes Luckies because they are mild and mellow. A full-page version appeared on the back cover of the October 26, 1928, issue of *Life* magazine. Another version adds an intriguing incentive: "For a slender figure—Reach for a Lucky instead of a sweet." There is also a print ad featuring Lazzeri in uniform in the act of making a throw. In this version Lazzeri offers a longer written endorsement above his signature: "After a tough day at the ball park one needs mental as well as physical relaxation. I get mine smoking 'Lucky Strike' cigarettes. I smoke one of them; two of them; three of them; and I like 'em. They never bother my throat." As for Lazzeri's personal smoking habit, a brief bio in a 1932 *Sporting News* column ends with: "Smokes very little, does not drink."[17]

The selection of Lazzeri to represent what would be the top-selling cigarette brand in the United States during the 1930s and '40s was an indication that this son of immigrants had achieved not only fame on the diamond, but also some measure of acceptance by mainstream America.

Lazzeri was enjoying another great year when suddenly his season was turned upside down. On July 11, in the sixth inning of the first game of a doubleheader with Detroit, after drawing a walk, Lazzeri injured his right shoulder diving back to first base on an attempted pickoff. (To add insult to injury, he was called out.) One report called it a wrenched muscle, another a ripped muscle.[18] At first it was estimated that he would be out of the lineup for a few days, but that prognosis was overly optimistic. Except for a pinch-hit appearance on July 18, he did not return to the lineup until July 22. In his absence Durocher again filled in at second. After he returned to the lineup, Lazzeri hit .357 for the remainder of July, but ultimately the strain caught up with him, especially after he played in nine games in six days between July 22 and 28 thanks to three doubleheaders.

After starting in eleven straight games, Lazzeri was out of the lineup for the July 31 game against Cleveland. When the Yankees went to St. Louis on August 1 for a series against the Browns, on the advice of Dr. Robert W. Hyland, team physician for the

Browns and a specialist in athletic injuries, Lazzeri entered St. John's Hospital to undergo several days of diathermy treatment. (A relatively new form of physical therapy at the time, diathermy uses high-frequency electrical current to treat tissue damage.) An X-ray of the shoulder had shown the injury to be more serious than previously thought, and Dr. Hyland warned Lazzeri that if left untreated, it threatened to end his career.

In mid-August James Harrison discussed Huggins's frustration over some aspects of his team: "Mr. Huggins has had some bitter disappointments. His reserve strength, for one thing, failed to materialize. When Lazzeri was hurt, the infield collapsed for lack of capable substitutes. Durocher can field but he is a miserable hitter. Cy Moore has been worthless, Meusel has disappointed and the catching has been decidedly minor-league-ish."[19]

Following his treatment in St. Louis, Lazzeri made his first appearance on August 11 as a pinch hitter but did not return to the starting lineup until August 15. Over the next nine games, including two doubleheaders, all as a starter, he went 5 for 29 (a .172 average) with one double and one home run, his tenth and last of the season. It was apparent that Lazzeri was still hurting and that something had to be done to minimize the risk of permanent damage. In late August the headline of Harrison's story in the *Times* announced: "LAZZERI FORCED OUT FOR REST OF SEASON." Huggins was quoted as saying: "He is practically through for this year. I gave him two weeks' rest with medical treatment; then he played a week and now the old trouble has returned. I consider that conclusive proof that he cannot play regularly. Besides affecting his throwing, Tony's sore shoulder has interferred [sic] with his hitting and fielding. A long rest will cure him; abuse of the shoulder might result in permanent injury." Harrison added that "Lazzeri will be used as a pinch hitter and might go to the keystone sack for an inning or two. His loss will be a body blow to the Yanks in their efforts to stave off the Athletics."[20]

At the time Lazzeri began the diathermy treatment in St. Louis, he was hitting .356, third best in the AL. But as the season progressed, the effects of his injury became more evident. He appeared in only twelve games in August and hit a paltry .194. But being the competitor that he was, Lazzeri was not ready to give up on the season. Acting on the advice of Huggins and coach Art Fletcher, he went to Philadelphia in late August to be treated by Dr. Charles J. Van Ronk, an osteopath. "The doctor said I tore a set of tendons in the upper part of the shoulder," said Lazzeri. "He said it would hurt a lot to put them back, but that it had to be done if I was to be able to throw a ball again. So I said, 'Go ahead.' But it sure hurt. Worse than when I hurt the shoulder sliding back to first during that Detroit game." The doctor ordered Lazzeri not to pick up a bat or ball for five days, but said that after that he would be able to play "without feeling any effects of the injury."[21] However, a *Daily News* photo showed a shirtless Lazzeri, who had been out of the lineup since August 26, being treated with a heat lamp. The caption: "Tony Lazzeri, young Kid Lightning, will play only [a] few more games this season, they say. Doc Woods, Yankee trainer, is baking Tony's bum shoulder with the torn ligament, but it doesn't help much. Yanks will miss this boy."[22]

Notwithstanding the physical setbacks he endured in 1928, Lazzeri did not lose his sense of humor or his love of pranks. In mid-August Bill Dickey, a twenty-one-year-old catcher from Louisiana, made his debut with the Yankees. He would earn his way into the Hall of Fame over his seventeen seasons with New York, but in 1928 he was just a raw rookie, and an easy target for Lazzeri. Years later he would tell the story: "Tony was a fellow who liked to play jokes on people. I went out to the clubhouse—this was my first year with the Yankees—and my shoes was nailed to the floor. You know, shoes in those days cost $17, or something like that. That was a lot of money and it kind of made me mad. Tony said to me, 'Ruth done it.'" The next day Dickey brought an egg to the clubhouse and put it in one of Ruth's shoes.

In comes the Babe and off comes his clothes, and everybody's sitting there watching. He put on the shoe without the egg in it first, and then he put on the second. He took that shoe off, held it up, and poured the egg out. It seemed like it took a minute to get the egg out of the shoe. His face got red and he said, "I can lick the dirty so-and-so that put that egg in my shoe." He walked up and down the clubhouse, still cussin'. I waited till he got way down to the other end and I said, "Babe, I put that egg in your shoe." He walked back and got real close to me, and then he busted out laughing. You should have heard that clubhouse laugh. And the funny part of it was that it was Lazzeri that nailed my shoes to the floor. I found that out a little later.[23]

One of Lazzeri's favorite targets was none other than his good friend, Babe Ruth. Waite Hoyt recounted this story in his foreword to H. G. Fleming's history of the 1927 Yankees:

It was the custom of the regulars, after two were out in their turns at bat, to scale to the second step of the dugout, ready to charge out to their positions when the third out had been made. . . . Ruth usually carried a large bandana handkerchief in a rear uniform pocket, and one day the rag was hanging over the rim. Tony Lazzeri, who enjoyed needling the Babe, borrowed a match from a spectator in an adjacent box seat and set fire to the rag. After the third out had been made, Ruth trotted to right field with actual smoke issuing from his rear. It took the big guy several moments to discover the joke, and the "bench" was hysterical.[24]

Lazzeri's mischievous side was also noted by columnist John Kieran: "If a player thinks it's bad luck to lend a glove, Tony always manages to mistake it for his own as he goes out to practice. If a player is cherishing a valuable bat, Tony is caught with it half way to the plate in batting practice."[25]

While the Yankees' 13½ game lead over the A's on July 1 looked insurmountable, that month Philadelphia fought back, winning

25 of 33 to close the gap to 5½ games, and one month later the A's stood within 2½ games of the faltering Yanks. By the end of June the Yankees had amassed their huge lead by winning 50 and losing only 16, but in July they slipped to a 20–15 record, followed by 14–11 in August. When the dust cleared on September 7, following a twin loss to the Senators by the Yankees and a twin win over Boston by the A's, the teams were deadlocked at 87–47. And when the A's again beat the hapless Red Sox twice the next day, they slipped into first place, setting the scene for yet another doubleheader on September 9, this one matching the two pennant contenders at Yankee Stadium.

The crucial series was portrayed in the press as a meeting not only of the top two teams in the AL, but also between their two managers: the venerable sixty-eight-year-old Cornelius McGillicuddy, the "Tall Tactician" with perfect posture and starched collar, fighting for his first pennant since 1914, and Huggins, the "Mighty Mite" who had led the Yanks to five pennants and two World Series titles in the previous seven seasons. The Mackmen versus the Hugmen. While the veterans (Cobb, Speaker, and Collins) were still on the A's roster, Mack had chosen to bench them and go mainly with his younger players down the stretch, led by Jimmie Foxx, Al Simmons, and Mickey Cochrane. (Both of the senior citizens in Mack's outfield—Cobb [forty-one] and Speaker [forty]—would retire at the end of the season.) Even though the Yankees had beaten the A's in thirteen of their eighteen meetings, going into the series the odds seemed to favor the A's; their pitching was better, and their young sluggers had been recently outhitting the Yankees.

Three days before the fateful matchup, Walter Trumbull placed part of the blame for the Yankees' slump on the absence of Lazzeri: "The San Francisco Italian was the kingpin which held the team together. Both his spirit and his bat are missed. Without Lazzeri, Koenig isn't within 30 per cent of his full efficiency. Durocher is a good fielder but he can't hit with Lazzeri nor is he as inspirational to his team."[26] In his syndicated column Joe Williams concurred about the domino effect of Lazzeri's absence. Without Lazzeri, the Yankees infield "became slow and sluggish. Not only was there a weakness at second, . . . there was a more striking weakness at short, where Koenig, missing the co-operation of his injured team mate, floundered and staggered." In Williams's opinion, Lazzeri, "who shouldn't even be in a uniform," returned to the lineup "chiefly because he wanted to steady his buddy and coax him back into playing the kind of baseball that made him a standout among the shortstops earlier in the season." Williams also addressed the idea, suggested by some, that Lazzeri had come back because of the money he and his teammates would lose if they didn't make it to the World Series. "Yes, this may have been a consideration, though I am pleased to doubt it. Lazzeri is one of those youngsters who like to play ball. And he has a lot of pride in the Yankees, the only big league team he has ever played with."[27]

On the morning of the September 9 doubleheader an AP story expressed surprise at the unexpected return of Lazzeri, who had made his first start since August 25 the previous day against the Senators: "Quite the most surprising move by Miller Huggins in his desperate stand to save the American League championship and another chance at the world's title was sending Tony Lazzeri back to the wars. Not two days ago the little Miller was declaring he would rather lose a dozen pennants than chance a permanent injury to his Italian star—but there was Tony at second, lame shoulder and all, apparently the beneficiary of [a] remarkably rapid cure."[28]

Exactly what condition Lazzeri was in remains unclear, but it is certain his shoulder was still a major concern. Nevertheless, he had been lobbying hard to get back in the lineup. In his account of the September 8 game, Marshall Hunt wrote that "there was life in that Yankee skeleton yesterday, and the Yank array looked more like the Varsity team than it had in a long while, for the fiery Wop, Tony Lazzeri, had begged Mr. Huggins to let him put on his red underwear again and see if that would have any benefitting effect on the Senators."[29] In spite of the limitations caused by Lazzeri's bum shoulder—he was forced to throw underhand, and his power was greatly diminished—not to mention the threat of permanent injury, Huggins obviously wanted his second baseman in the lineup, knowing that regardless of how he performed with his bat and glove, his very presence on the field provided a measure of stability and inspiration to a team that was struggling without him.

The doubleheader had generated so much excitement among fans that police had to be called in on September 6 to quell the crowd rushing the Yankees ticket offices on Forty-Second Street. In anticipation of a crowd of over eighty thousand, emergency seating was installed in Yankee Stadium, and extra subway service was provided. The turnout was repeatedly identified as the biggest crowd in baseball history. Early newspaper accounts estimated the crowd as high as ninety thousand before later citing the official attendance as 85,265 (81,622 paid), including thousands of fans who had come from Philadelphia on special trains. (To put that figure in perspective, the average AL attendance in 1928 was 6,841.) As many as 50,000–100,000 more without tickets were estimated to be outside the stadium, where mounted police worked to control the crowd. That same day newspapers announced the death of Urban Shocker at the age of thirty-seven.[30]

In the opener of the doubleheader Lazzeri was in his usual sixth spot, behind Meusel. He had gone hitless in five at bats in the Washington series, but in the opener against the A's he more than justified his desire to be back in the lineup. He went 3 for 4 and drove in two runs in the Yankees' 5–0 win behind the shutout pitching of George Pipgras. In the fifth he hit a leadoff double, then drove in Gehrig in the sixth and Ruth in the eighth with singles. The *Philadelphia Inquirer* called him "the motor of the Yank team in this game. He made his presence felt every minute."[31] Lazzeri was hitless in the second game, which the Yankees won 7–3 on the strength of Meusel's eighth-inning grand slam, pushing them back into first place by 1½ games. William J. Chipman of the AP wrote that the presence of Lazzeri "patently perked up the play of the champions, both defensively and offensively, but the gallant signor was playing largely on his grit. He had to give way to a substitute in each contest and there is no telling how long he will be able to continue playing even in parts of games."[32]

Seated in the grandstand behind home plate that day, and presumably every day of the series with the A's, was Maye Lazzeri, along with the wives of Combs and Meusel. Paul Gallico, writing about the doubleheader that drew "the biggest crowd that baseball has ever known," concluded his column with a "Fashion Note." "Mrs. Anthony Lazzeri was attired becomingly in a brown suit with lace collar and brown hat to match," he wrote, adding that she "clapped her hands almost all of the time."[33]

Following a day off on Monday, the series resumed on September 11. The Yankees were shut out over the first six innings by Grove and trailed 3–0 but came back with one run in the seventh when Lazzeri scored after reaching on a fielder's choice. Then in the eighth, after New York tied the score at 3–3, with Gehrig on second, Ruth hit his forty-ninth homer to win the game, 5–3.

Norman Macht wrote that the verbal abuse that the two teams had been exchanging during the series turned physical following the game. When the A's headed into the Yankees dugout to get to the tunnel that led to their locker room, Lazzeri approached pitcher Howard Ehmke:

> There had been ill will between them last year when, Lazzeri later claimed, Ty Cobb had tipped him off that Ehmke intended to throw at him in a game at Yankee Stadium. . . . As they reached the steps, Lazzeri said, "Hey, what are you riding me for?" Ehmke, who was not a bench jockey, replied, "I haven't even been thinking about you, much less riding you." Lazzeri pushed against him and continued ranting. "Say, if you're looking for trouble," Ehmke said, "I'm not the guy to run away." He threw down his glove and sweater and started after Lazzeri. Just then [Mickey] Cochrane tackled Lazzeri and brought him down. Babe Ruth picked up Lazzeri and dragged him into the clubhouse.[34]

Philadelphia avoided a sweep by taking the fourth game, 4–3. Lazzeri was 1 for 3 and drove in a run on a bases-loaded walk in the eighth to tie the game at 3–3 before Max Bishop gave the A's the win with a ninth-inning homer.

After overcoming a 13½ game deficit to reach first place, the A's fell from the mountaintop and left town trailing the rejuvenated Yanks by 1½ games, never to take back the lead. The Yankees would play the final fifteen games of the season on the road, winning ten. The A's faced a more daunting season-ending schedule, playing their last twenty-four games away from home. Before arriving in New York on September 9, they had won five of their first seven on the road. After losing three of four to the Yankees, they went 8–5, finishing the season at 98–55, 2½ games behind New York. The Yankees clinched their third straight pennant on September 28 with a win over the Tigers. It was not yet time for Mr. Mack to return to the top of the baseball world.

After limping to the pennant, the Yankees faced the Cardinals in a rematch of their 1926 epic World Series battle. As they had been in 1927, the weary and wounded Hugmen were considered the underdogs, even though the common perception was that they were, on paper at least, the better club. But they were hardly a healthy bunch. Lazzeri continued to play in severe pain, Koenig had a sore ankle, Ruth a sore knee, and Dugan, whose knee continued to bother him and who was in a bad slump, had been replaced at third by Gene Robertson. To make matters worse, in the nightcap of a doubleheader at Detroit on September 27, Combs suffered a broken right wrist when he collided with the outfield wall and appeared to be out for the rest of the season. As for the pitching staff, Pennock continued to be out of action due to neuritis, and Wilcy Moore, the surprise star of 1927, was hampered all season with a sore arm, won only four games, and placed himself on the voluntary retired list before the season ended. The Cardinals, who featured two power hitters in NL MVP Jim Bottomley (who led the league in RBIs and tied for the lead with thirty-one homers) and Chick Hafey (who hit twenty-seven home runs), as well as a keystone combination of two future Hall of Famers, Rabbit Maranville at short and Frankie Frisch at second, had also struggled to win the pennant, edging the Giants by two games. Nevertheless, given the multiple injuries to the Yankees lineup, J. Roy Stockton boldly predicted that "the Cardinals are going to have a short but pleasant journey to the championship of the world."[35]

Stockton was right about the brevity of the Series, if not the outcome. For the second consecutive year the Yankees swept the Series in lopsided fashion. Led by record-setting performances by Ruth and Gehrig, they outscored the Cardinals 27–10. In the opener, with the exception of a solo home run by Bottomley, Hoyt shut them down with a 4–1, complete-game gem. Grover Cleveland Alexander, the hero of the 1926 Series, was the starter in Game Two, with twenty-four-game winner Pipgras pitching for New York. Now forty-one, "Old Pete," who had posted a 16–9 record in the regular season, lasted only 21/3 innings, giving up six hits and eight runs, as the Yanks won, 9–3. Lazzeri, facing his nemesis for the first time since the 1926 Series, grounded out twice before Alexander left the game.

When the Series moved to St. Louis for the next two games, a political sidebar was introduced at Game Three. Babe Ruth had created a brief furor in September when he refused to have his photo taken with Herbert Hoover, the Republican presidential candidate, claiming that he was a supporter of New York governor Al Smith, Hoover's Democratic opponent. (Lazzeri also supported Smith, as did several other teammates, and on at least one occasion he and Ruth promoted Smith's candidacy on radio in New York City.)[36] A photo in the *St. Louis Post-Dispatch* showed Ruth, Lazzeri, and seven other players, as well as Eddie Bennett, the Yankees batboy and mascot, lined up next to the stands at Sportsman's Park before the start of the game. Each of them was holding up a long stick with a single letter attached to the top. From left to right the letters spelled out "FOR AL SMITH." The caption read: "The Yankees do a little boosting for another New Yorker before the game."[37]

The Yanks completed the sweep in St. Louis. In the first game Gehrig hit two home runs and drove in three while Tom Zachary pitched the third consecutive complete game in the 7–3 win. When rain forced a postponement of Game Four, Huggins was able to start Hoyt after four days of rest. St. Louis held a 2–1 lead after six, but the Yankees scored six runs in the next two innings. Ruth hit three home runs (as he had done in the fourth game of the 1926 Series) and Gehrig one, with Hoyt pitching his second complete game as the Yanks won again by a score of 7–3 to close out the Series. In addition to hitting three home runs and avoiding soda bottles tossed at him from the stands, Ruth closed out the game with a spectacular catch of a fly ball down the left-field line. As of this writing, Gehrig's slugging percentage of 1.727 remains the all-time best in a World Series, with Ruth's 1.375 in third place. Gehrig's four homers are one off the record of five, and Ruth set a World Series record (which stood until 2013) with a .625 batting average, while Gehrig hit .545.

In spite of the persistent shoulder pain, Lazzeri started all four games, with Durocher replacing him toward the end of each game. To make matters worse, in the opening game he injured the middle finger on his right hand while fielding a grounder. "That finger turned black and was so swollen Tony couldn't grip a bat," said Joe Dugan. "He didn't get a hit for three games then socked out three in the last one. That's what I call the old fight."[38]

In the seventh inning of the final game, Lazzeri got another chance to face Alexander. After starter Bill Sherdel had given up home runs to Ruth and Gehrig (giving the Yankees a 3–2 lead) and a single to Meusel, Alexander was brought in specifically to face Lazzeri, who had hit two singles earlier in the game. Marshall Hunt noted the déjà vu moment: "Who was at the plate but Signor Lazzeri, the very wop Alexander struck out with the bases filled two years ago!"[39] Lazzeri lifted a high fly to left that fell in for a double when Hafey lost it in the sun, sending Meusel to third. After Meusel scored and Lazzeri advanced to third on a fielder's choice, Combs, making his only appearance in the Series, pinch-hit for Benny Bengough and hit a sacrifice fly that scored Lazzeri, making the score 5–2.

Noting that "those two ancient enemies" were unlikely to face each other again, Gallico wrote that he was pleased that Lazzeri got that double since "it was not good that young Lazzeri should go through his major league career with the memory of a mocking old man with a cap that perched on top of his head like a wart on a melon, whom he could not hit. Professional ball players must take happy memories to their winter quarters with them, and whenever Anthony looks back over the series of 1928 he will smile and think of that hit and the jinx he conquered. It's going to make him a tough man for pitchers next year."[40]

Dealing with a serious injury, especially one that could prove to be career-ending, is stressful for any athlete. And in Lazzeri's era much less was known about the cause and treatment of shoulder injuries than would later be the case, only adding to the uncertainty of the outcome. But for Lazzeri that stress was layered on top of his daily concern about the possibility of an epileptic seizure, making his ability to be in the lineup every day during the intense pressure of the late-season pennant race and the World Series all the more remarkable. Following the Series, Huggins praised Lazzeri for his dedication: "The public may not appreciate that here was a man who was playing strictly on his nerve—playing out the string when he had no business in the line-up at all. His arm was sore and aching all the time. He could not grip his bat properly. But he held on. And when it comes to sheer courage there's no man in the whole series who showed more than Tony."[41]

Going into August, Lazzeri was hitting .356 and trailing only Gehrig and Goslin for the league lead, but by the end of the season his average had fallen to .332, second on the team to Gehrig's .374. Even more obvious was the impact on his power. While he had a slugging average of .614 in July, he fell to .387 in August and .339 in September, when two doubles were his only extra base hits. His home run on August 24 was the last of ten for the season, and the only one he hit in forty-four games after the injury. Nevertheless, his batting average and on-base percentage were both higher than in his first two seasons. More surprising, perhaps, is that his slugging average of .535 surpassed his .482 in 1927; though he hit fewer home runs, he hit more doubles and triples in fewer at bats. And he continued to hit in the clutch. His average with runners in scoring position was .372, compared to .272 and .348 the previous two seasons. And in spite of his limited playing time, he led the Yankees with fifteen stolen bases.

Over the final three months of the 1928 season and in a pennant chase that proved much closer than it had been prior to his injury, Tony Lazzeri faced the biggest challenge of his young career. (Given all that he had achieved in his first two seasons, it is easy to forget that he was only twenty-four years old.) His damaged shoulder not only diminished his ability to hit for power or even throw the ball overhand, but it also threatened to end his career. In a column that appeared after the World Series, George W. Daley of the *New York World*, writing under the pseudonym of "Monitor," noted that Lazzeri "never recovered the use of his arm which had kept him out of the line-up in the closing days of the season, until he went back and played the last dozen games on his nerve alone, and the pennant was saved." He then concluded that "Lazzeri shouldn't have been in the World Series at all. In every inning of every game played he ran the risk of ruining his future."[42]

But while Lazzeri's power productivity fell off, his determination and courage never wavered. His willingness to play through the pain when the season was on the line, even at the risk of doing permanent damage, reconfirmed his role as a selfless team leader whose very presence on the field provided inspiration and a much needed sense of stability and calm to a team plagued by numerous injuries. Perhaps all of this explains why, even though he missed thirty-eight games, he finished tied with Joe Judge of the Senators for third place in the MVP vote, trailing only Mickey Cochrane of the A's and Heinie Manush of the Browns. A January 1929 story recounted an interview with Lazzeri and Koenig in late September 1928, when the Yankees were in Chicago. Koenig was quoted as saying he thought Lazzeri should win the AL MVP Award. "You have shown you were our most valuable player," he said. "When you were out of the game we could not win. We would be in second place if it were not for you." But Lazzeri demurred. "Mickey Cochrane should get the most valuable player award," he said. "I have been out of the game too much with this bum shoulder of mine."[43]

7

Peak Performance

Soon after the end of the 1928 World Series, Lazzeri sought treatment for his damaged shoulder, but reports of the exact nature of that treatment were vague and even contradictory. He checked into St. Vincent's Hospital in New York, reportedly for repairs to torn ligaments. A photo in the *Brooklyn Standard Union* shows Lazzeri seated and wearing a robe, with his right shoulder bandaged and a caption indicating that "an operation for a water sack may follow preliminary treatments."[1] The next day the *New York Times* reported that Lazzeri left the hospital on October 19, "following an operation on his right shoulder," with no further details.[2] However, a story with a dateline of New York, October 21, reported that "it has been decided that Lazzeri's arm will be better with rest instead of an operation."[3] In any case by October 21 Lazzeri had returned to his home in San Francisco.

Throughout the postseason writers expressed concern about the state of Lazzeri's arm and whether he could come back in 1929. As it turned out, there was good cause for concern. Apparently neither the treatment Lazzeri had received in New York—whatever it was—nor the prescribed rest in San Francisco resolved the issue. A Newspaper Enterprise Association dispatch datelined San Francisco, January 18, appeared in several newspapers across the country with the headline "Rubber Saves Lazzeri's Arm" and a photo of Lazzeri's shoulder being massaged. According to the story, Lazzeri, who was still in pain and could not lift his arm above his head when he returned from New York, was despondent. He was quoted as telling Dutch Ruether, a former Major Leaguer who was now pitching for the San Francisco Seals in the PCL that "none of the doctors did any good."[4]

Ruether suggested that Lazzeri see the Seals trainer and "rubber," Denny Carroll, calling him "the best arm guy in the business." Lazzeri took the advice and went to Carroll, who provided daily massages to the shoulder. The ligaments reportedly responded almost immediately, and within a month the pain was gone. When Lazzeri tried out the arm, he found that he could throw overhand without pain. The story concluded by saying that Lazzeri "feels sure that the injury has been corrected" and that when he reports to spring training "he will be able to go to work at once with the squad."[5] Meanwhile, he primarily rested in anticipation of heading back to Florida.

In January Lee Scott of the *Brooklyn Citizen* claimed that "the Walloping Wop" had recently sent a telegram to the Yankees in which he stated that "he has gained full control of his throwing arm" and had even played in a game on the coast "and after a short workout declared that his arm felt as good as ever." Scott added: "Now that Tony has pronounced himself fit Huggins is greatly relieved."[6] However, an unsigned story in the *Brooklyn Standard Union* the very next day reported that "Lazzeri himself has sent no report to Yankees officials regarding the strength of his arm."[7] And there is other evidence suggesting that Huggins, ever the pessimist, remained skeptical about the condition of Lazzeri's arm and took a wait-and-see approach. He was quoted as saying "in cases of this sort there is no way of predicting complete recovery unless the players have had a thorough trial," which would occur in spring training.[8]

In early February Lazzeri and Maye drove from their home to St. Petersburg well before the official start of spring training, apparently in response to Miller Huggins's suggestion that bathing in the Florida sun would help the shoulder to heal. Huggins was finally convinced in late February that Lazzeri's shoulder had healed when he watched his second baseman make a strong throw to first base. "Tony again threw as hard and as accurately as he ever could," reported Marshall Hunt, "under hand, side arm or over shoulder."[9] There was renewed concern when, in the first few days of March, Lazzeri felt some discomfort in his right elbow, prompting one journalist to remind readers that in his three years with the Yankees "the San Francisco young man had made himself the vital driving force of the Yankee infield and the stalwart bulwark that kept it from crumbling in a hundred critical situations."[10] To the relief of all concerned the elbow issue cleared up after a few days rest, and Lazzeri returned to regular workouts.

On March 30 the Yankees began a two-week exhibition tour of the South, playing both Major and Minor League opponents. The game in Oklahoma City on April 7 resulted in a scene that only the presence of Babe Ruth could generate. A record crowd of eighteen thousand turned out to see the Yanks play the Oklahoma City Indians of the Western League, and in the eighth inning a few of those folks, anxious to get a closer look at the Bambino, rushed onto the field hoping to get autographs. Their audacity soon triggered "a general stampede and in no time the Babe scarcely could be seen in the midst of a milling mob of several thousand." The fans remaining in the stands, eager to see Ruth hit again, became frustrated when those on the field refused to leave and began hurling cushions at them. The fans in the field, in turn, threw the cushions back so that "the scene took on the aspect of a gigantic pillow fight." Finally the Babe, "still beaming good nature though his uniform was almost in shreds, gained the exit aisle and rushed for his automobile." But in the parking lot he encountered a crowd that almost turned his car over "while a steady downpour of cushions" rained down from the back of the grandstands. The "jubilee" was finally brought to a close by a sudden rainstorm.[11] The tour ended on April 12 with a 9–4 win over the Charlotte Hornets that featured two home runs by Lazzeri, who "has recently been hitting at a terrific pace."[12]

Heading into the 1929 season, the power-laden Yankees, much like the American stock market, seemed to be invincible and set for another triumphant run. They had, after all, won three consecutive pennants and eight straight World Series games, a first in Major League history. So intimidating had they become that opposing teams were suggesting it was time to "break up the Yankees," a cry that would be echoed in later decades by fans and opponents frustrated by the success of what has often been called the most storied franchise in sports history. (Between 1921—Ruth's second year with New York—and 1964 the Yankees played in twenty-nine World Series, winning twenty of them.) How could any team compete against a squad that had both Ruth and Gehrig in the lineup? And even with several key players injured, the 1928 squad had swept the Cardinals.

Management of course scoffed at the notion that it should weaken the team to provide a more even playing field for the rest of the league. "I not only have no thought of breaking up the Yankees," said Colonel Ruppert, "but Ed Barrow, Huggins, and myself will exert our best efforts to strengthen them. . . . In every sport the object should be to win on your own merits and not ask the other fellow to weaken himself deliberately to aid your cause."[13] Huggins offered a different perspective in a statement that would prove to be eerily prophetic, not just for the Yankees' near future, but also for that of the nation's economy: "It won't be necessary to break up the Yankees. No matter what we do, the law of averages will take care of us. We can go on, trying to improve the team to the best of our ability. But the time will come when we will crash."[14] Not many would have guessed that Huggins's prediction would come true in less than a year, when both the Yankees and the stock market would crumble at the same time. Lazzeri, on the other hand, would have what may have been the best year of his entire career. After all the concern about whether he would ever be the same or even if he would be able to play again, not only did he prove that his shoulder problems were behind him, but, like the soaring bull market on Wall Street prior to the October crash, his numbers reached new heights in 1929.

For all their recent success the Yankees continued to make efforts to improve their team in the offseason. They cut ties with Joe Dugan, who had appeared in only ninety-four games in 1928 and was claimed on waivers by the Boston Braves. But it would prove to be difficult to replace the twelve-year veteran at third base. The plan was to shift Koenig to third and bring up Lyn Lary, the highly touted prospect who had been acquired from the Oakland Oaks the previous season, to play at short. But in spite of Hunt's late March prediction that with the quartet of Gehrig, Lazzeri, Lary, and Koenig, the Yankees "will have one of the most formidable infields in the history of the team," the plan soon went awry, at least at third and short.[15] When both Lary and Koenig fell short of expectations, Gene Robertson and Leo Durocher were given a chance. The end result was a season-long juggling of those four players in the left side of the infield with limited success.

The Yankees had much better success with the catcher's position, which had been the weakest link in their lineup for some time. The answer was twenty-two-year-old Bill Dickey, a Louisiana native who had appeared in 10 games in 1928 after being called up in mid-August. In 1929 he played in 130 games and hit .324 with 10 home runs and 65 RBIs in his rookie season. He then played in more than 100 games in each of the next twelve seasons, was chosen to play in ten of the first eleven All-Star Games, and compiled a lifetime average of .313 with 202 home runs in a seventeen-year career, all with the Yankees. In 1949 he became a Yankees coach and is credited with turning a struggling young Yogi Berra into one of the game's greatest catchers. They would both end up in the Baseball Hall of Fame.

In 1929 the Yankees became one of the first two teams, along with the Cleveland Indians, to permanently place numbers on the backs of uniforms so as to make it easier for fans to identify the players. Considering all the switching that took place among the

Yankees playing at third and short that season, the numbers must have been particularly helpful. Initially the numbers, at least for the starters, corresponded to the player's position in the batting order: Accordingly, Lazzeri wore no. 6, following Combs, Koenig, Ruth, Gehrig, and Meusel in the lineup. The idea caught on, and by the end of 1932 all teams were wearing numbers.

New York Times columnist John Kieran expressed the prevailing opinion about the upcoming season: "The Yankees seem stronger this year," while their primary rivals, the Athletics "have been unsettled if not actually upset by maladies and misfortunes in the training season." The conclusion? "If Pennock's arm and Lazzeri's shoulder are in shape for a season's play, all odds favor the Yankees."[16]

Following a one-day weather delay and the usual rituals, including raising the World Series flag, the season got off to a familiar start on April 18. Ignited by a first-inning homer by the Bambino, who only the day before had married his longtime companion, Claire Hodgson, the Yankees beat the Red Sox, 7–3. When they went on to win thirteen of their first seventeen games, it seemed like the juggernaut was rolling once again. But then a speed bump popped up, and they lost five straight. By the end of May their record was 20–16, which put them in third place, 7½ games behind Philadelphia. An eight-game winning streak gave them a 44–26 record on July 6, but that left them 8½ games behind the A's, who were coasting with a record of 53–18. And so it would go for most of the season. When the Yankees surged in July, winning 22 of 29 games, the A's kept pace, going 24–9 and leading by 9½ games by the end of the month. And when the Yankees fell to a 13–18 record in August, putting them 12½ games back, the race was essentially over.

It was Connie Mack's turn to step back into the spotlight. The A's clinched the pennant on September 14, finishing the season eighteen games ahead of New York, then went on to win the World Series, beating the Chicago Cubs in five games. With old timers Ty Cobb and Tris Speaker gone and Eddie Collins appearing in only nine games, Mack's team was young and powerful, featuring four future Hall of Famers: first baseman Jimmie Foxx, outfielder Al Simmons, catcher Mickey Cochrane, and ace pitcher Lefty Grove, who led a strong pitching staff with a 20–6 record and a league-leading 2.81 ERA. It was, in fact, a team on its way to becoming a dynasty.

As for Kieran's proposition that the success of the Yankees depended on both Pennock's and Lazzeri's being healthy, only Lazzeri got through the season unscathed. Pennock continued to be plagued by a sore arm and was relatively ineffective with a record of 9–11. He and Hoyt had won a combined forty games in 1928, but in 1929 they won only nineteen. Of the starters only George Pipgras lived up to expectations with eighteen wins. Tom Zachary posted a 12–0 record but started only eleven games.

Overall the offense was more effective. Their home run, runs scored, and batting average numbers were almost identical to those of 1928, when they had won thirteen more games. As the A's prepared to face the Cubs in the World Series, eighteen-game-winning southpaw Rube Walberg said, "What I'm glad about is that we don't have to face Ruth, Lazzeri and Co. in the coming series. I'd rather face the Cubs any day than those clubbers."[17] In spite of missing seventeen days in June due to illness, Ruth once again was the home run king, hitting 46, with a robust .345 average and 154 RBIs (3 fewer than league leader Simmons). While Gehrig's average dropped to .300, 74 points below that of 1928, he hit 35 homers and drove in 125 runs. Meusel, however, was showing signs of slowing down. He played in only 100 games, and both his batting average (.261) and RBI total (57) were the lowest of his career. Part of the slack was picked up by the rookie Dickey's 65 RBIs.

But it was Lazzeri who showed the greatest improvement in offense. Playing in 147 games, he had a career-high average of .354, 70 points above the league average. He also posted career highs in hits (193), doubles (37), total bases (306), on-base percentage (.429), slugging percentage (.561), and OPS (.991) and tied his career high in home runs (18). (His slugging average and OPS were higher in 1939, his final season, but he played in only fourteen games.) In addition, his 101 runs scored were the second highest of his career. He was among the league leaders in several offensive categories: fourth best in batting average and on-base percentage; fifth in OPS; sixth in home runs; and eighth in slugging percentage, extra base hits, total bases, and RBIs. The only blemish on his career-year season was on defense, where he finished second in the league in errors by a second baseman with 27. But he was also third in the league in double plays and putouts.

In the ten games the Yankees played in April, Lazzeri hit a modest .257, but by the end of May he had jumped up to .346. He then hit .416 in June, reaching his high-water mark of .392 on June 18. He "slumped" to .317 in August but finished strong with a .367 average in September. Even though he was wearing no. 6 on his uniform because of what had been his usual spot in the batting order, by May 22 Lazzeri had moved up to the fifth position, presumably because of his productivity and the lack of it from Meusel, who was hitting .243 at that point with a .379 slugging percentage compared to Lazzeri's .330 and .520 respectively. On the last three days of the season he even hit in the cleanup spot, behind Ruth, and went 7 for 14.

One factor in Lazzeri's offensive surge was his improved plate discipline. For the first time he had more walks than strikeouts. The once notorious free swinger who had led the league with 96 strikeouts in his rookie season—striking out at a rate of 14.4 percent of his plate appearances—struck out only 45 times in 639 plate appearances in 1929, a rate of 7 percent. At the same time his walk rate increased from 8.2 percent in 1926 to 10.6 percent in 1929. Correspondingly his .429 on-base percentage in 1929 was his highest of any full season.

In 1929 the AL abolished the MVP vote, but two unofficial polls were taken, one by *The Sporting News* and another by the BBWAA. In *The Sporting News* vote, taken by the same eight writers who formed the official MVP selection committee in 1928, Lazzeri finished second with thirty-three points, seven fewer than Al Simmons. The BBWAA selected first baseman Lew Fonseca of the Indians, the AL batting champion. He received only one first-place vote but collected enough second-, third-, and fourth-place votes to garner forty-six points. Lazzeri finished sixth with twenty-two points, three ahead of Ruth.[18] In an otherwise undated 1929 story found in the Lazzeri Scrapbooks, cartoonist/writer Feg Murray of the *Los Angeles Times* wrote: "Isn't it just Tony's tough luck for them to go and abolish the most valuable AL player prize, when he was the logical man to win it this year? This is only the Walloping Wop's fourth year in the majors, yet each year he has one better than the last, and given even more evidence of his skill, gameness and alert mentality. The Italians are rightfully proud of this native son."

What was already a disappointing season for the Yankees took a much darker turn on September 25, when the team, then in Boston for a series with the Red Sox, learned that their beloved manager had died at the age of fifty-one. Huggins, who had not been well for some time, had finally been convinced to seek treatment for an ominous looking growth beneath his left eye. By September 20 he was in St. Vincent's Hospital being treated for an infected carbuncle, but in spite of several blood transfusions the infection spread quickly, and he died five days later. When the news reached Boston in the middle of the game, both teams gathered at home plate for a moment of silence. Huggins's death prompted AL president Ernest Barnard to cancel all games scheduled for September 27, the day of the funeral. With their game in Washington postponed, the Yankees returned to New York for the services at the Church of the Configuration. Lazzeri was one of eight Yankees to serve as an honorary pall bearer, along with Ruth, Gehrig, Combs, and Pennock and coaches Bob Shawkey, Art Fletcher, and Charlie O'Leary. (Fletcher would manage the team for the final eleven games of the season.) Following the services, Huggins's body was taken to Grand Central Station and placed on a train to his hometown of Cincinnati, where he would be buried. An estimated ten thousand people lined the streets to view the funeral cortege.

Hired in 1918 to manage a Yankee team that had finished last the previous season, Huggins, who had spent his entire career in the NL, thirteen years as a second baseman with Cincinnati and St. Louis and five managing the Cardinals, was met with a cool reception in New York by his players, the press, and fans. Players were initially skeptical of their pint-sized skipper, none more than Ruth, who threatened to quit in 1925 when Huggins fined and suspended him. Fans also had a hard time warming up to the seemingly humorless and grumpy guy in the dugout. But in time the man who gave his all to the team and led the Yankees to six pennants and three World Series wins in twelve years won over the skeptics and became beloved by his players. When Ruth learned of Huggins's death, he told reporters: "It is one of the keenest losses I have ever felt. You know what I thought of Miller Huggins and what I owe to him." That same day Lazzeri said: "I can't talk about it. You could tell the man he was by bringing along a kid player hopeless for anyone but Huggins."[19]

None of the Yankees was more touched by the loss of Huggins than Lazzeri, who credited his manager with teaching him how to play second base. When Lazzeri, who had primarily played at short in the Minors, was assigned by Huggins to play second in his rookie year, he struggled to the point where he feared he might be demoted to the Minors. "Guess I might have been sent back," he said, "if Manager Huggins had not been a star second baseman in his day. He knew how second ought to be played and he coached me until I became familiar with the work. My previous work in a boilershop gave me the power to hit the ball but it was Miller Huggins who taught me to be a second baseman."[20]

Nine weeks after Huggins's death, there was momentous news that would affect not just the baseball world, but the nation as a whole. The euphoria of the unprecedented boom in stock prices came to a sudden end on October 29, "Black Tuesday," when the market crashed, wiping out thousands of investors and triggering America's plunge into the Great Depression. Within four years 30 percent of the workforce would be unemployed, and about half of America's banks would be closed. Exactly what effect the crash may have had on Lazzeri and his wife remains unclear. In a story on the postseason plans of Yankees players Pat Robinson wrote: "Mark Koenig and Tony Lazzeri are going back to the coast to dabble in the stock market and take life easy."[21] To what extent Lazzeri did in fact dabble in the market is unknown. In any case the economic impact of the Depression on baseball would not be felt immediately, nor did it have any immediate effect on Lazzeri's income. Given his outstanding season, his salary was boosted to $16,000, a 20 percent increase over his 1929 salary of $12,500.

Nor was Babe Ruth's salary immediately affected by the Depression. On March 8, 1930, he signed a two-year contract for $160,000. When someone pointed out that his salary was higher than President Hoover's, he supposedly offered the oft-cited and possibly apocryphal reply: "I had a better year than he did." But beginning in 1932 even the Sultan of Swat would have to face the economic reality of the Depression and accept lesser amounts.

8

A Major League Mystery

The death of Miller Huggins, tragic enough in itself, would prove to be a harbinger of the Yankees' descent from dominance. While Connie Mack's A's were just approaching their prime, the Yanks were heading in the opposite direction. There were several indications in 1929 that changes were soon to come. Veterans Bob Meusel, Waite Hoyt, and Herb Pennock all had shown signs that their best years were behind them; Mark Koenig, only twenty-five years old, continued to be inconsistent at short; and no adequate replacement for Joe Dugan at third base had been found. It was also the last season for the Murderers' Row quartet; Meusel, who had slumped to the lowest average of his career at .261, was sold to Cincinnati soon after the 1929 World Series.

The first order of business for Colonel Ruppert and Ed Barrow was to find a new manager, a task that proved to be more difficult than they expected. Who would not want to manage the Yankees, the richest franchise in baseball? Their first choice was Donie Bush, who had more than three years of managerial experience with the Senators and Pirates. But the very same day that they called with the offer, Bush had signed to manage the White Sox. They next approached future Hall of Famer Eddie Collins, who had managed the White Sox for two years before returning to the field to play for Connie Mack, but Collins said he did not feel he was ready to manage the Yankees. Third on the list was an in-house candidate, popular third base coach Art Fletcher, who had managed the Phillies for four years and served as the Yankees' interim manager for the final eleven games in 1929. He too begged off, saying he preferred to remain in the less stressful position of coaching. That brought Ruppert and Barrow to another in-house candidate, thirty-nine-year-old Bob Shawkey, a thirteen-year veteran of the Yankees pitching staff and a four-time twenty-game winner between 1915 and 1927 who had served as the pitching coach in 1929. On October 17, 1929, Colonel Ruppert officially announced that Shawkey would be the new manager.

The announcement surprised many since Shawkey, whose service in the navy during World War I had earned him the nickname of "Bob the Gob," had no managerial experience. Marshall Hunt offered this modest vote of approval: "Retiring, sincere, intelligent and always a hard worker, Shawkey has been held in high esteem by every one in baseball." The next day he added this caveat: "But I wonder, knowing Shawkey as I do, whether he has the firmness, the driving power so often needed in the long, tedious stretches of a baseball season, to keep his men burning with the fire of dogged determination and aggressiveness."[1] At his first press conference Shawkey revealed his plans for the coming season, which included moving Lazzeri to third and giving Jimmie Reese, the PCL phenom signed two years earlier, a chance to prove himself at second, with Gehrig and Koenig at first and short respectively.

At the time that Shawkey was being introduced in New York, Lazzeri was back in California, where, once again, he was being honored by the Italian American community of Los Angeles. On October 19 he appeared in the lineup of the Pirrone All-Stars at White Sox Park for a California Winter League game against the Philadelphia Royal Giants, a barnstorming Negro League team. (The Giants' top star was Biz Mackey, the future Hall of Fame catcher who was playing for the Philadelphia Hilldale Giants, which had faced the Pirrone All-Stars in October 1927, when Lazzeri was in the lineup.) Both Lazzeri and Mackey hit home runs in a slugfest won by the Giants, 12–6. The next day was

"Lazzeri Day" at White Sox Park when, according to the *Los Angeles Times*, "the Italian colony will be there en masse" to honor its hero. "A brass band will be on hand for the occasion," and "preparations have been made to handle the biggest crowd in the history of the park."[2]

Looking ahead to the 1930 season, one writer, noting that other teams had rebuffed the efforts of Ruppert and Barrow to bolster their lineup through trades, predicted that the Yankees would have to rely on some rookies if they hoped to catch the A's. Among those expected to make the team were outfielder Allen "Dusty" Cooke, infielders Ben Chapman and Reese, and pitchers Vernon "Lefty" Gomez and Louis Polli.[3] Of those prospects only Chapman would appear in more than a hundred games in 1930. Gomez, however, after a modest 2–5 record as a rookie, would go on to be a four-time twenty-game winner for New York in a fourteen-year career that would take him to the Hall of Fame. Basically the Yankees would be entering the season with an inexperienced manager and a number of hopefuls.

Lazzeri, like Ruth and Hoyt, refused to sign the team's initial contract, which reportedly offered him $15,000. Some writers speculated that he may have felt that the possible shift to third base merited more money. Abe Kemp wrote that it was Lazzeri's intention to negotiate in person when he arrived at St. Petersburg.[4] But on February 20 Barrow was quoted as saying that "Lazzeri is not a holdout, as his terms were accepted several days ago and his signed contract is probably on its way back, or will be turned in when Tony arrives at St. Petersburg."[5] The terms of the contract were not revealed by Ruppert, but Lazzeri's salary was $15,000, reportedly the same sum as the contract he initially had refused to sign. By February 22, just prior to the start of spring training, Shawkey was now planning to put rookie Chapman at third and keep Lazzeri at second.[6] Meanwhile, it was reported that Lazzeri, along with his buddy Lefty O'Doul, was keeping in shape by playing four rounds of golf a week in San Francisco.[7] Lazzeri arrived in St. Petersburg on March 4, and that same day he was work-ing out at second base alongside Koenig, his double-play partner.

It came as no surprise that Connie Mack's A's were favored to repeat as AL champs, but Mack himself was sounding cautious during spring training: "Everyone tells me I have the strongest team in the American League, but the boys will have to win for me this year to convince me we did not have all of the luck in the league last year." For his part Shawkey was confident the offense would produce but knew that his chances of success depended on a rebound by the pitching staff: "If I can bring Pennock, Hoyt and Pipgras back to their stride of 1928 I'll beat out the Athlet-ics."[8] It's a challenge for any rookie manager to quickly gain the respect of his players, and it was even more so for someone like Shawkey, who had so recently been one of their teammates. And as it turned out, several of the Yankees took advantage of their manager's reluctance, or inability, to be a disciplinarian.

As expected, the Yankees opened the season with two rookies in the starting lineup: Chapman at third and Cooke in left. To say that the refurbished team under its new manager got off to a sluggish start would be generous. They played their first four games on the road and lost them all, including a 6–2 loss to the A's in the season opener. Then, before more than sixty-six thou-sand fans, they lost their own home opener to the A's, 7–6. At the end of April they were mired in last place with a 3–8 record. The Yankees did boost their faltering pitching staff on May 6, when Shawkey managed to acquire from the Red Sox—the same sup-plier that eleven years earlier had provided New York with Ruth—Charles "Red" Ruffing in return for outfielder Cedric Durst and cash. Ruffing, who just a year earlier had lost twenty-two games, following a twenty-five-loss season in 1928, won fifteen games in 1930, would spend fifteen years with the Yankees, and ended up in the Hall of Fame.

Also early in May, Shawkey, "thoroughly irritated at the per-sistence at which his charges have been dropping the close games," decided to shake up the lineup.[9] On May 10 Koenig was replaced at short by Lary, and Chapman and left fielder Sam Byrd were dropped to the seventh and eighth spots in the order. In what was likely the most surprising move Lazzeri, who had been hitting fifth—behind Combs, Koenig, Ruth, and Gehrig—was put in the cleanup spot, as "a reward for his vigorous attack with the stick this season," while Gehrig dropped to the fifth spot.[10] The move paid immediate benefits as the Yankees won seven of their next eight games.

The revised batting order worked particularly well on May 22, when the Yankees, in fourth place with a 14–14 record, and the A's, one game out of first with a 20–10 record, met in a doubleheader in Philadelphia. In the first game, a 10–1 New York win, Lazzeri went 2 for 5 with two RBIs, and Gehrig was 4 for 5 with one RBI. Then in the nightcap, a 20–13 win, Lazzeri had four hits, scored five runs, and drove in four, three coming on a home run, while Gehrig had an even better game, hitting three homers with eight RBIs. Over the course of the season both of them produced better results hitting in their new positions than they had in their original slots. Gehrig's batting average was .439 when hitting fifth, compared to .312 as the cleanup hitter, and Lazzeri hit .326 in the cleanup spot and .263 hitting fifth. Their on-base percentages and slugging averages were also higher when they hit in their revised positions.

Shawkey wasn't done making changes. On May 30 the Yankees traded Hoyt (who disagreed with his manager's pitching philosophy) and Koenig to Detroit. For a while things came together for the team as a whole following Shawkey's lineup revisions. A 19–9 record in May followed by 20–8 in June put them in a second-place tie with the Senators and only two games behind the A's. But eventually the lack of pitching did them in, and they reverted to the mean, becoming a .500 team in August and September, with a combined 27–25 record. The pitching staff did not meet Shawkey's preseason hopes. Ruffing and Pipgras each won fifteen games, and Hank Johnson won fourteen, but the staff's 4.88 ERA tied Cleveland for the second worst in the league. The Yankees finished the season in third place at 86–68, eight games behind the Senators and sixteen behind the defending champion A's.

Other than the pitching woes, Shawkey's primary challenge was finding the right combination in his infield. He tried to mix and match throughout the season but without much success. *New York Times* columnist John Kieran suggested that "the hapless pitchers could have filed suit against their fielders for non support. The fielding of the Yankees wasn't even 'adequate.' It was mediocre."[11] According to Frank Graham, there were so many changes in the lineup that one of the veterans observed that "the trouble with this club is that there are too many fellows on it who aren't Yankees."[12] The rookie Chapman hit .316 with ten homers but struggled on defense and was replaced at third by Lazzeri. Once Koenig was traded, Lary got the bulk of the playing time at short. Over the course of the season six players played third base, four as starters, with Chapman and Lazzeri starting in a total of 149 games. Five started at short, headed by Lary (112), and three started at second: Lazzeri (77), Chapman (43), and Reese (34). As he had in 1927, Lazzeri displayed his defensive versatility by starting at second, third, and short, as well as appearing in one game each at first and left field.

As Shawkey had predicted, the Yankees' offense was potent, but then that was true throughout the big leagues that year. While the stock market dropped like a rock, baseball's offensive numbers reached unprecedented heights in 1930, with new highs in home runs and runs scored. The effects of the long-ball era that Ruth had inaugurated in the early twenties were increasingly evident as several sluggers in addition to Gehrig were now challenging the Babe's home run superiority. Whereas in 1927 only two players (Hack Wilson and Cy Williams) other than the Yankees' duo hit 30 or more homers, in 1930 three hit 40 or more, and six more hit at least 35. Wilson of the Cubs led both leagues with 56 home runs and set a still-standing record of 191 RBIs. The AL batting average was .288, surpassed by the NL's .303 average. As a team the Yankees led the league with a .309 batting average and 1,062 runs scored, the first time any team had reached 1,000. They also led the league in hits, triples, and RBIs. Gehrig led the league with 173 RBIs, hit 41 homers, and batted .379. Combs hit .344 and led the league in triples. Ruth, now thirty-five years old, hit .359, led the AL with 49 homers, and drove in 153 runs.

According to J. Harold Sommers, Lazzeri played a minor role in Ruth's "rejuvenated power" in 1930. In a story titled "Mrs. 'Babe' Ruth at the Plate," he attributed Ruth's resurgence to his wife, Claire: "It's just a simple little story of the right girl coming along at the right time. Babe Ruth's wife has made a better man out of him—and made him like it." Featuring a photo of Claire washing dishes with Ruth sitting on the kitchen counter next to her while drying a dish, the story credits Claire—who cooks for him "when necessary"—for the Babe's "trimmed-down physique." His favorite dish was a spaghetti recipe Claire got from Lazzeri: "Tony's wife cooks the elastic for him, and if it isn't real, undisguised Italian spaghetti, Tony's a Chinese laundryman."[13]

As for Lazzeri's own performance in 1930, after a career-high of .354 in 1929, his average fell fifty-one points to .303, the third lowest among the Yankees' starting position players but still fifteen points above the league average of .288. After hitting eighteen homers in three of his first four seasons—he hit ten in 1928, when he suffered the shoulder injury—he hit only nine in 1930. At the same time he drove in a career-high 121 runs, thanks to a .337 average with runners in scoring position together with 175 at bats with runners in scoring position, the third highest of his career.

While no injuries were reported that would account for his decline, following the season there were several reports that Lazzeri had been hampered by health issues in 1930. In January a note in the "Fuel for Hot Stove League Sessions" segment of *The Sporting News* indicated that Lazzeri "was handicapped last season by ill health," but it offered no details as to what the problem may have been. The story added that Lazzeri "will report for spring training in excellent condition," according to a letter received by New York friends from Maye Lazzeri. "She reports that Tony has been particularly careful of his diet, hasn't done any hard work and has abandoned those long automobile tours he usually took after the close of the ball season."[14] In March, in a preview of the 1931 season, Fred. Lieb predicted that Joe McCarthy, the new Yankees manager, would leave Lazzeri at third base: "For some reason or other, Lazzeri, who was not in good health last season, did not pivot well on double plays."[15] Then in September 1932 Westbrook Pegler noted that "although he has been a professional athlete for a dozen years, his health is not always good."[16]

Whatever the issue might have been in 1930, it seemed to affect mainly Lazzeri's speed and agility rather than keep him out of the lineup since he played in 140 games. He stole only four bases, fewer than eight other Yankees and the lowest number of any of his full seasons. (In every previous season he was either first or second on the team in steals.) But if in fact the fifty-one-point drop in average and the decline in home runs were due to "ill health," why the secrecy as to its nature? This is a question we will return to below in the chapter.

As was his custom, Lazzeri spent the offseason playing golf in San Francisco and occasionally participating in benefit games in California. On October 25 he, together with Koenig, Joe Cronin, and other area Major Leaguers, squared off against an All-Star team of PCL players in the Alameda Elks charity game in Oakland. (On September 24, 1929, Lazzeri and Koenig had been initiated into the Elks Lodge in Winthrop, Massachusetts, an oceanside suburb of Boston.) Sponsored by the Alameda Elks Lodge until 1954, the annual charity games featured some of the biggest stars in the game and drew large crowds. And on November 9, along with Lefty O'Doul, the reigning NL batting champion, Lazzeri served as an umpire for a charity game between the San Francisco Police and Fire Departments to help the St. Vincent de Paul Society build a soup kitchen for the needy.

Given the Yankees' third-place finish in 1930, it came as no shock to most observers that Ruppert and Barrow chose to move on and find another manager. This time they turned to an experienced candidate. Joe McCarthy had recently been let go by the Cubs after five years at the helm, despite leading them to the pennant in 1929 and a second-place finish in 1930. It was a poorly kept secret that even before the World Series ended, the Yankees had been pursuing McCarthy, so it came as no surprise when the official announcement was made on October 15 that he had been signed to a two-year contract. Whereas Shawkey had been lenient with his players, McCarthy was known to be a strict disciplinarian. He established a dress code that required players to wear coats and ties when on the road and to be in the dining room for break-fast by 8:30. He also banned card playing in the clubhouse. In fact, to make his point clear and with the players in the room, he ordered the clubhouse attendant to get an ax and smash the card table. Given his recent track record, McCarthy was gener-ally well received in New York, certainly more so than Huggins had been initially. Kieran, however, did offer this caveat: "Marse Joe will have his hands full of work in overhauling the Yankee machine and making a front runner of it again."[17]

While the response to McCarthy's hiring was generally posi-tive, there was one notable exception. Ruth had long had aspi-rations of becoming a manager, but Barrow and Ruppert were opposed to the idea. While Ruth had tempered some of his more extravagant exploits, especially after marrying Claire Hodgson, Barrow and Ruppert remained convinced that he lacked the dis-cipline to be a manager. "After all," wrote Barrow in his memoir, "Ruth couldn't manage himself."[18] Bitter about being rebuffed, Ruth openly resented McCarthy, who wisely overlooked Ruth's disdain and did his best to maintain a respectful working rela-tionship with his star.

There were, according to Graham, some players who resented McCarthy, believing Ruth should have been given the manag-er's job. Knowing Lazzeri to be a close friend of the Bambino, as well as the team leader, McCarthy was concerned about how his infielder would relate to him. Graham recounts an incident in the

Yankees clubhouse that occurred one day when one of the players who didn't care for McCarthy showed up late for batting practice. As the manager was giving the player a vicious tongue lashing, Lazzeri, who had come back into the clubhouse to grab a bat, walked in on the scene and was shocked by McCarthy's behavior. In what appears to be a loose reproduction of the encounter, Graham recounts McCarthy's explanation for his harsh behavior, telling Lazzeri that he was hoping to scare the player, who was not playing up to his potential because of his negative attitude, into changing his behavior. According to Graham, Lazzeri responded: "I've known all along how he felt about you—and how some of the others feel. I didn't know just how I felt about you myself. But I do now. I want you to know that from now on, I'm on your side." Graham concluded the segment by relating that Lazzeri not only was now on McCarthy's side, but also let his teammates know about it. "And since they had a great regard for him and a profound regard for his judgment, those who, like himself, had wavered in their loyalty to their manager, followed him into McCarthy's camp."[19]

In January 1931 Abe Kemp wrote that "Lazzeri is not at all perturbed over reports that McCarthy has him slated to toil around third the coming season, a position that 'Poosh-'em-up' was shifted to last year. The hot corner is not as difficult in Tony's opinion as second, which requires a greater degree of fielding skill."[20] However, Joe Sewell, a thirty-two-year-old eleven-year veteran infielder acquired as a free agent in January after being released by the Indians, was performing so well in spring training that on March 20 he started at third, with Lazzeri moving back to second base for the first time. On March 22 Kieran noted in his column that "Joe McCarthy has been trying Tony Lazzeri at his old position at second base. It was decided last year that Tony couldn't play that position any longer. The complaint against Tony was that he was too slow on double plays."[21] By March 29 Lazzeri was back at third, with Chapman at second.

Lazzeri was at third on April 2 when the Yankees were in Chattanooga to play the Lookouts of the Class A Southern Association. For that game Lookouts president Joe Engel had signed a local seventeen-year-old pitcher named Jackie Mitchell, reportedly the first girl ever to sign a professional baseball contract. After the starting pitcher for the Lookouts had given up a double and single to Combs and Lary in the first inning, Mitchell, a 5 foot 8 inch left-hander, came in to face Ruth. According to William E. Brandt, "Ruth performed his role very ably," swinging and missing on the first two pitches, then taking a called third strike, after which "he flung his bat away in high disdain and trudged to the bench." Next, "Gehrig took three hefty swings as his contribution to the occasion." Lazzeri then fouled off the first pitch on a bunt attempt before watching four outside pitches. At that point Mitchell was replaced by the starting pitcher, who gave up ten hits and five runs in four-plus innings.[22]

For the remainder of spring training the starting lineup had Lazzeri at third and Chapman at second, as it would be on April 14, opening day, with the Yankees hosting the Red Sox in front of a crowd of seventy thousand. In his game story of the opener Hunt expressed his surprise at the large turnout in light of the poverty that gripped the city: "The settlement is supposed to be suffering from the anguishing effects of a general financial depression, and the bony, grasping fingers of Want are pictured throttling the scrawny throats of the community's famished and ragged inhabitants, a stark, revolting visualization indeed." He leaves unanswered the question as to how so many men, women, and children "poured happily into the vast Yankee stadium [sic] to welcome heartily the return of the baseball team that performs therein."[23]

The starting team the fans welcomed on opening day included, in addition to Lazzeri and Chapman, veterans Combs, Ruth, and Gehrig, together with relative newcomers Lary, Cooke, and Dickey. As the season progressed, Chapman was moved from third base to the outfield, alternating with Ruth in left and right, depending on the venue, with Lazzeri moving back to second base and Sewell replacing Lazzeri at third. The Yankees had two outstanding months in 1931, going 22–9 in July and 21–6 in September, but they were more or less a .500 team the rest of the season. Their record of 94–59 was an eight-game improvement over their third-place 1930 mark, but their second-place finish still left them 13½ games behind the A's, whose third consecutive pennant had clearly established them as the reigning AL dynasty. Led by Ruth and Gehrig, the Yanks once again led the league in batting average, runs scored, and homers, but the A's had a potent lineup of their own. While Ruth and Gehrig shared the home run title with 46 each, Jimmie Foxx was fifth in the AL (30) and Al Simmons eighth (22). Mickey Cochrane, whose stern competitiveness earned him the nickname "Black Mike," was the best-hitting catcher in the game. But it was in pitching that the A's now had clear superiority. For the third straight year Lefty Grove led the league in ERA (2.06) while posting an astonishing record of 31–4, and George Earnshaw won 21 games after winning 22 and 24 the previous two seasons. The A's dynasty would be short-lived, however, as the economic collapse forced Mack to sell off his star players as he had done in 1914.

Now in his fifth season of covering Lazzeri for the *Daily News*, Marshall Hunt continued to relentlessly remind readers of the infielder's Italian ancestry. Three weeks into spring training in 1931, Hunt reassured New York's Italian fans that Signor Lazzeri was doing well, in spite of a lack of quality Italian dishes available to him in the south: "It is very true that Signor Lazzeri has been complaining frequently about the quality of the pastafazoula served in these parts and has aften [sic] remarked that the output of Florida raviola [sic] vats is hardly sufficient to supply his demand, but he is, none the less, in high spirits generally."[24]

Lazzeri's high spirits would be tested early in the regular season. If the 1931 season proved to be a lackluster venture for the Yankees, it was a near disaster for Lazzeri. The offensive decline that began in 1930, when his average dropped to .304 following his .354 mark in 1929, worsened in the early months of the 1931 season. Lazzeri, who was back at third base as the season opened and hitting in the fifth spot—accordingly he wore uniform no. 5 in both 1930 and 1931—got off to the worst start of his career. He went hitless in five of his first ten games, giving him a season-low average of .158 on April 25. Beginning in the second game of the May 25 doubleheader, when his average stood at .217, he was benched for a few days. Even more stunning was the decline in power. He did not hit his first homer until May 30, when he pinch-hit for Pennock in the ninth inning and hit a solo shot off "Sad Sam" Jones of the Senators. That home run was the topic of a ghostwritten story under Ruth's name that appeared on June 7:

> It meant more to him than just one more home run, and it meant a lot to all of us to see Tony hitting again. . . . Tony had been having a tough time this spring, and it finally got so bad that he was benched. Lazzeri had always been a .300 hitter or better since his first year in the big leagues, and here he was way down around .230. . . . Lazzeri is a powerful hitter, one of the best in the game. Few players who hit right handed can drive a ball into right field the way I've seen him hit 'em. In other years a homer by Lazzeri was taken as a matter of course, and here he was almost up to June without getting one.[25]

> It is interesting that "Ruth" offers no explanation for Lazzeri's power outage.[26]

On June 19, now hitting .231 and playing second base with Sewell at third, Lazzeri, who began the season in the fifth spot, was dropped to seventh. Then on July 19, with his average at .229, he was dropped to the eighth spot. In his first five seasons he had hit eighth in only two games, but now, except for a few occasions, he would stay in that spot for most of the remainder of the 1931 season. Even in early June at least one trade rumor was still circulating. A sidebar in the *San Francisco Examiner* announced that

Colonel Ruppert "today flatly denied that Tony Lazzeri, star Yankee second baseman, had been traded to the Washington American League club."[27]

In mid-July, when Lazzeri had two home runs and a .322 slugging average, Kieran, who had been the *Times* sports columnist since 1926, offered this somber assessment of Lazzeri's season:

> The Yanks have been hitting well and have scored plenty of runs. It's easy to show by fancy figures that the trouble with the Ruppert Rifles is the pitching staff. But there's another item that might be considered. Antonio Lazzeri. Tony has been holding down a seat on the bench for much of this season. Three or four years ago he was one of the greatest players in the game and just a youngster, too. He was on his way to take a place with Cobb, Wagner, Speaker, Hornsby, Ruth and players of that order. Now he has a hard job breaking into a game.
>
> When a team loses a player of that class, it's bound to show in the long run. The Yanks still have Ruth and Gehrig, but Tony was giving them a brisk race for batting honors when he was in his stride. The Yanks haven't won an extra inning game all season. They've lost plenty of close ones in the regulation nine innings. The Lazzeri of three or four years ago would've turned the tide with his bat in some of those games; perhaps in enough to have made this a pennant race instead of a parade in the American League. Nobody knows what has come over Lazzeri. He doesn't know himself. It's a major league mystery.[28]

One week earlier an unidentified writer for the *Brooklyn Times Union* had been less diplomatic: "Tony Lazzeri, once a dangerous right-hand hitter, is through at 27. Sewell will not play third next season nor will Lazzeri be with the Yankees."[29]

After struggling mightily in the first three-plus months of the season, hitting .226, .242, and .200 respectively, Lazzeri began to bounce back in late July, when he had at least one hit in eleven of the final twelve games of the month. That raised his average to .240, the first time since May 15 he had reached that mark. He followed with a .296 average in August and .302 in September, enabling him to finish the season with a .267 average. That figure, which was eighty-seven points lower than his .354 mark in 1929 and forty-six points below his aggregate average of .313 over his first five seasons, matched his 1934 average as the lowest of any full season in his fourteen-year career. It was also the first time since his rookie season that he hit below the league average (.279 in 1931). His eight homers and .401 slugging average were the third lowest of his career. Recognized from his rookie season on as a hitter who delivered in the clutch, Lazzeri's average with runners in scoring position was .230 in 1931, a far cry from his numbers in the previous five seasons: .348, .272, .354, .365, and .360. While the decline in both average and power suggests a loss of strength, timing, and hand-eye coordination, he apparently had not lost his speed; he stole eighteen bases, the second most of his career.

How, then, do we account for such a precipitous decline by a twenty-seven-year-old who, in Kieran's words (noted above), until recently had been "one of the greatest players in the game"? In the span of two seasons Lazzeri went from being one of baseball's elite players to trade bait. Beginning in his rookie year, he had been the Yankees' bellwether, the man his teammates looked to for guidance and stability; now suddenly his career was crumbling. His 1931 performance was such an anomaly that both journalists and teammates were left scratching their heads. In December 1931 John B. Foster of the Consolidated Press Association wrote: "Lazzeri was a mystery to ball players of both leagues in 1931. They couldn't understand why that wiry, aggressive, impetuous ball player was not making a better showing."[30]

Then in September 1932 Colonel Ruppert was quoted as having said prior to spring training that year: "Lazzeri probably will be all right again this season. He lost a lot of money in stocks last year and it worried him. It takes time to get over those things.

Lazzeri will learn that he has plenty of time to make more money and then he will be himself again."[31] In other words, Lazzeri had performed poorly in 1931 because he had been preoccupied about his finances. Three weeks after Ruppert's statement appeared in print, Westbrook Pegler, in a story about the upcoming World Series, wrote of Lazzeri: "This will be his fourth world series [sic] and one of the reasons for his temporary decline in 1931 was that he was sorrowing over the investments that he made with the money from the three previous series and his routine savings."[32] Why Pegler first revealed this information a year after the 1931 season had ended is unclear, nor does he reveal his source. *The Sporting News* reiterated the claim that Lazzeri's 1931 slide was due to worrying over his losses.[33] It is curious that these financial explanations for Lazzeri's failure in 1931 surfaced in 1932. If in fact Lazzeri had lost money prior to or during the 1931 season, were Colonel Ruppert and the others not aware of the issue until 1932? If in fact Lazzeri did lose a substantial amount of money, did he keep the matter to himself throughout the 1931 season? Or did he reveal it to Ruppert, who chose to keep it quiet until the following year? If so, why reveal it at all?

Many years after the fact others would claim that Lazzeri lost money during the Depression years because of a bank failure, though none of the statements I have seen provide details as to which bank failed, or when, nor do they indicate the original source of their claims.[34]

On the other side of the ledger are statements that contradict those assertions of major financial losses by Lazzeri. There is anecdotal evidence from members of the Lazzeri family that Tony and Maye did not suffer serious losses due to the Depression. Tony's daughter-in-law, Marilyn, said that according to Maye, "they didn't panic during the crash; they kept what they had instead of trying to sell it. What they kept were blue chips, so they did quite well."[35] Lazzeri's grandson, Matt, verified that it was Maye who invested in the market: "My grandmother never mentioned getting wiped out. I think they were pretty cautious and, even so, probably took a hit like everyone else. She was the one in the family that managed the money and made the financial decisions. She was the type of woman who would spend a lot of her spare time learning about and investing in the stock market. She just said they were always careful with their money. She made some pretty wise choices along the way, so she had no worries financially ever that I'm aware of."[36]

Furthermore, Graham, who was the Yankees' beat writer for the *New York Sun* at the time of the stock market crash, reported that Huggins talked to his players regarding their investments: "A sound student of finance, he warned them against the increasing lure of the stock market, which seemingly everyone, in all walks of life, was playing in the spring of 1928. 'If you're in the market, get out,' he dinned. 'It can't last.' Most of them, fortunately, took his advice. When the crash came in the fall of 1929, very few of the players were affected, and those few but lightly."[37]

Given the dire financial circumstances at the time, it is possible, even likely, that the Lazzeris' finances were negatively impacted. But without specific evidence beyond the anecdotal references cited above, it is impossible to know with any certainty the extent of their losses. Moreover, Lazzeri's salary of $16,000 in 1931, and even his diminished salary of $12,000 in 1932, were well above the average income for those who were employed during the Depression years.

One event in 1932 raises further questions regarding the allegations of a major financial loss in 1931. A few weeks before the end of the 1932 season, Tony and Maye purchased a six-room house at 427 Hazel Avenue in the recently opened upscale Millbrae Highlands development, a suburb featuring Spanish- and mission-style homes along tree-lined streets. (Millbrae is a small community in San Mateo County located about fifteen miles south of the home on Missouri Street where they had lived since their marriage in 1923.) If, as reports suggested, they had lost a large amount of money less than two years prior, would they have been able to recoup enough of their losses in the height of the Depression to enable them to make such a purchase?

The suggestion that Lazzeri's struggles on the diamond in 1931 were due to his financial situation raises some perplexing questions. Lazzeri had established himself as the leader of the team, a fierce competitor with a keen baseball mind who remained calm in dire situations and came through in the clutch. Keep in mind Paul Gallico's description (cited in chapter 5): "Tony is all temperament, fire, fight and push, a natural competitor and a natural born ballplayer." Lazzeri had proven his tenacity late in the 1928 season when he played in crucial games in spite of a shoulder injury that threatened to end his career. How likely is it that such a consummate professional would allow his concerns over financial matters, however serious, to distract him to such an extent, and for so long, as to dramatically affect his play over a good part of the 1931 season and, consequently, the success of his team?

Of course there is always the possibility that Lazzeri may have been hampered by an injury without revealing it or without the Yankees publicizing it. At the time, with big leaguers lacking the protection of long-term contracts and knowing there was always someone waiting to replace them—which would have been especially true during the lean years of the Depression—it was not uncommon for them to play hurt. And it seems unlikely that an injury serious enough to explain Lazzeri's struggles in 1931 would not have been noticed and discussed by the sportswriters. Instead they were at a loss to explain what was wrong, with Kieran going so far as to say in July (as noted above) that "nobody knows what has come over Lazzeri. He doesn't know himself."

Even if the suggestion that Lazzeri's poor play in 1931 was due to his being distraught because of financial losses were credible, how do we explain his 1930 performance? There were no indications that he had suffered losses prior to or during that season. The only explanations that surfaced then were the vague references to health issues. Is it possible that the causes of his 1931 struggles were related to the "health issues" that hampered him in 1930? If so, what exactly were those health issues?

Any vague mention of an otherwise unspecified health issue regarding Lazzeri suggests the possibility that the "issue" may be a veiled reference to his affliction with epilepsy. In light of the comments by someone as well informed as Kieran on the mystery surrounding Lazzeri's struggles, together with the absence of any reported injuries that might account for his poor performance, as well as the rather secretive reports indicating that he had been hampered in 1930 by poor health, it seems fair to ask whether Lazzeri's epilepsy may have been a factor in his struggles in 1930 and 1931. Is it possible that his illness had become more troublesome than in previous years, when there seemed to be no public mention of any health problems? If that was the case, Lazzeri certainly would have known but would have never admitted it publicly. Since his shoulder injury in 1928 was given wide press coverage, why was so little known, at least publicly, about the cause of his relatively poor performance in 1930 and a good part of 1931? The statement by Pegler cited above— "although he has been a professional athlete for a dozen years, his health is not always good"—suggests that Lazzeri's health was an ongoing issue. If so, why was the nature of the problem not addressed more directly by the press? Was the secrecy due to a lack of knowledge as to what the problem was or to an unwillingness to publicly discuss the issue of epilepsy? Even though sportswriters never publicly revealed Lazzeri's illness, it seems highly unlikely, given his teammates' awareness of his condition and the amount of time writers spent with ballplayers then, that none of the writers knew about it.

Regarding Lazzeri's struggles with epilepsy, baseball historian Charles Alexander wrote: "Lazzeri experienced frequent seizures. Always in the morning, according to Ed Wells, and never during games. [Wells was a teammate from 1929 to 1932.] On train trips, Wells was assigned a seat across the aisle from Lazzeri, who told Wells that if he felt a seizure coming on, Wells was to put a wet towel on his forehead, hold his tongue down, and not get upset if his mouth began to foam; it would be over in four or five minutes. After Wells left the team, others would look after Lazzeri on trains, as would his roommates in hotels."[38]

There is no doubt that the Yankees were committed to keeping Lazzeri's epilepsy secret, as Ed Barrow confirmed: "I don't believe the public ever knew this about him. Certainly we took every precaution we could to see that the public never did, and in this the sports writers traveling with the club were likewise as considerate of Tony's feelings and welfare."[39] Since Colonel Ruppert's comment quoted in September 1932 appears to be the first public announcement of Lazzeri's alleged financial woes, is it possible that the Yankees' brass was providing an excuse for Lazzeri's poor play in 1931? The only justification for suggesting such a scenario is that, given the stigma attached to Lazzeri's affliction, if Ruppert wished to offer a rationale for Lazzeri's performance, it would be more acceptable to the public to attribute it to mental distress over finances than to suddenly reveal to the public that Lazzeri was an epileptic.

When asked about the possibility that Lazzeri's decline in 1930 and/or 1931 might have been due to his illness, Dr. Chad Carlson of the Medical College of Wisconsin replied as follows:

> It is common for people to have good periods (even periods of remission for extended periods of time) along with worsened periods with more frequent and/or more disruptive seizures. It would be impossible to know without direct records whether this was actually true, but a reasonable hypothesis is that seizures began worsening and this combined with changes to his medication resulted in changes in performance. Having seizures will leave people with sore and tired muscles and will often leave them feeling tired and with less focus. The two most likely treatments would have been phenobarbital or bromides and increasing either could have had associated cognitive or psychomotor effects that would impact his coordination and performance.[40]

The reference to sore and tired muscles as a consequence of seizures seems particularly relevant to Lazzeri's situation in 1930 and even more so in 1931. The most startling aspect of the 1931 slump was his decrease in power. Whereas in his first five seasons his previous low in slugging average was .462, with highs of .535 and .561, in 1931 his average fell to .401, his second lowest in any full season. (In 1937, his last year with the Yankees, his average was .399.) In 1930 he hit nine homers and in 1931, eight, compared to eighteen in three of his other four seasons. (The drop to nine in 1928 was due to his severe shoulder injury and diminished playing time.) In the June 7, 1931, article ghostwritten under Ruth's name and cited above regarding Lazzeri's first home run of the season, Ruth seemed puzzled by his teammate's sudden inability to hit the long ball. How was it that this "powerful hitter, one of the best in the game," had gone two months into the season without a homer when "in other years a homer by Lazzeri was taken as a matter of course"? Furthermore, Maye Lazzeri, in the letter cited above in which she guaranteed that Tony would report to 1931 spring training in "excellent condition," based her claim on the fact that "Tony has been particularly careful of his diet, hasn't done any hard work and has abandoned those long automobile tours he usually took after the close of the ball season." These would seem to be precautions against fatigue rather than a response to injuries. According to Dr. Carlson, "Fatigue (sleep deprivation in particular) can increase the risk of seizures and that would have been the expectation in that era as well, so I could certainly envision a physician recommending avoiding any excess activity."[41]

As for the drop in batting average in both 1930 and 1931, if there were an increase in Lazzeri's seizures at that time, he may have increased his use of medication. If so, the corresponding increase in sedation and cognitive slowing referred to by Dr. Carlson may have contributed to a decrease in reflexes and hand-eye coordination needed to consistently hit the ball squarely. All this, of course, is conjecture, necessitated by the lack of any definitive evidence to explain Lazzeri's downward spiral. However, in 1932 at least one writer did make a specific reference to illness as the cause of Lazzeri's poor showing in 1931. In a preview of the 1932 World Series, Harold C. Burr wrote: "The story of the comeback by the terror of Telegraph Hill is old by now—how he became sick and discouraged, how the Yanks attempted to trade him during the past Winter, and how he strode out on the field this year, brown and healthy."[42]

Kieran, who had been critical of Lazzeri in his July 14 column, offered a general overview of the big league season in late September. Here he acknowledged Lazzeri's improvement and even expressed optimism for the future: "The Yankees have done as well as anyone could expect [in light of a disappointing season by the pitching staff]. That hurt the Yankees, as did the surprising slump of Tony Lazzeri. But Tony staged something of a comeback in the last month or two of the season and may be the Lazzeri of old in 1932."[43] Apparently the Yankees' brass was less confident of a comeback. A profile photo of Lazzeri graced the front page of *The Sporting News* on December 10, under the caption "Yanks' Bait for a Pitcher." According to the note below the photo, the Yankees, with "a wealth of brilliant young talent coming up for the infield," were hoping to trade Lazzeri in return for pitching strength, perhaps in a deal with the White Sox or Indians.

Baseball can be cruel. Three years after his 1928 shoulder injury had threatened to end his career, it looked as though Lazzeri's future in baseball was again in jeopardy. Without explicit documentation, it is impossible to determine a definitive answer as to the cause, or causes, of Lazzeri's diminished performance relative to his first four seasons with the Yankees, a performance that in turn motivated management to consider trading the man who had been such a vital part of the team. Was this a temporary hurdle or the beginning of an irreversible downward trajectory? Wherever the truth may lie, the reason for Lazzeri's decline at such a young age remains, in the words of Kieran, "a major league mystery," as was his fate heading into 1932.

1. Lazzeri home at 142–44 Missouri Street, San Francisco. Courtesy of the Lazzeri family.

2. Agostino Lazzeri on the steps of the Missouri Street home. Courtesy of the Lazzeri family.

3. Lazzeri at age eighteen. National Baseball Hall of Fame Library, Cooperstown, New York.

4. Lazzeri with the Salt Lake City Bees, in his record-setting 1925 season. David Eskenazi Collection.

5. Lazzeri and double-play partner Mark
Koenig, 1926. Courtesy of the Lazzeri family.

6. Lazzeri at the 1926 World Series with Cardinals outfielder Ernie Orsatti, a former stunt man who worked for silent film star Buster Keaton. Courtesy of the Lazzeri family.

7. Lazzeri on Tony Lazzeri Day at Yankee Stadium, with Lou Gehrig and Babe Ruth, September 8, 1927. Rucker Archive/Transcendental Graphics.

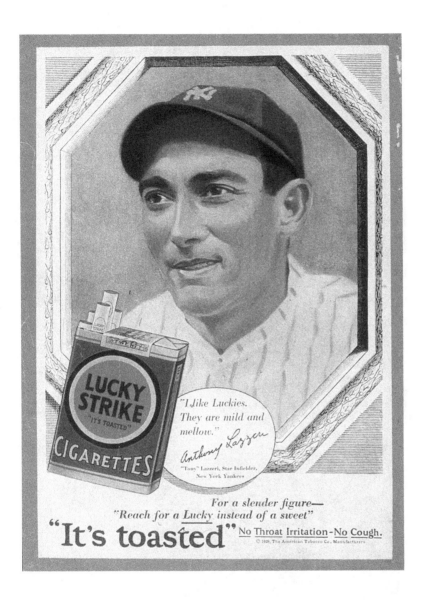

8. In 1928 Lazzeri was chosen to be part of the first national ad campaign by Lucky Strike cigarettes. Rucker Archive/ Transcendental Graphics.

9. Lou Gehrig, Babe Ruth, Earle Combs, and Lazzeri at Fenway Park. Courtesy of the Boston Public Library, Leslie Jones Collection.

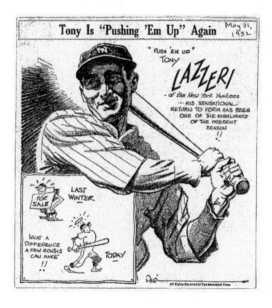

10. Cartoon by Thomas "Pap" Paprocki celebrating Lazzeri's comeback in 1932. Rucker Archive/Transcendental Graphics.

11. Frank Crosetti and Lazzeri with rookie Joe DiMaggio (center) in
Fenway Park dugout, 1936. Courtesy of the Boston Public Library, Leslie
Jones Collection.

12. Lazzeri and DiMaggio with Red Sox manager Joe Cronin (center), who
idolized Lazzeri when both were playing sandlot baseball in San Francisco.
Courtesy of the Boston Public Library, Leslie Jones Collection.

13. (*opposite top*) Lazzeri receives 1936 Player of the Year
Award from New York chapter of BBWAA, February
7, 1937. Left to right: NL president Ford Frick, Travis
Jackson (recipient of Player of Most Meritorious Service
Award), Lazzeri, and AL president William Harridge.
William Hoff/*New York Daily News*.

14. (*opposite bottom*) Maye Lazzeri plays the piano as
Tony and son David sing along at their residence in the
Concourse Plaza Hotel in the Bronx, July 1937. Ossie
Leviness/*New York Daily News*.

15. (*above*) Lazzeri crossing home plate after hitting a
home run at Yankee Stadium, with Frank Crosetti on
deck, 1937. Rucker Archive/Transcendental Graphics.

16. Five Italians in 1937 World Series versus the Giants. Left to right: Gus Mancuso, Joe DiMaggio, Lazzeri, Frank Crosetti, and Lou Chiozza. Courtesy of the Lazzeri family.

17. (*opposite top*) Gabby Hartnett, who replaced Charlie Grimm as Cubs manager in midseason, with player-coach Lazzeri, 1938. Rucker Archive/ Transcendental Graphics.

18. (*opposite bottom*) Lazzeri, managing the Toronto Maple Leafs, 1939–40. City of Toronto Archives, Fonds 1257, Item 3350.

19. David, Tony, and Maye Lazzeri in their Toronto residence. Courtesy of the Lazzeri family.

20. Lazzeri and Babe Dahlgren, Yankees first baseman who replaced Lou Gehrig on May 2, 1939, the day Gehrig ended his consecutive-game playing streak at 2,130. Courtesy of the Lazzeri family.

21. Lazzeri in Olympic Club portrait.
Courtesy of the Olympic Club, San Francisco.

22. Lazzeri golfing at the Olympic Club, January 1939, with Ty Cobb, a member since 1935. National Baseball Hall of Fame Library, Cooperstown, New York.

23. Player-manager Lazzeri with Frank Lawrence, owner of the Portsmouth Cubs of the Piedmont League, 1942. Courtesy of Sargeant Memorial Collection, Norfolk Public Library.

24. Always a snappy dresser, Lazzeri was
managing the Wilkes-Barre Barons of the
Eastern League when this photo was taken
in 1943. Courtesy of the Lazzeri family.

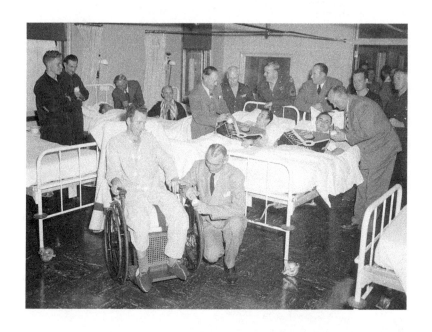

25. Lazzeri, Ty Cobb, Lefty O'Doul, and
Walter Mails visit war casualties at
Letterman Hospital, San Francisco, July
1946. Fang Family *San Francisco Examiner*
photograph archive negative files, BANC
PIC 2006.029:105938.02.02—NEG, Box
838, USO-*Examiner* baseball tour at
Letterman Hospital, © Regents of the
University of California, Bancroft Library,
University of California, Berkeley.

9

The Big Revival

W hile the Yankees leadership was somewhat pleased that the team had moved up to second place in its first season under Joe McCarthy, Ed Barrow and Colonel Ruppert were anxious to return to the elite status they had enjoyed from 1926 through 1928. And for a long time it appeared that Tony Lazzeri was not part of their plan. Rumors regarding possible trades were swirling around like so many dark funnel clouds during the 1931 offseason. So much so that Harold C. Burr wrote: "Life in his California retreat holds many uncertainties for Tony Lazzeri this Winter. He has been a greatly traded infielder."[1] Among the teams reportedly interested in acquiring the veteran were the Red Sox, White Sox, Indians, and Senators. Some of the trade rumor reports suggested the extent to which Lazzeri's star status had fallen. He was described in one story as "a competent second baseman" and in another as "the slightly shop-worn Italian second baseman."[2]

According to the rumor mill, slated to replace Lazzeri was Jack Saltzgaver, a seven-year Minor Leaguer who had hit .340 in 1931 for St. Paul in the American Association. One report in December indicated that "there is little doubt that Lazzeri is on the market, in view of McCarthy's plan to play Jack Saltzgaver at second base as a starter next year."[3] One AP report sounded like a forecast of someone's imminent demise: "Saltzgaver's introduction to a Yankee uniform, it is predicted, will mark the passing of the illustrious Lazzeri at second."[4] Burr, however, reminded his readers that

Lazzeri had something that anyone who replaced him might not have: "He has more than his share of color on a team that has always been noted for its bizarre ballplayers, from Kid Elberfeld down to Babe Ruth. Lazzeri is the most popular of all the Italian players in the big league. He is to baseball what Franco Georgetti was to bicycle racing, a crowd getter and a crowd pleaser. The Yankees would be a little bit duller to watch without Poosh 'Em Up, Tony."[5]

Nevertheless, it seemed to be a certainty that Lazzeri's time with the Yankees was coming to an end after his disappointing performance in 1930 and a good part of 1931. A week after Burr's story appeared, his colleague Tommy Holmes reported that Ruppert and McCarthy were hoping to repeat the unexpected success of Miller Huggins's decision in 1926 to start two rookies—Koenig and Lazzeri—in the middle of the infield: "That was only a few years ago, but already Koenig, now with Detroit, and Lazzeri, still with the Yanks, seem well on their way to the cleaners."[6] Trade rumors persisted well into the season. Less than a week before the trade deadline in June, the *Washington Post* reported that Senators owner Clark Griffith had contacted McCarthy regarding a deal for Lazzeri.[7]

One blatant indication of Lazzeri's uncertain status going into the 1932 season was the dramatic change in his uniform number. In 1929, the first year the players wore numbers, Lazzeri was wearing no. 6, corresponding to his primary place in the batting order. In both 1930 and 1931 he wore no. 5 for the same reason. But in 1932 he was assigned no. 23, the last available number since teams had cut the number of active players from twenty-five to twenty-three, suggesting either that the Yankees expected to trade him, perhaps even after the season opened, or that if he were still with the team, he wasn't expected to be in the starting lineup.

But, to paraphrase Mark Twain, reports of Lazzeri's demise would prove to be greatly exaggerated. From his uncertain status as trade bait, he would bounce back in 1932 to have one of his best years, enjoying what Westbrook Pegler described as "a big revival all season."[8] It would prove to be a revival season for the Yankees as well. Meanwhile, while others were speculating about Lazzeri's fate, he and Maye became the parents of a nine-pound baby boy; David Anthony Lazzeri was born in San Francisco on December 16, 1931. A photo of Lazzeri visiting Maye and the baby in the hospital bearing gifts of a baseball and glove for the newborn—who was sleeping soundly—appeared in newspapers across the country. Soon after, Lazzeri sent a card to Yankees GM Ed Barrow wishing him a Merry Christmas and informing him that "henceforth two Bambinos will be identified with the Yankees."[9]

It took a while, but inevitably the harsh reality of the Great Depression took its toll on Major League Baseball. Following record-high attendance in 1930 of over ten million, there was a drop-off of more than 15 percent in 1931, and by 1932 attendance would fall to roughly three and a half million, a drop of nearly 70 percent since 1930. This prompted owners to lower the number of players on the active roster to twenty-three in 1932—the reduction would remain in effect until 1939—and to begin to cut their payrolls in order to survive the hard times. (Given the reserve clause, which required a player to sign with his current team unless he were traded, sold, or released, players had no options other than to accept what was offered or leave the game.) Holmes called it "the almost universal salary war in the major league baseball ranks."[10]

In spite of his subpar performance in 1931 and the trade rumors, once again Lazzeri was a holdout. In late January 1932 a story about New York Major Leaguers who were dissatisfied with the contract offers they received described Lazzeri as the "former kingpin second sacker of the Yankees but last year a reservist."[11] In mid-February the *San Francisco Examiner* reported that Lazzeri "would be satisfied if he was mailed the same contract he had last season, but the Italian star found his earnings almost cut in two." Lazzeri was quoted as saying, "It is true I got off bad last year, but I came back and played as good ball as I ever did. The Yankees have always treated me fine, and I am confident we'll be able to get together." The story also noted that "no less than seven clubs are eager to take Lazzeri away from the Yankees in a trade or by purchase."[12]

By the end of February Ruth and Lazzeri were reported to be the only two Yankees to have not signed a contract. One story quoted McCarthy as saying of Lazzeri, "I fail to see how he figures he's so important in our plans that he can buck at terms." The anonymous writer goes on to say that the manager's "present plans for the infield don't include the Wollopin' [sic] Wop, and it is still the general opinion among the players that Lazzeri will be wearing another uniform before opening day arrives."[13] Regardless, on March 1 Lazzeri came to terms with the Yankees for a salary later disclosed to be $12,000, a 25 percent cut from his 1931 salary. Ruth also signed for a lower figure, but his cut from $80,000 to $75,000 amounted to a mere 6 percent reduction. Paul Gallico poked fun at the steep cut in the Bambino's salary: "That five thousand makes all the difference in the world," he wrote. "It may be the means of bringing back prosperity."[14]

Once everyone had reported to St. Petersburg, it was time to figure out who would be playing where in the Yankees infield. "So crawling with infielders is the Yankee training camp this Spring that your correspondent is afraid he will spoon one from his vegetable soup one day. The hotel lobby is alive with them, and at unexpected moments a second sacker is flushed from under a potted palm and a shortstop is sighted peering furtively from behind a divan."[15] So begins Marshall Hunt's colorful report from St. Petersburg on the six infielders who were competing to play at second, third, and short. In addition to Lazzeri and Saltzgaver, the contenders included Lyn Lary, Joe Sewell, Eddie Farrell, and rookie Frank Crosetti.

Like Lazzeri, Crosetti was a San Francisco native of Italian descent; his father was an immigrant, and his California-born mother was a second-generation Italian American. Crosetti's childhood illness forced the family to move to a farm in Los Gatos, California, when he was two years old. It was there that he and his older brother improvised their own brand of baseball: "We used the big end of a corn cob as a ball. For a bat we'd take a board and shave it down. Baseball came naturally to me. I wanted to play as long as I can remember."[16]

Crosetti played the game so well when the family moved back to San Francisco that by 1928 the seventeen-year-old was playing third base for the San Francisco Seals of the PCL. Also on the Seals roster that year was forty-one-year-old former Major Leaguer and San Francisco legend Ping Bodie (known to his parents as Francesco Pezzolo). Crosetti recalled some advice he received from the veteran: "He told me, 'Go to the butcher shop and get a large meat bone. Have your mother boil the meat off and use that to bone your bats.' I did that; then when I went to the Yankees, I took the same bone with me." After hitting .248 and .314 in his first two seasons with the Seals, in 1930 Crosetti raised his average to .334 and hit twenty-seven home runs, making him one of the most sought-after Minor Leaguers in the country. In August, while the season was still in progress, the Yankees purchased the contract of the 5-foot-10-inch, 165 pound infielder for three players and $75,000—a huge sum at the time—with the proviso that the nineteen-year-old would remain with the Seals through the 1931 season, when he would hit .343.

When the 1932 season opened on April 12 at Philadelphia, Lazzeri was still wearing a Yankees uniform. The prevailing opinion was that while several teams were interested in acquiring him, none was willing to give up the front-line pitcher the Yankees were looking for. However, Lazzeri was not in the starting lineup. McCarthy had settled on Saltzgaver at second, Crosetti at third, and Lary at short. But Saltzgaver failed to get a hit in his first four games, and by April 19 Lazzeri was starting at second. Saltzgaver played sparingly thereafter, never hitting higher than .132, and after appearing in twenty games, he was sent down to the Yankees' Double AA affiliate in Newark. Lazzeri, meanwhile, hit .303 in April, then took off in May, hitting .397. By the end of May the man few expected to see in a Yankees uniform was second in the AL in average (.368) and on-base percentage (.481) and fourth in slugging average (.613).

Another shift in the infield alignment occurred in the second game of a doubleheader on June 1. Lary was removed from the shortstop spot, and Crosetti, who had been starting at third, took his place, while Sewell—a thirty-one-year-old veteran infielder who had hit .320 in eleven years with the Indians—stepped in at third. From that moment Crosetti and Lazzeri—the first Major Leaguers of Italian descent to form a double-play combination in the big leagues—began the Yankees' keystone combo that, with few interruptions, would last through the 1937 season, Lazzeri's last with the Yankees. Crosetti, who would be in the Yankees lineup for another eleven years after Lazzeri left, was a player-coach in his final two seasons, then spent another nineteen years as the third base coach. He ended up wearing a Yankees uniform for thirty-seven years, longer than anyone in franchise history.

A mid-September story noted that the two middle infielders would communicate in Italian while on the field: "Both come from San Francisco and often jabber away in their native tongue in the infield to the discomfiture of the enemy on the bags. Lazzeri was Crosetti's boyhood hero, and Tony from Telegraph Hill has taught him many tricks in English and Italian."[17] Lazzeri was indeed a mentor to his fellow San Franciscan, as he later would be to Joe DiMaggio. "When I was called up by the Yankees, I looked up Tony at his home, and he took me under his wing," said Crosetti. "He told me what to expect when I joined the team. He was a big help to me."[18]

On June 30 Lazzeri and Crosetti were initiated into the Orient Heights Lodge of the Sons of Italy at East Boston High School, and the following day, "Sons of Italy Day" at Fenway Park, they were honored prior to the game. Or as Marshall Hunt described the scene: "Members of the Sons of Italy Society indigenous to South Boston left their vermicelli vats, raviola [sic] foundries and shoe shine stalls long enough to bestow emblems, bouquets and other symbols of esteem upon two of their illustrious countrymen."[19] The tribute failed to ignite Lazzeri, who went 0 for 5 in an 11–6 loss to the Red Sox. Crosetti never got into the game.

Crosetti was given the obvious nickname of "Crow," but he noted that one teammate had yet another name for him: "Babe Ruth used to call me 'Dago Bananas,' probably because he couldn't remember my name." But Crosetti didn't object. "Babe was a wonderful person," he said. "He did more for the game of baseball than anybody."

With their infield now set and with Dickey behind the plate and Chapman, Combs, and Ruth in the outfield, the Yankees got off to a strong start, as did Lazzeri. On May 21 they held a half-game lead over second-place Washington when the teams met in a doubleheader. Lazzeri went 6 for 7 with a double, triple, and home run as the Yankees won both games to stretch their lead to 2½ games. At the end of the day Lazzeri's batting average stood at a season-high .422, second in the AL only to Jimmie Foxx at. 452. He led the league in on-base percentage and was second in slugging average.

Following that outburst Lazzeri fell into a slump; with nine hits in thirty-seven at bats in his next ten games, his average fell from .422 to .333. Then on June 3 the Yankees faced the Athletics in Philadelphia in what would prove to be not only one of the more memorable games of the season, but also one with historical significance for Lazzeri. The final score was 20–13 in favor of the Yankees, who rapped out twenty-three hits compared to thirteen for the A's. Nine home runs were hit, seven by the Yanks. Amazingly an additional seventeen runners were left on base. The A's used five pitchers, the Yankees four. The game also featured six errors, five by the Yankees. Hunt called the epic slugfest a "three-hour brawl" and an "insane affair."[20] However, the game is best remembered not for the final score but for remarkable individual achievements.

In this game Lazzeri was playing third base while Saltzgaver was at short in one of his rare starts. After striking out in the second inning, Lazzeri singled to center in the fourth, doubled to left in the sixth, tripled to center in the seventh, singled to right in the eighth, and hit a home run in the ninth to make the score 20–12 in favor of New York. Not only did Lazzeri hit for the cycle, but he also made it a "natural" cycle by hitting the single, double, triple, and homer in that order. As if that weren't enough, the home run came with the bases loaded, making it the first, and to date the only, natural cycle capped by a grand slam. In the only game of his career in which he had five hits Lazzeri drove in six runs and scored three times. His performance boosted his average from .333 to .357, third best in the AL, as was his slugging average of .619.

On most days such an offensive display would command significant coverage, but on this particular day Lazzeri's feat was overshadowed by another rare achievement by one of his own teammates. Gehrig hit four home runs, a feat achieved only twice before, in 1894 by Bobby Lowe and in 1896 by Ed Delahanty. After hitting four homers in his first four at bats, followed by a single, Gehrig came very close to hitting a fifth homer in the ninth inning. His four round trippers gave him eleven for the season, good enough for third place in the AL, behind Ruth and Foxx, both of whom also homered in that game. (Foxx, who would go on to win the Triple Crown, hit fifty-eight homers, the most at that time by anyone other than Ruth.)

But even Gehrig's historic barrage was cast into the shadows that day by the sudden announcement by John "Mugsy" McGraw, the Giants' legendary manager of thirty years, that he was retiring. His was the story that made the front page of the *New York Times*, where McGraw was called "as dominating a figure as ever stepped upon a diamond." The Gehrig story appeared on page 10. None of the stories I have seen referred to Lazzeri as hitting for the cycle, a term that was not yet in common usage.

With their record of 107–47 challenging that of their 1927 Murderers' Row mark of 110–44, the Yankees coasted to the pennant, ending the three-year stranglehold of their old nemesis, Connie Mack's A's, who finished thirteen games behind. Along with Lazzeri, the three other holdovers from the 1927 squad all played key roles. Gehrig led the team in average (.349) and RBIs (151) and added 34 homers. Ruth, now thirty-seven years old, no longer dwarfed all others but was still a powerhouse, hitting 41 homers with a .341 average and 137 RBIs. Leadoff hitter Earle Combs scored the most runs (143) and hit .321. In addition, Chapman drove in 107 and led the league with 38 stolen bases, and Dickey, now in his fourth full season, hit 15 homers and drove in 84 runs, in spite of being suspended for thirty games after punching Washington outfielder Carl Reynolds, who had crashed into him at home plate, and breaking his jaw. The pitching staff led the league with a 3.98 ERA, while the top four starters won a combined 75 games. Red Ruffing (18–7) led the rotation with a 3.09 ERA, followed by rookie Johnny Allen at 3.74 and a 17–4 record. Lefty Gomez posted a 24–7 record and veteran George Pipgras went 16–9.

The Yankees' World Series rival Chicago Cubs had posted a more pedestrian record of 90–64, making New York a heavy favorite. One of the sidebar stories of the 1932 Series was the encounter of Lazzeri and his former double play partner, Mark Koenig. Like Lazzeri, he had been written off. Traded to Detroit in 1930, after two lackluster seasons with the Tigers, he was back in the Minors at the age of twenty-seven, his big league career seemingly ended. But when he flourished with the San Francisco Missions of the PCL, hitting .335, he was signed in mid-August by the Cubs to fill in for Billy Jurges at short.[21] Koenig played a key role in helping the Cubs win the pennant, hitting .353 in thirty-three games.

A cartoon in *The Sporting News* prior to the World Series illustrated the irony of the two supposedly over-the-hill former infield partners reunited as foes. The cartoon featured a portrait sketch of Lazzeri on the left and a sketch of Koenig in full swing on the right. Above Lazzeri's portrait was the caption: "The Yanks couldn't give Tony Lazzeri away last March," and below it was: "Now, he is the main spring of the champions' infield." Next to the sketch of Koenig the caption read: "Voted no dice by the Yanks and the Tigers and kicked to the bushes . . . Mark Koenig bounced back with the Cubs a month ago, and look at them now." The story beneath the cartoon noted that the Series "will bring into the spotlight a little personal drama culminating in the come-back of two personal pals."[22] But, as it turned out, there was more drama to come regarding Koenig's appearance in the World Series.

When the Cubs met to decide how to share their World Series money, they voted to give Koenig a half share. Years later Koenig told historian Norman Macht how he felt about his Cubs teammates: "The way the Cubs treated me, I was glad the Yankees beat us. I just wasn't accepted by that bunch of players. I had no friends on the team."[23] The snub of Koenig provided the context for what would become the biggest story of the Series: the legendary "called shot" by Ruth in Game Three. As the story goes, at least some of the Yankees were resentful of what they considered the Cubs' unfair treatment of their former teammate, and they displayed their anger verbally and relentlessly from the moment the Series began, none more so than Ruth. The Cubs, in response, hurled intense abuse at the Yanks from their dugout, much of which was not fit for sensitive ears, with Ruth the primary target of the most vitriolic and vulgar bench jockeying.

The Series, which opened on September 28, did not get off to a promising start. A disappointing crowd of 41,450 showed up at Yankee Stadium, the start of the game was delayed by rain, and the game itself was a pedestrian affair. In addition to being the targets of Ruth's harangue, the Cubs had to endure an embarrassing 12–6 loss. Game Two was a repeat performance; more tongue lashing by the Bambino and a 5–2 Yankees win. Following the first two games, writers were lamenting the lack of drama. Paul Gallico called the opener "a ragged, harum-scarum sort of ball game that looked a lot like a Broadway show opening cold," while Irving Vaughn made this prediction following Game Two: "Unless somebody puts a new complexion on this world series it will go down in the baseball books as one of the poorest spectacles staged at inflated prices."[24]

Who better to provide that new complexion than Ruth, the inimitable showman? When the Series moved to Chicago for Game Three, a hostile crowd of 49,986 jammed into Wrigley Field to greet the Yankees. (Temporary bleachers had been erected to accommodate the large turnout.) Cubs fans were ready to let Ruth know how they felt about the man who had been so openly berating their players, not only jeering him lustily, but even tossing lemons at him on the field. The players continued to exchange barbs, if anything at a more intense and personal level than in New York.

Facing Cubs starter Charlie Root, Ruth opened the festivities with a three-run homer in the first inning. The Cubs scored a run in the bottom of the inning, but a homer by Gehrig in the third made the score 4–1. By the time Ruth came to bat in the fifth inning, with none on and one out, the Cubs had rallied to tie the game at 4–4. With both players and fans heaping abuse on the Bambino, he laughed, took a strike from Root, and then held up one finger as he looked toward the Cubs dugout, reminding the hecklers that it was just strike one. He took two pitches that missed the plate, looked at a second strike, then held up two fingers. Now came the "Did he or didn't he?" moment. Before Root delivered his next pitch, Ruth made a gesture of uncertain direction or meaning. According to some, he was pointing at Root; according to others, he was pointing at the Cubs dugout, perhaps alerting it to what he was about to do with the next pitch, but to others he was pointing to center field as if to predict where the next pitch would end up. Predicted or not, that is exactly where the ball ended up. Root threw a changeup, and Ruth drove the ball far into the center-field bleachers; more than one writer called it the longest homer ever hit at Wrigley. Ruth laughed as he trotted around the bases, then made a pushing gesture with both hands toward the Cubs dugout as he rounded third base. Gehrig, who had homered in the third inning, shook the Babe's hand as he crossed the plate, then stepped into the batter's box and ended

Root's day by hitting the first pitch into the right-field stands to extend the Yanks' lead to 6–4. Each team tacked on a run in the ninth to make the final score 7–5.

While Ruth's "called shot" is not the most decisive or dramatic home run in World Series history, it is certainly the most debated. In any case, who else but Ruth, in a crucial moment of a World Series game, would exchange loud barbs with the opposing team without losing focus and enjoy every moment of it? But would someone even as exuberant and confident of his ability as was the Sultan of Swat be foolish enough to predict a home run? Yet even if he did not point to center field, his incredibly bold act of signaling to the Cubs bench that he still had one strike left would seem to be a reminder that he was still in charge of the situation and a "watch-what-I-do-now" message to his hecklers.

While not claiming that Ruth had pointed to center field, Westbrook Pegler, in his syndicated column, clearly interpreted Ruth's gesture as a prediction of a home run: "Nor will you ever see an artist call his shot before hitting one of his longest drives." Whether or not Ruth did call his shot, Pegler aptly captured the essence of the moment, writing that the people who saw Ruth hit those two home runs "came away from the baseball plant with a spiritual memento of the most gorgeous display of humor, athletic art and championship class any performer in any of the games has ever presented."[25] The Series as a whole was generally regarded as a dud. Writing as Walter W. Smith, the byline he used early in his career, Red Smith called it "the worst slaughter in World Series history" and "a dismal flop."[26] Nevertheless, with his showmanship and singular moment, the Babe put his personal stamp on his tenth, and last, postseason appearance, creating one of the most celebrated moments of Ruthian folklore.

Among those who witnessed Ruth's artistry that day was New York governor Franklin Delano Roosevelt, recently nominated as the Democratic presidential candidate to run against Herbert Hoover, and future Supreme Court justice John Paul Stevens. Roosevelt watched the game from a front row box seat alongside

Chicago mayor Anton Cermak after throwing out the ceremonial first ball. Another eyewitness was the legendary tap dancer
and actor Bill "Bojangles" Robinson, a staunch Yankees fan. The
Chicago Tribune reported that he visited the Yankees locker room
after the game, shook hands with the players, then "jumped on
a trunk and began to dance while the players surrounded him,
hollering and clapping their hands."[27]

After that game a Yankees sweep seemed inevitable, and they
delivered with a salt-in-the-wound 13–6 win, giving them an
unprecedented twelve-game winning streak in World Series games
dating back to 1927. Lazzeri, hitting fifth throughout the Series,
had gone 2 for 12 in the first three games, scoring two runs and
driving in one. But in the clincher he stole the spotlight from
Ruth and Gehrig, and capped his comeback season, by going 3 for
5 and driving in four runs on a pair of two-run homers. The *Salt
Lake Tribune* paid fond tribute to the former Bees' star with this
headline: "Our Tone Helps Yanks Put Riotous End to Series."[28]

The Yankees punished Cubs pitching, scoring thirty-seven runs
on forty-five hits and hitting a record eight homers. Gehrig led
the way with nine hits in seventeen at bats, including three homers and eight RBIs. But even though he outperformed Ruth (two
homers and six RBIs), Gehrig was once again overshadowed by
the Babe, whose dramatic performance in Game Three was the
big story. The Series win was especially sweet for McCarthy, who
gained some measure of revenge against his former employers
for letting him go near the end of the 1930 season.

By June 30 the Yankees were 9½ games ahead of the Tigers with a
48–19 record, and from there they coasted to the pennant. Along
with Dickey and Gehrig, Lazzeri was a spark plug for the Yankees' success through the first half of the season; all three were
at or near the top of the AL batting statistics. Regarding Lazzeri's comeback from 1931, Graham wrote: "He made the journey
from the rim of obscurity. He was, everybody said, all through,
washed up and ready for shipment to the Red Sox, the White Sox,

or some other second division outfit." While noting that Lazzeri was third in the AL in hitting, Graham acknowledged that he had slowed up—"he can't cover ground like some of his rivals and he doesn't often turn off a double play"—but "for intelligence, for steadiness and for sheer courage Tony has an edge on all the others. Seeing Tony at work around second base every day calls up memories of the years from 1926 to 1928. . . . This is the same Lazzeri who, grim and silent, in deadly earnest, was the prop on which Miller Huggins pinned his pennant hopes in 1926."[29]

An International News Service dispatch regarding Lazzeri's comeback indicated his standing with his peers: "Ballplayers throughout the country are pleased by the remarkable comeback of Tony Lazzeri, veteran second baseman of the New York Yankees. . . . Making sparkling plays afield, and walloping the horsehide with his old-time vigor, 'Poosh 'em Up' Tony has molded the club together just as he did in the halcyon days of 1926."[30]

Soon thereafter, however, Lazzeri fell into a temporary slump. He hit .237 in July, dropping his average from .341 to .302. Nevertheless, he managed to score 22 runs, more than in any other month, and his 4 homers and 22 RBIs were exceeded only by his numbers in August: 5 and 27 respectively. He then bounced back with averages of .287 and .315 in August and September to finish the season at an even .300, thirty-three points higher than his 1931 average. He regained his position at second base, and after having been relegated to the number eight spot in the order for most of 1931, he forced his way back to the heart of the order in 1932, hitting in the fifth spot in more than half of the 142 games in which he played. The most marked improvements came in his power numbers; his 15 home runs almost doubled his 1931 output of 8, and his 16 triples put him in a tie for second-most in the AL. He also finished near the top of the league in several other offensive categories: seventh in OPS (.905), eighth in RBIs (113) and slugging average (.506), and ninth in on-base percentage (.399) and walks (82). By comparison, in 1931 Lazzeri finished in the AL top twenty only in RBIs (83). Just as he had in his rookie year, he confounded those critics who had doubted him. By any measure Lazzeri's 1932 season was a dramatic revival by a player considered to be washed up by many and put unceremoniously on the trading block by his team.

In early September 1932 Joe Williams acknowledged that in 1931 Lazzeri "was a bad ball player. . . . He couldn't hit and he couldn't field." But then, in terms reminiscent of what had been written about Lazzeri in his rookie season, Williams added: "Lazzeri has been the mainspring of the new champions' infield this year. It's no cinch they would have won without him. Besides a fine mechanical ability, he brought a steadying influence to the middle of the diamond that was vitally needed."[31] The inside cover of the November 1932 issue of *Baseball Magazine* consisted entirely of a photo of Lazzeri and this caption: "Tony Lazzeri, Who Is Playing the Game of His Life for the New York Yankees."

So impressive was Lazzeri's performance that the man who seemed destined to not even appear in a Yankees uniform in 1932 finished eighth in the vote for the AL MVP Award, one slot behind Ruth. In 1930, and even more so in 1931, he had faced challenges that tested both his talent and his will. Whether the issue was mental, physical, or both will never be known with certainty. What is certain is that as he had done before, Tony Lazzeri confronted those challenges and overcame them. In the end his startling 1932 renaissance remains as mysterious as were the struggles he had endured in the previous two seasons.

Immediately after the World Series ended, Lazzeri boarded a train in Chicago and headed to California to join Maye and their nine-month-old son, David, in their recently purchased home in the Millbrae Highlands, south of San Francisco.

10

Pennant Drought

I n 1933 the Great Depression reached what most historians consider to be its worst year. Almost thirteen million people were out of work as unemployment rose to 25 percent, and many lost their homes. The average annual wage, for those getting one, was about $1,500. Hundreds of thousands of homeless were living in tent cities called Hoovervilles. The unemployed and destitute flocked to bread lines and soup kitchens, and many rode the rails in search of work. In the baseball world attendance had fallen drastically in 1932, and only the pennant-winning Yankees and Cubs were believed to have turned a profit. In an attempt to survive, baseball owners continued to cut back on expenses in 1933. Rosters were again limited to twenty-three players, and several clubs trimmed their coaching staffs. Even the Yankees, the richest franchise in baseball, had to economize. They released Jimmy Burke, one of their three coaches, and trimmed a week off the normal spring training schedule. As Marshall Hunt reported: "Determined to cut expenses in numerous ways, [the Yankees] decided that the performers, archaic specimens with squeaking hinges as well as robust youth fresh from the furrows, will have to attend to their Spring training in an unusually short space of time. . . . When times were good, the Yankees could have stayed profitably in the provinces for several months. . . . But those days are gone."[1]

The biggest savings of course would be gained by further slashing salaries. One writer predicted that when Major League contract letters go out, "the slaughter will be terrible"[2] As expected, many players protested what they considered excessive cuts, though it is likely they got little sympathy from those struggling to survive. None protested more loudly, or more publicly, than the Bambino. As noted, his 1932 salary had been cut from $80,000 to $75,000, but the expectation was that a much bigger slice was coming in 1933. Ruth was indignant when he received an offer of $50,000, telling reporters that "lopping off $25,000 at one smack is no cut. It's what you fellows might call an amputation."[3] That would be only the first salvo in an ongoing skirmish between the Babe and Yankees brass.

Lazzeri was one of the other key Yankees who held out, along with Gehrig, Dickey, and Ruffing. In light of the offer he received, which remained undisclosed, Lazzeri suggested he might have to go back to his old job, even if it meant forsaking his favorite hobby. "I was given a stiff salary cut last year," he said. "Now they're trying to cut my pay again. I guess I'll go back to the boiler factory. I would have to quit playing golf if I go back to the factory, but, then, I'll have to quit many things if I can't get better money playing baseball."[4] On March 6 it was announced that Lazzeri, as well as Dickey, had signed their contracts. (It was later revealed that Lazzeri was signed for $12,000, the same amount he received in 1932.) Meanwhile, Ruth was threatening to quit baseball if he did not receive $60,000, the lowest amount he was willing to accept. Finally, after receiving an ultimatum from Colonel Ruppert, he signed for $52,000. One New York wag referred to Ruth as "the well-known wage slave who used to be a high salaried artist."[5]

In spite of the strained economic conditions, heading into the 1933 season the outlook was bright for the Yankees. After all, they were coming off their World Series sweep with their lineup essentially unchanged. Soon after the Yanks clinched the 1932 pennant, columnist Jimmy Wood predicted a glorious future for the Yankees: "Yes, seems as if the Yanks are going to have a monopoly on the bunting for a while."[6] The monopoly, as it turned out, began and ended with the 1932 World Series. Over the next three seasons the Yankees would be good but not quite good enough to win another pennant, finishing second each year. It would also prove to be a challenging stretch for Tony Lazzeri.

Prior to the season several writers saw a real danger in the Yankees' decision to stand pat going into 1933, given the age of several key players. First and foremost on the list was Ruth. Now thirty-nine, he had slowed down considerably in 1932 and was a liability on defense, requiring frequent late-inning replacements. He remained, however, a powerful threat at bat. Future Hall of Famer Eddie Collins, who became general manager of the Boston Red Sox in 1933 under new owner Tom Yawkey, put it this way: "One slap and away goes your ball game. He hangs over you like a bucket of dynamite."[7] Both Earle Combs and Joe Sewell were also identified as senior citizens who would require time off during the season. And once again there were suggestions that Lazzeri would be replaced by Jack Saltzgaver. The headline above one AP report was blunt: "Chances Are All against Tony Lazzeri, Joe Sewell and Earl [sic] Combs Repeating Success of 1932."[8] While noting that "Signor Tony Lazzeri's work last Summer was satisfactory enough," Hunt concluded that the veteran "is on the down grade, and may have to be supplanted at second base before another pennant race will be decided."[9] Yet again there were doubts about Lazzeri's ability to perform at a high level, with some even ready to close the curtain on his career. So the question going into the new season was: Could Lazzeri replicate his comeback season of 1932, or would he revert to his disappointing 1931 level?

During spring training Lazzeri provided what was, for him, a rather lengthy interview with Harold C. Burr, who offered a more positive outlook for the coming season. Burr opened his story by noting that Lazzeri "plays the batters so uncannily and rams those long drives between the fielders so frequently that the bleacher bug at once thinks of him as a natural ball player."[10] But Lazzeri acknowledged, as he had done previously but at less length, that he didn't know a thing about playing second base when he came to the Yankees and was fortunate to have learned how to play the position from Miller Huggins and Joe McCarthy, both of whom had been second basemen. He also gave credit to Fred Merkle, a Yankees coach in 1926, for improving his hitting. "He was a great hitter, and smart up there," said Lazzeri of the former Giants outfielder better known for his notorious "boner" in a game that ultimately cost the Giants the pennant in 1908.[11] Lazzeri continued: "It didn't take him too many games to see that I was too choked up. So I lengthened my swing and began to pole the long hits. Then he recommended that I straddle out more at the rubber. I was standing with my feet too close together."

Lazzeri also admitted that he preferred to hit on the road rather than at Yankee Stadium, where "after the fifth inning you're in the shade and the pitcher is in the sun. Just try and hit with this glare between you." Then, in what sounds like the kind of veiled allusions to Lazzeri's struggles with epilepsy that appeared in 1931, Burr reached this conclusion: "Lazzeri, after a spell of sickness that nearly ended his baseball career, looks set for one of his best years since becoming a Yankee."

In spite of the doubts expressed about some of the carryover players from 1932, the Yankees' starting position players were exactly the same in 1933, with Dickey catching; Gehrig, Lazzeri, Crosetti, and Sewell in the infield; and Chapman, Combs, and Ruth in the outfield. They got off to a hot start, winning their first seven games and going 11–4 in April. But on April 25 in Washington they and the Senators were involved in one of the nastiest brawls in many seasons, one that involved fans as well as players, prompting several newspapers to call it a riot. Tensions between the rival clubs that had been smoldering since July 4, 1932, when Dickey broke the jaw of Carl Reynolds, suddenly erupted in the fourth inning. Chapman slid hard into second baseman Buddy Myer in an attempt to break up a double play, spiking him and knocking him over. (One of the fastest runners in baseball, Chapman had led the Majors in steals in 1931 and 1932 and would do so again in 1933.) After Myer got up and kicked Chapman in the thigh, they started trading blows. As is wont to happen on such occasions, players from both dugouts rushed onto the field. Umpires soon broke up the fight, and all seemed resolved until Chapman, who was ejected from the game along with Myer, headed to the Senators dugout, where the ramp to the Yankees locker room was located. There he was confronted by Senators pitcher Earl White-hill, who said something that inspired Chapman to punch him.

A new melee broke out in and near the dugout as several Senators jumped on Chapman, and several Yankees, including Lazzeri, sprinted across the diamond to come to his aid. To add to the fun hundreds of fans poured out of the stands to join in the festivities, fighting both with Yankees players and among themselves. According to Hunt's eyewitness account, the fans "closed in on a knot of Washington and New York players. Arms were swinging briskly, police were forcing their way into the melee, spectators were pounding their closed palms on the heads of New York players."[12] After about fifteen minutes the police broke up the brawl and arrested a few civilians. An AP story reported that when Lazzeri got involved in the melee, "some feminine fan yelled from the grandstand: 'Don't let Tony Lazzeri get in there, he'll kill somebody.'" The story quoted Lazzeri as saying: "I didn't know I was supposed to be a tough guy. I didn't kill anybody but I threw a few punches and for a minute I had a lot of fun."[13]

If the fight on the field was more or less a draw, the game itself was a KO by the Yanks, who had lost the first two games of the series. They smashed twenty-one hits off four Washington hurlers, including home runs by Lazzeri (his first of the season) and Gehrig, while rookie Russ Van Atta pitched a five-hit shutout. On April 28, three days after the brawl in Washington, the Senators were at Yankee Stadium for a two-game series. With AL president Will Harridge—who that same day inflicted a five-day suspension and $100 fines on Crenshaw, Myer, and White-hill—in attendance, the Senators edged the Yanks 4–3 in what the AP called "a mild ball game" in which both teams "leaned over backward being polite to each other."[14] When the first month of the season came to a close, the Yankees held a 1½ game lead over the Senators and White Sox.

Compared to the Yankees' fast break out of the starting gate, Lazzeri's start was decidedly slow. While the Yanks were winning their first seven games, Lazzeri had four hits, all singles, in twenty-six at bats, for a .154 average. Through the first thirteen games, his average stood at .200, with an on-base percentage of .286 and a slugging average of .340. Then he broke out of the slump in a big way in a home doubleheader with Boston on April 30, with what John Drebinger called "an astonishing show of versatile swatting."[15] Lazzeri logged seven hits in a row, going 4 for 5 in the opener, with a double, a triple, and two RBIs, then 3 for 4 with two homers and five RBIs in the nightcap as the Yanks swept the Sox, 11–2 and 8–3. That surge raised his slash line to a more robust .288/.354/.559.

That twin bill also provided the background for one version of a prank Lazzeri pulled on Ruth, who himself got a kick out of nailing Tony's shoes to the floor of his locker. The Yankees slugger was fond of using an eye wash called "Eye-Lo" to clear his eyes before a game. Prior to the opener, according to an undated clipping in the Lazzeri Scrapbooks, Lazzeri and Gehrig grabbed the eye wash and drank it in front of Ruth, saying, "That stuff puts the old pep into you." Lazzeri then went out and posted the seven consecutive hits. Only later was Ruth told that his teammates had earlier emptied the bottle and filled it with water. In another version, after a long night on the town, Ruth asked the trainer for something to clear his bloodshot eyes. After using the eye wash, Ruth got three hits, then continued to use the eye wash for several days. After observing this, Lazzeri got a bottle of the eye wash, filled it with water, drank it in front of Ruth, then got three hits that day. The next day Ruth followed Lazzeri's lead and drank a bottle of the eye wash. He then said to his teammate, "Sure tastes terrible, doesn't it, Tony?"[16]

The Yankees continued to play well in May with a 14–9 record that put them three games ahead of the Senators, who had now replaced the A's as New York's primary challengers. Philadelphia was no longer the dynasty it had been from 1929 to 1931, when it won two World Series and three consecutive pennants. The impact of the Depression had convinced Connie Mack that it was time to sell off his best players, as he had done with his power-house team that had won four pennants in five years from 1910 through 1914. By the end of 1933 he had sold Al Simmons, George Earnshaw, and Mickey Cochrane, along with several others. The A's finished the season in third place, 19½ games out of first.

The Yankees and Senators remained neck and neck through July, when the Yankees trailed by one game. But after a 13–15 record in August put them 8½ games behind, they never seriously challenged the Senators, finishing in second place, seven games behind. (It would be the last pennant for a Washington team until 2019.) With Ruth and Gehrig leading the charge the Yankees continued to produce on offense, leading the league in homers and runs scored and finishing third in batting average. While his numbers were far from "Ruthian," the Bambino led the team with 34 homers, drove in 104 runs, and hit .301. Gehrig, who set a record by extending his consecutive games-played streak to 1,307, finished fourth in the MVP vote with 32 homers and 140 RBIs.

Unfortunately for the Yankees the pitching staff did not match its 1932 performance and bore the primary responsibility for the failure to win the pennant. After leading the league with a 3.98 ERA, the staff's 1933 ERA of 4.36 dropped it to fifth place. On the heels of his 24–7 record, Gomez, in spite of a 3.18 ERA, went 16–10, while Red Ruffing finished at 9–14. And the two pitchers with the best win-loss averages (Johnny Allen, 15–7, and Van Atta, 12–4) had unimpressive ERAs of 4.39 and 4.18 respectively. On October 1, the final day of the season, the Yanks added a new starter to their staff. In an attempt to boost attendance—the September 20 game against the White Sox had drawn two thousand fans to Yankee Stadium—Ruth took the mound against the lowly 63–86

Red Sox. (He had last pitched on the final day of the 1930 season, a complete-game 9–3 win, also against Boston.) Before a crowd of twenty thousand the "rookie," as he was called by the press, pitched five shutout innings before yielding four earned runs in the sixth on his way to a complete-game, 6–5 win. He also hit his thirty-fourth home run. Paul Gallico, now sports editor of the *Daily News*, lamented the absence of Ruth—"the most colorful and dynamic figure that baseball has ever known"—from the World Series. But in anticipation of Ruth's return to the mound, he sent his entire sports staff to cover the game.[17]

Over the first three months of the season Lazzeri displayed the kind of power he had been known for in his first four seasons and again in 1932, when he averaged 16 home runs and 104 RBIs. (These figures include his 1928 record, when his shoulder injury limited him to 116 games.) From April through June he hit 13 homers with 55 RBIs. But in the second half of the season he hit only 5 more homers, suggesting that some fatigue may have set in. On the other hand, his batting average in each of the final three months (.296, .316, and .327) was higher than in any preceding month, accounting for his ability to drive in 51 runs, almost equaling his first-half production. Lazzeri played his last game on September 20, in which he hit his eighteenth and last homer. For some unknown reason with eight games left in the season, Lazzeri requested, and received, permission to leave for his California home. Hunt explained the departure as only he could: "The eminent Fascist . . . begged leave to be excused from classes for the rest of the season, basing his plea on a desire to be in California to superintend the harvesting of his macaroni crops."[18]

Overall Lazzeri's statistics for 1933 were very similar to those of his comeback season of 1932. His 1933 slash line was .294/.383/.486, compared to .300/.399/.506 in 1932. He scored more runs (94 vs. 79), hit more home runs (18 vs. 15), and drove in 9 fewer runs (104 vs. 113). In both years the once strikeout-prone free swinger, who led the league with 96 strikeouts in his rookie season, had more walks than strikeouts (73 and 62 respectively in 1933, 82 and 64 in 1932). His 15 stolen bases put him in a tie for eighth place in the Majors. After finishing eighth in the MVP vote in 1932, he finished fourteenth in 1933. By any measure Lazzeri had proven that his comeback season of 1932 was not a fluke.

Lazzeri also earned a new distinction in 1933 when he was selected to play in the first-ever All-Star Game. The brainchild of *Chicago Tribune* sports editor Arch Ward, the unprecedented contest, initially conceived as a one-time event, was called "The Game of the Century." One of Ward's selling points in pitching the idea to the league presidents was that the game was a way to boost public support for baseball since all proceeds from the event would go to the Baseball Players Charity Fund. Rosters of eighteen players from each league were selected by managers and fans, who submitted about five hundred thousand ballots appearing in fifty-five newspapers across the country. John McGraw came out of retirement to manage the NL while Connie Mack managed the AL squad.

Lazzeri was one of five AL infielders selected for the game, along with Gehrig, Charlie Gehringer, Jimmie Foxx, and Joe Cronin. Gehringer, who was hitting .293 at the time—compared to Lazzeri's .282—was Mack's choice to start at second base. Known as the "Mechanical Man" for his consistency and durability, Gehringer was challenging Lazzeri for the title of the premier second baseman in the AL. Now in his eighth full season with the Tigers, the future Hall of Famer would be the starting second baseman in the first six All-Star Games. He would also finish in the top ten in the MVP vote in each of those years, winning the award in 1937, when he led the league with a .371 batting average. In his sixteen full seasons with the Tigers, he hit above .300 thirteen times, compiling a .320 lifetime average. Four of the five other Yankees selected were in the starting lineup: Gehrig at first, Ruth and Chapman in the outfield alongside Al Simmons, and Lefty Gomez on the mound. Dickey sat out the game after injuring his thumb in batting practice.

The game, which took place on July 6 at Comiskey Park, was a huge success, with a reported forty-nine thousand fans on hand to watch the parade of future Hall of Famers. Tabbed as 8–5 favorites, the AL came through with a 4–2 win. Rising to the moment, as usual, was the aging Bambino. In the third inning, with the AL leading 1–0 and Gehringer on first, he became the first player to hit a home run in an All-Star Game, providing what would prove to be the winning runs. Lazzeri did not make an appearance, as Gehringer, like every AL starting position player except Ruth, played the entire game. (Ruth was on the field until the ninth, when Sam West of the St. Louis Browns went in as a defensive replacement.) Not even Jimmie Foxx, the reigning AL MVP—he would win the award again in 1933, as well as the Triple Crown—made it onto the field.

The game was featured on the front page of the *Chicago Tribune*, which labeled the contest "the baseball game of the century." In the *Daily News* Paul Gallico called it "the most interesting and exciting game I have ever seen. . . . If the Leagues don't play this game every year, magnates should be examined psychopathically."[19]

Notwithstanding his solid performance in 1933, for the second time in three years Tony Lazzeri's future was once again a consistent topic of speculation at the end of the season. According to Dan Daniel of the *New York World-Telegram*, he would likely be a victim of a Yankees' rebuild: "Once more Tony Lazzeri—he who is called, with true affection and admiration, Nino by his teammates—finds the wedge of a Yankee reconstruction edging toward his position at second base. For eight years Lazzeri has been one of the bulwarks of Yankee defense and a strident power in the winning of pennants. . . . But with the dismal collapse of 1933, Lazzeri has been carried away by the flood of failure."[20]

George A. Barton concurred that the Yankees' failure to win the pennant would likely seal Lazzeri's fate: "Rumors along the baseball rialto in New York are to the effect that the Yankees will be rebuilt for 1934. It is reported that Colonel Jacob Ruppert, keenly disappointed over the failure of his high-priced team to win the pennant this season, has decided to get rid of a number of play-ers and fill the vacancies with younger athletes."[21] Among those reportedly "ticketed to go" were such stalwarts as Ruth, Lazzeri, Combs, Sewell, Ruffing, and Pennock. This time the apparent heir to Lazzeri was no longer Jack Salzgaver but Don Heffner, a twenty-two-year-old infielder purchased in August from the Baltimore Orioles of the International League.

In late October a story by New York writer Bud Nelson appeared under the title "Lazzeri, Yank Infielder, Has Doubtful Future." Acknowledging that "Lazzeri is a valuable man [who] rates with any second baseman in the big leagues today," Nelson concluded that "it may be all for the best if he becomes a member of another club next season. . . . The Yankees must mold a new club and Lazzeri is one of those slated to play in other pastures."[22] By the time Nelson's prediction was published, it briefly appeared that Lazzeri was already heading to other pastures. Citing an exclusive story appearing in the *Detroit Times* on October 23, newspapers across the country printed the announcement that "Tony Lazzeri, of the New York Yanks, has been signed by the Detroit Tigers, and comes here in exchange for Elon Hogsett, Tigers southpaw."[23] The report was immediately and emphati-cally denied by both Ed Barrow and Colonel Ruppert. In the midst of all the trade rumors (and the one false report) Sam Byrd, a reserve outfielder since 1929 known as "Babe Ruth's Legs," came to Lazzeri's defense: "Tony hits 'em in the clutch. Look over his record and you'll find he consistently drives in over a hun-dred runs a season. We could have never won a pennant with-out Tony Lazzeri"[24]

So once again Lazzeri headed to his California home uncertain about the next season. Would he be playing in other pastures, or if he were with the Yankees, would he be at second, third, or on the bench?

In what was becoming an annual ritual Lazzeri was again rumored to be on the trading block following the 1933 season, especially when the owners gathered in Chicago for the winter meetings in early December. At that time the *Daily News* predicted that Lazzeri's future would be known "during the next three days."[25] Mickey Cochrane, the newly appointed player-manager of the Tigers, was quoted as saying, "I really had hopes of getting Al Simmons and Tony Lazzeri. But the Yanks wouldn't let Lazzeri go and the Sox couldn't let Simmons go."[26]

As it turned out, the housecleaning that many predicted for the Yankees going into the 1934 season proved to be minimal. Of the six players that George Barton identified as ticketed to go, only Sewell and Ruffing were not on the scene, both having been released. However, as teams were going into spring training, a recurring motif among the writers was that Gehrig was the only infielder assured of his position. Otherwise there was wide open competition for the other three spots among Lazzeri, Crosetti, Heffner, Saltzgaver, and rookie Red Rolfe. Even the outfield positions were undetermined since the durability of both Ruth and Combs was in question.

By March 20 Joe McCarthy had reportedly settled on his infield: Heffner at second, Rolfe at short, Lazzeri at third. Hunt was convinced that this would be the best Yankees infield since 1926. When a preseason poll of writers revealed that the Senators were favored to win a second consecutive pennant, he disagreed, asserting that McCarthy "has devised an infield that may be the most sensational in the league."[27]

McCarthy's original infield alignment proved to be well short of sensational. Less than five weeks into the season Saltzgaver, who had been shipped to the Yankees' farm team in Newark, was recalled, triggering yet more trade rumors about Lazzeri, who was struggling at the plate. But once again the trade rumors were unfounded. Instead of being traded, on May 24 Lazzeri was moved back to second base, with Saltzgaver taking over at third. Heffner, known for his defense, was not hitting and beginning to be erratic in the field, so he was sent to the bench.

Through much of the season the infielders shifted like the sands of the Sahara. Saltzgaver and Crosetti alternated at third, and Crosetti was sometimes at short. When Lazzeri was out for a week between June 11 and 18 after splitting a finger in a game, Crosetti was at third, Rolfe at short, and Heffner back at second. Shifting occurred in the outfield as well. Ruth was sitting out or being replaced late in games more frequently. Byrd appeared in 104 games, primarily in left and right, in only 42 as a starter (Ruth alternated between both positions, depending on which was the sun field.) Another backup for the Babe was Myril Hoag, who appeared in 97 games. As predicted, the thirty-five-year-old Combs, one of his era's best leadoff hitters, was showing signs of reaching the end of the road. But, after appearing in 63 games, his season came to a sudden end on July 24, when, in the seventh inning, he crashed into a concrete wall at Sportsman's Park in St. Louis trying to catch a fly ball. He was carried off the field unconscious and spent two months in the hospital recovering from a fractured skull and broken collarbone.

Though not close to the severity of Combs's injury, Lazzeri incurred a potentially season-ending setback of his own. In the June 20 doubleheader at home, when the Yankees were in first place by a half game over Detroit, Lazzeri twisted his knee. At first the injury did not appear to be serious and was expected to keep him sidelined for only a week. But then it was reported that Lazzeri was facing a critical situation. Ordered to bed by the team doctor, he was told an operation might be needed to remove the displaced cartilage, a procedure that would keep him out of the lineup for the remainder of the season.[28]

Other sources offered a more dire outlook. On June 28 the *St. Louis Star and Times* ran a front-page photo of Lazzeri resting in bed with his two-year-old son, David. The caption reported that "the injury is said to be so serious that he may never be able to play ball again." Under the ominous headline "Future Is Dark for Tony Lazzeri," the *Pittsburgh Press* wrote: "One of the most brilliant careers in baseball may be halted by an injured knee."[29]

However, after learning that no surgery would be needed, Lazzeri was back at the ballpark by July 3. But he did not appear in a game until July 16, when he pinch-hit for Saltzgaver, after almost a month on the sidelines. Following two more pinch-hit appearances, he was back in the starting lineup at second base on July 21, where he stayed the remainder of the season.

As they had in 1933, the Yankees got off to a fast start. They were in first place from April 30 to May 30, then seesawed between first and second until a crucial four-game road series in mid-July with the surprising Tigers, whose potent lineup featured Gehringer, Cochrane, Goose Goslin, and twenty-three-year-old Hank Greenberg. (A future Hall of Famer and one of the game's greatest right-handed hitters, Greenberg acknowledged in a 1938 interview that he had taken a tip from Lazzeri, who advised him to stand closer to the plate so as to follow the ball better and hit the outside pitches.)[30] With Lazzeri sidelined by his knee injury and the Yankees holding a half-game lead going into the series, the contenders split the first two games. By the middle of the fourth inning in the third game the Yanks had surged to a 9–1 lead, which looked safe with ace Lefty Gomez, sporting a 14–2 record, on the mound. But by the end of the sixth the Tigers had cut the lead to 9–8. A two-run homer by Crosetti in the seventh stretched the lead to 11–8, but the Tigers stunned the visitors with a four-run rally in the bottom of the ninth for a dramatic 12–11 victory. After winning the next day to take a 1½ game lead, Detroit never fell out of first the remainder of the season. New York stayed close, even tying for the lead on three occasions, but by mid-August the Yankees fell back and finished in second place, seven games out, just as they had in 1933. After winning their first pennant since 1909, the Tigers fell to the scrappy "Gas House Gang" Cardinals in seven games.

While Colonel Ruppert and Ed Barrow had hoped that the aging Ruth would retire after the 1933 season, the Bambino, still clinging to the naive hope that the Yankees would hire him as manager, hung around for one more year. It was far from a triumphant exit. Playing in only 125 games, he hit .288 with twenty-two homers, both low-water marks of his fifteen years in pinstripes. Gehrig, on the other hand, was at the peak of his career, winning the Triple Crown and leading the league in on-base percentage, slugging average, and total bases. But overall the Yankees offense was disappointing, leading the league only in walks. Not even the outstanding performance by the pitching staff, led by twenty-six-game winner Gomez, was enough to get the Yankees back to the top of the AL.

After a slow start in April—.225, with 1 homer and 5 RBIs—Lazzeri picked up the pace in May, hitting 5 homers and driving in 19 runs. Then, limited to twelve games in June due to his split finger, he posted some of the worst numbers of his career in that brief span. He hit .154 (6 for 39) with no home runs and 2 RBIs, a .283 on-base percentage, and a .256 slugging average. But as he had done so many times, he bounced back. After returning on July 16 from the knee injury that had kept him out of the lineup for twenty-five days, he went on a tear. In 15 games in July he compiled a slash line of .395/.527/.605, which enabled him to raise his average to .252 by the end of the month. In August he hit a season-high 6 homers with 17 RBIs and had a .295 average, and while his average fell off to .269 in September with only 1 home run, he drove in 18 runs. But overall it was a disappointing season. Injuries limited him to 123 games, his fewest with the Yankees other than the 116 games in the injury-riddled season of 1928. His .267 average tied for the second lowest of his career with the Yankees, and his 67 RBIs were the fewest of any season with the Yanks, but he hit 14 homers, tied for the third highest of his career.

Six Yankees—Ruth, Gehrig, Dickey, Chapman, Gomez, and Ruffing—were selected to play in the second All-Star Game, scheduled for July 10 at New York's Polo Grounds. The *Tampa Bay Times*, noting that Lazzeri, "long one of our baseball idols," was left off the roster, conceded that Gehringer "has finally arrived at the peak of his powers, and is deserving of the rank as the leading second-baseman in the American league [sic]."[31] In late September statistician Al Munro Elias provided a comparison of Gehringer and Lazzeri, the second basemen from the two AL teams contending to appear in the World Series: "When you talk about second basemen in the American League, you mention Charlie Gehringer's name, followed by an exclamation point, then stop."[32] The 1934 game, won by the AL, 9–7, featured one of the most memorable achievements in All-Star history. In the first two innings the Giants ace lefty, Carl Hubbell, struck out five future Hall of Famers—Ruth, Gehrig, Foxx, Simmons, and Cronin—in succession.

While Lazzeri's numbers were not as impressive as they once had been, he remained the most notable Italian American player in the game. But by 1934 several others had joined the ranks of big leaguers. Whereas only twenty-two players of Italian descent had ever appeared in the Majors by 1929, at least fifty-four would make their debuts in the 1930s. The influx prompted *Boston Globe* writer and cartoonist Gene Mack—a nephew of Connie Mack—to write a story titled "Some New Baseball Dishes, Done Italian Style." "Early returns on the 1934 baseball season indicate that spaghetti may soon become the national dish of the national game," Mack wrote. "Oscar Melillo will vary the diet now and then with large helpings of spinach but Cuccinello, Puccinelli, Crosetti, Lazzeri, Bonura, Orsatti, [Vince] Di Maggio [sic] and a host of other 'walloping Wops' can't be wrong. The Italians are in this business to stay." In his accompanying cartoon, which includes a caricature of Mussolini giving a Fascist salute and saying, "Viva baseball," Mack illustrated his benign stereotypical portrayal by depicting thirteen Italian ballplayers, past and present, seated around a large table. In the middle of the table sits a large bowl labeled "spaghetti," while several cloves of garlic hang above the table.[33]

As he did each year while at home in San Francisco during the offseaon, in 1934 Lazzeri participated in several benefit baseball games, along with many other Major and Minor Leaguers from California. And when he wasn't appearing in the occasional charity game, he was most likely to be found on a golf course. Like Ruth, Lazzeri was almost as passionate about golf as he was about baseball. By the time he entered the big leagues, the sport had become popular with baseball players. No one did more to popularize golf among ballplayers than Ruth, who spent much of his leisure time during spring training on the links. While it is not clear exactly when Lazzeri took up the sport, he became an avid golfer and was known to be one of the better players among Major Leaguers. On November 16, 1934, for example, he played in the professional baseball players tournament at Berkeley Country Club in El Cerrito for the championship of Northern California, along with two other future Hall of Famers, Ty Cobb and Joe Cronin.

The course where Lazzeri spent the bulk of his golf time during the offseason was the Millbrae Golf and Country Club, close to the Millbrae home on Hazel Avenue that he and Maye had bought in the autumn of 1932. (Originally known as the Union League Golf and Country Club when it opened in 1930, the course was designed by Alister MacKenzie, co-designer of Augusta National and Cypress Point. Following financial setbacks, the club reorganized in 1933 as the Millbrae Golf and Country Club; then, after another reorganization, it reopened as the Green Hills Country Club in 1945.) According to the club's archives, Lazzeri's involvement went well beyond being a member and playing an occasional round. "Millbrae Country Club actually became Lazzeri's winter training facility. In the course of any given year he would spend more time at our club than he would at Yankee Stadium. His daily routine was to go to the club, play 18 to 27 holes of golf (he was one of the best professional baseball golfers), chop firewood for the clubhouse fireplace, and hand mow the greens!"[34] (Lazzeri's grandson Matt told me that as part of his offseason conditioning, Lazzeri would cut out sheets of lead and put them into his golf shoes.)

What must have been the golfing highlight of Lazzeri's 1934 postseason occurred on December 20. After making a birdie on the fourteenth hole at Millbrae, he pulled out a spade mashie at the 150-yard fifteenth hole and dropped in a hole-in-one.[35] That shot may have alleviated some of the frustration he must have felt at the end of a disappointing season on the diamond, both for him personally and for the Yankees. According to one newspaper report, some time after that hole-in-one Lazzeri scored another, less conventional, hole-in-one at Millbrae when he hit a slice off the ninth tee and found the ball in the cup of the adjacent seventh green.[36]

Lazzeri was instrumental in the establishment of a series of golf tournaments at Millbrae featuring professional ballplayers. "During December of 1936, lured by Lazzeri, other baseball greats began to play the first of what would be many Professional Baseball Players tournaments to be held at Millbrae, and eventually Green Hills Country Club."[37] The inaugural tournament, held on December 20, 1936, attracted twenty-nine current and former Major and Minor League players, including Ty Cobb, Lazzeri's former teammate Mark Koenig, Babe Pinelli, and Lefty O'Doul. Lazzeri shot 81 and Cobb, 83. Lazzeri's teammate Myril Hoag led all the ballplayers with a three-over 75.[38] The 1937 tournament, held on November 11, again featured Cobb, along with Lazzeri, O'Doul, and Willie Kamm. The tournament grew in popularity over the years but was not held during the war years. Then, beginning on January 23, 1949, it became known as the Babe Ruth Professional Baseball Cancer Tournament. Alameda resident Dick Bartell, a former Major League infielder and a Tigers coach at the time, was its initial chair. In 1951 J. G. Taylor Spink, publisher of *The Sporting News*, donated trophies to be awarded to the winners of the active and inactive flights in the tournament, which raised funds for the American Cancer Society of San Francisco.[39] Reports on the tournament were published in newspapers across the country.

The Green Hills archives post also noted that singer Bing Crosby, one of the most famous celebrities of that era, became a regular at the event, adding: "It is more than a coincidence that Crosby's Monterey 'Clambake' would usually be held the week before or after the Babe Ruth event at Green Hills, with many of the same celebrities attending both events."[40] The Babe Ruth event at Green Hills came to an end in the mid-1950s, when there was no longer adequate parking space for spectators due to the local housing boom.

Lazzeri continued to play, and train, at Millbrae until 1940, when the family moved to Rosewood Drive in San Francisco and he became a member of the nearby Olympic Club.

For the first time in sixteen years the Yankees went into spring training in 1935 without the man who had built Yankee Stadium. They had faced a dilemma at the end of the 1934 season when Ruth insisted that he would not wear a Yankees uniform again unless he were the manager. While Colonel Ruppert was by now anxious to be rid of Ruth, he planned to make a token offer so as not to appear that he was discarding his aging superstar, still the biggest drawing card in baseball. The dilemma was resolved when, in February 1935, Boston Braves owner Emil Fuchs, who desperately needed someone who would attract fans to his floundering franchise, asked Ruppert to release the Babe so that he might sign him. Ruppert didn't hesitate to provide the release, asking nothing in return from Fuchs.

In order to make the three-year deal more appealing, Fuchs gave Ruth the titles of assistant manager and vice president, giving him new hope that what he understood to be positions in management would lead to the manager's job that he so much coveted. But it didn't take long for the would-be executive to realize that those titles were smoke screens and that his real job was to be a part-time player and gate attraction. Ruth ended up playing in twenty-eight games for the Braves, batting .181 with six homers and twelve RBIs. The one bright spot came on May 25 in Pittsburgh when he belted three homers and drove in six runs. Five days later he played the final game of his twenty-two-year career.

With Ruth gone, the only regulars remaining from the Murderers' Row lineup were Lazzeri, Gehrig, and Combs, who would appear in only eighty-nine games as he attempted a comeback from his near-fatal injury in 1934. Ben Chapman started in center in place of Combs, who shared left field with twenty-eight-year-old rookie Jesse Hill. The man with the unenviable job of replacing Ruth in right was Canadian-born George Selkirk, who had been called up from Newark in July 1934 following Combs's injury. In 1935 he inherited Ruth's third spot in the batting order, as well as his uniform number. But the resemblance ended there. He hit a solid .312 and drove in ninety-four runs but had little power, hitting only eleven home runs. As if the pressure to replace the Bambino weren't enough, he also had to live with the nickname "Twinkletoes," given to him because of his habit of running on his toes.

After getting off to fast starts the previous two years, the Yankees struggled early in the season, languishing in third or fourth place for much of April and May. But by the end of May they had clawed their way into first place. They remained there until the surging Tigers, who had been in fourth place as late as June 25, pulled ahead on July 24 and never relinquished their lead. Led by Hank Greenberg, who would be the 1935 AL MVP, Detroit steadily pulled away, leading the second-place Yanks by ten games on September 7. Only an end-of-the-season streak in which New York won eight of its final nine games while Detroit lost six of its last seven enabled the Yankees to finish three games out, runners-up for the third straight year. The Tigers went on to win their first World Series, beating the Cubs, whose twenty-one-game winning streak had propelled them to the pennant.

Although Gomez, the Yankees ace who led the league with twenty-six wins in 1934, fell off to a 12–15 record, the pitching staff compiled the league's best ERA at 3.60. Ruffing topped the starters with sixteen wins, followed by Johnny Broaca with fifteen. The offense, however, was no longer dominant, finishing third in home runs, runs scored, and slugging. Gehrig had a solid year, finishing fifth in the MVP vote, but he hit nineteen fewer homers and drove in forty-six fewer runs than in 1934, when he won the Triple Crown. In 1935 he led the league in walks as opposing teams pitched around him. Ed Barrow was convinced that Gomez and Gehrig were worn down because they had taken part in Babe Ruth's eighteen-game barnstorming tour in Japan following the 1934 season.

Beneath a photo of Lazzeri on the front page of the April 25, 1935, issue of *The Sporting News* appeared a brief article regarding his early season performance. "Three years ago they said Lazzeri was nearing the end in select society. Everybody seemed to agree that he was slowing down. . . . They said the same thing a year ago." The story noted that during the 1934 season he had put on weight, but after adopting a strict dietary program, he reported to spring training "reconditioned and revitalized," with his job at second base "sewed up." With Lazzeri's return to form "the Yankees hold a much higher rating as a pennant possibility than they would have otherwise commanded. Much of Tony's old speed has returned, he has no trouble getting down on grounders and he is a valuable aid to the youngsters, Crosetti at short and Rolfe at third."

Lazzeri had indeed reclaimed his old position at second base, where he played in 118 of his 124 starts. Hitting primarily in the fifth position, he improved slightly over his 1934 performance in batting average, hits, runs scored, and RBIs, and he was third on the team in home runs, RBIs, and stolen bases. Overall, however, he hit with less power, finishing sixth on the team in slugging average and OPS. And in several offensive categories his numbers were well down the final list of his twelve-year record with the Yankees, with his on-base percentage, slugging average, and OPS ranking third lowest.

Apparently the Yankees' third straight failure to win the pennant frustrated not only the players and management, but the fans as well. Perhaps the absence of Ruth also contributed to their disappointment, but in any case the average attendance at Yankee Stadium in 1935 fell by 20 percent, from 11,100 to 8,826, the lowest figure since 1925. (By comparison, the average attendance across the AL fell by only 2 percent.) While second place may have been acceptable for most AL teams, it wasn't for the richest and most successful franchise in baseball.

Joe McCarthy had entered the season finally free of Ruth, who had not only coveted his job, but had also openly criticized his worth as a manager. Never close, by 1934 the two had reached the point where they barely spoke to one another. But as long as Ruth was in uniform, McCarthy had to tread lightly. While the Bambino had become too old and slow to provide significant offense or defense, he was too much of a draw to bench. Now McCarthy could run the team as he chose. But after a third season without a pennant the burden was on him to prove that he could win without the greatest star in baseball history. What no one could know as yet another disappointing season came to an end was that the Yankees were about to embark on the greatest dynastic run baseball had ever seen, led by a young man destined to be the successor of Ruth as the Yankees superstar.

11

Snubbing Father Time

I n 1933, his first full season as a professional ballplayer, eighteen-year-old San Francisco Seals outfielder Joe DiMaggio captured the attention of scouts everywhere by hitting safely in sixty-one consecutive games. His potential sale price increased in the early part of the 1934 season, but a knee injury in June raised questions about his durability and future productivity, causing many teams to lose interest. But just as he had done with Lazzeri, Ed Barrow, once additional scouting had convinced him that DiMaggio's knee would not be an ongoing issue, was willing to take a chance on signing him. (It is likely that the success of both Lazzeri and Crosetti in drawing Italian fans to Yankee Stadium played a role in the Yankees' decision.) Prior to the injury the Seals' expected asking price for their prize prospect was $100,000. Instead the Yankees got him for the bargain price of $25,000 and five players, and they hedged their bet by requiring that DiMaggio stay with San Francisco in 1935 to prove that he was healthy. He more than passed the test by hitting thirty-four homers, batting .398, and being named MVP of the PCL.

For the third time in eleven years—Lazzeri in 1926, Crosetti in 1932, and now DiMaggio—a highly sought-after young Italian ballplayer from San Francisco made his way across the continent to the Yankees' spring training camp in St. Petersburg. The new-comer had the privilege of making the trip with his two veteran predecessors. Lazzeri, who had never met DiMaggio, invited the rookie to join him and Crosetti in his brand-new Buick roadster for the long cross-country road trip. The story of this car ride has been retold many times and, for reasons that will be obvious, in few words. This is the version told to me by Crosetti: "In Joe DiMaggio's first year with the Yankees, Tony Lazzeri and I invited him to go with us to spring training. We pooled our money, then I would pay for the gas, food, and hotels. We got to about Florida, and Tony and I were doing all the driving. So Tony says, 'Let's ask this guy to drive.' Joe said, 'I don't know how to drive.' We didn't say much on the whole drive. The three of us were quiet."[1]

Confirmation of the San Francisco trio's preference for limited conversation was provided that summer by Jack Mahon of the International News Service, who happened to be sitting near them in the lobby of the Hotel Chase in St. Louis. Noticing after a while that none of them had said a word, he began to time them. "Believe it or not," he wrote, "they didn't speak for an hour and twenty minutes. At the end of that time, DiMaggio cleared his throat. Crosetti looked at him and said: 'What did you say?' And Lazzeri said: 'Shut up. He didn't say nothing.' They lapsed into silence and at the end of ten more minutes I got up and left. I couldn't stand it any more."[2]

Few if any Major League players had ever entered their rookie season burdened with as much hype and high expectations as did DiMaggio, who was hailed as the second Babe Ruth. The original Ruth, while saying he hoped that the kid would succeed, also expressed some doubt. "He'll be nervous and pressing," he said. "Only one phenom out of a hundred makes good and they all look like $1,000,000 under a palm tree." Ruth also predicted that their lack of pitching would once again keep the Yankees from winning the pennant.[3]

Given the fervor over DiMaggio's arrival in camp, it was no wonder the writers covering the Yankees were anxious to get their first look, and fire their first questions, at the rookie. With Ruth out of the picture they were anxious to have a new hero to extol. But they would soon discover that DiMaggio was as taciturn as Ruth was gregarious. Lazzeri and Crosetti, fully aware of what awaited their young passenger and wanting to protect him, at least on his first day in camp after such a long trip, purposely delayed their arrival in St. Petersburg until late in the evening, enabling DiMaggio to avoid the writers until the official start of spring training the next day. They had also advised the young man to be wary of the writers and say as little as possible so as to prevent them from putting words into his mouth. Not that the painfully shy youngster, who was dubbed "Dead Pan Joe" by the media, needed much encouragement to remain silent.

Facing "the most rigid scrutiny a Yankee rookie ever underwent," DiMaggio impressed the media in his first workout. "It is a distinct pleasure to report that California Joe hits the spot with the team and the writers. He exudes baseball, and if his performance today is a criterion, Joe is all they said he was on the coast."[4] If DiMaggio impressed the writers, it was strictly by his performance on the field; they got very little from him away from the diamond. Barrow recounted the scene when reporters first met him: "They found a slim, tall, black-haired young man, who was polite, but decidedly shy. Also, he was almost completely mum. . . . After that first meeting they didn't know whether they liked the new rookie or not."[5] According to Frank Graham, "DiMaggio convinced McCarthy, the players, and the newspapermen that the stories of his skill and power had not been exaggerated. Unmistakably, too, he was the number one man in camp. Gehrig, who had walked so long in the shadow of Ruth, now walked in the shadow of DiMaggio."[6]

Not willing to spend the kind of money or talent that other teams were demanding in return for their players, the Yankees, with the notable exception of DiMaggio, went into spring training with essentially the same squad they had fielded in 1935. (The Senators, for example, reportedly were asking $500,000 for second baseman Buddy Myer, the reigning AL batting champion and a potential replacement for Lazzeri.) According to a January report by Hugh S. Fullerton, the famed sportswriter best remembered for his role in uncovering the "Black Sox" scandal of 1919, McCarthy's primary concern for 1936 was his middle infielders. Crosetti was coming back from a knee injury that had kept him out of the lineup late in the previous season and required surgery. And while he expected to start Lazzeri at second once again, McCarthy noted that the veteran begins to weaken at the midpoint of the season, and neither Saltzgaver nor Heffner had proven they could do the job.[7]

After posting solid numbers in 1932 and 1933, Lazzeri struggled in the next two seasons. With the exception of home runs his composite numbers for 1934–35 declined significantly in all offensive categories compared to his 1932–33 record. He averaged 30 fewer hits, 28 fewer RBI, 20 fewer runs, and his average, on-base percentage, and slugging average fell by 27, 26, and 65 points respectively. Clearly the prevailing opinion was that Lazzeri's best days were in the rear-view mirror going into the 1936 season. And only one week into the season, when Lazzeri was batting .259 with no homers and 3 RBIs, an unsigned story in the *Brooklyn Times Union* concluded that he "finally appears to have reached the end of the trail as far as usefulness as a regular is concerned" and surmised that if Colonel Ruppert could have foreseen this earlier, he would have authorized Ed Barrow to acquire Myer from the Senators at any cost.[8] For several years Lazzeri had endured the litany of trade rumors, as well as occasional suggestions that his career was nearing an end. But the eleven-year veteran, routinely referred to as an aging ballplayer with diminishing durability and range, would once more show that predictions of his demise were premature by playing a significant role in the Yankees' return to glory.

One of the Yankees' holdovers from 1935 was right-hander Red Ruffing, who was entering his seventh year with New York after being acquired from the Red Sox in 1930. After winning nineteen games in 1934, he won only sixteen in 1935 but posted a lower ERA. When the Yankees refused his request for a salary increase, he became a holdout; that meant he was not allowed to work out with the team. In a postseason *Sporting News* article under the headline "Secret Workouts Helped Ruffing Rout 20-Win Jinx," Dan Daniel revealed the story of how Lazzeri, who was not staying at the team hotel but at a cottage outside of St. Petersburg, had convinced Ruffing that he needed to get into shape and invited him to work out with him every afternoon, which he did. According to Daniel, Lazzeri told his friend: "You look more and more like those fat little sausages they used to sell at the St. Louis ball park when I broke in." The story had not been revealed at the time "because the players did not know what attitude the front office would take in aiding, abetting and harboring an unsigned player."[9] Ruffing, who finally signed his contract on March 26, went on to win twenty games for the first time and was a key factor in the Yankees' pennant-winning season. As it turned out, the spring training workout partnership seems to have benefitted Lazzeri as well as Ruffing.

The eagerly awaited debut of DiMaggio was put on hold after a diathermy treatment he received following an ankle injury on March 21—at which time he was hitting .600—burned his left ankle so badly he missed the first seventeen games of the season. Meanwhile, the Yankees got off to a mediocre start. But Daniel noted that while the Yankees "muddled along with uncertain pitching and spotty hitting" over the first two weeks, "Tony Lazzeri has been playing fine ball every which way. He read that the chances of the Yanks, picked not to win the pennant, depended on his legs. Tony got sore. He said, 'I will make those writers eat their words in September.'"[10] That prognostication proved to be more accurate than those of the writers who predicted that the Yankees would again finish behind the defending World Series champion Tigers.

To the delight of both the writers covering the Yankees and the fans, DiMaggio made his debut on May 3 against the St. Louis Browns. Playing left field (with Ben Chapman in center and George Selkirk in right) and batting third, the rookie did not disappoint the largest Yankee Stadium crowd since opening day, going 3 for 6 with a triple and an RBI in a 14–6 rout. In the next game he went 3 for 5 with two RBIs in an 8–2 win over the lowly Browns. The Yankees won the first four games in which DiMaggio appeared, and fourteen of the first nineteen, giving them a 24–11 record on May 23 for a 1½-game lead over Boston. In that span DiMaggio compiled a slash line of .393/.420/.619, earning him praise as the dazzling rookie who was living up to the rave reviews that had preceded his arrival in New York.

But on Sunday, May 24, in the third of a four-game series in Philadelphia with the seventh-place A's, it was the veteran Lazzeri who stole the spotlight from his young teammate with the greatest power surge of his career and, quite simply, one of the most remarkable single-game offensive performances in baseball history. Hitting in the eighth spot, Lazzeri came up in the second inning with the Yankees trailing 2–0. After Gehrig grounded out, Bill Dickey, Selkirk, and Chapman all walked to load the bases. Lazzeri then hit a grand slam off starter George Turbeville to give the Yanks a 4–2 lead. The Yankees added five runs in the fourth to stretch the lead to 10–2. After they tacked on two more in the fifth, the A's brought in Herman Fink, their fourth pitcher of the game, to face Lazzeri, who again came to the plate with the bases loaded. This time he drove the ball over the center-field fence for his second grand slam, again scoring Dickey, Chapman, and Selkirk ahead of him for a 16–2 lead. With the score now 17–2 following a homer by DiMaggio in the sixth, Lazzeri led off the seventh with a solo homer into the second deck in left field off Woody Upchurch, the A's fifth pitcher. Then, with one out, Crosetti hit a solo home run to make the score 19–2.

But neither the team nor Lazzeri was finished yet. Selkirk and Chapman were once again on base when Lazzeri came up with one out in the eighth, again facing Upchurch. This time he hit a drive to deep center that looked as if it would clear the fence for his fourth homer, but it hit just below the top of the wall, and Lazzeri had to settle for a triple and two more RBIs, bringing his total to eleven. He then scored on a single by pitcher Monte Pearson before Crosetti ended the onslaught with his second home run, making the final score 25–2. Even though his record-setting performance occurred on the road, at the end of the game Lazzeri had to fight his way through a crowd of autograph seekers. (Incidentally, in spite of the twenty-seven runs and twenty-six hits amassed, the game lasted only two hours and thirty-four minutes.)

In his game story James C. Isaminger referred to Lazzeri as "the 33-year-old forgotten star of the Yankees" and the "old man of Joe McCarthy's new band of pennant contenders."[11] It was indeed a classic case of the old dog showing that he was still capable of performing some impressive new tricks. His tally for the day: 4 for 5, with three homers (including two grand slams), a triple, a walk, and a strikeout; eleven RBIs, four runs scored, fifteen total bases. The opening line of the *New York Times* account read: "Tony Lazzeri hammered his way to baseball fame today with an exhibition of batting unparalleled in American League history."[12] In fact he became the first player to hit two grand slams in one game, and his RBI total established a still-standing AL record, surpassing the previous mark of nine set by Jimmie Foxx in 1933. (The Major League record is twelve RBIs, jointly held by Jim Bottomley [1924] and Mark Whiten [1993], both with the Cardinals.)

A little more context is needed to fully comprehend the magnitude of Lazzeri's outburst on May 24. Prior to a doubleheader against the A's on the previous day, he had hit only two homers all season. In the first game of the doubleheader he hit his third homer, a solo shot in the fourth. Then, in the nightcap, he hit two-run homers in both the sixth and eighth innings as the Yankees swept the A's, 12–6 and 15–1, before a crowd of twenty-eight thousand. A's fans were so angered by the drubbing the Yankees were handing the home team that beginning in the eighth inning of the nightcap and lasting until the final out they "showered the field with pop bottles, seat cushions, torn papers, fruit and vegetables and whatever else came to hand, in a rowdy outburst that has had few parallels in organized baseball." Even after the final out the players had to run for the safety of the dugouts "as the angry fans continued throwing missiles."[13]

Lazzeri's six home runs in three consecutive games (May 23–24) set a Major League record that was later tied by four others, then broken by Shawn Green's seven homers in 2002. In addition, the home run Lazzeri hit in Detroit on May 21 gave him seven homers in four consecutive games, also a Major League record later tied by three others. His sixteen RBIs in Philadelphia almost equaled his season total of twenty-one prior to that series. Going into the four-game series, Lazzeri's slash line was .261/.375/.391; following his May 24 outburst it read: .295/.401/.566.

As the Yankees had hoped, the presence of Lazzeri, Crosetti, and DiMaggio in their starting lineup was a big gate attraction for local Italians. A week after the May 24 game in which Lazzeri hit two grand slams and Crosetti and DiMaggio also homered, Shirley Povich wrote of the large crowds of Italian fans cheering their trio of heroes: "New York's Little Italy is mildly nuts over the Italians in the New York line-up. In the past two days the Yankees have played to crowds of 74,000 and 40,000, and guttural Italain [sic] yells were easily audible throughout the stands. The red, white and green Italian flags were proudly displayed by fans in all sections of the enclosure."[14]

In an article that appeared three days before Lazzeri's record-setting game Daniel labeled the San Francisco trio the "Three Musketeers of the Roman Legion." Daniel's focus was on Crosetti's breakout season after returning from the surgery to repair the knee injury that had cut short his 1935 season. In his first four seasons with the Yankees Crosetti had struggled to live up to the offensive potential he had shown in the PCL that had motivated Colonel Ruppert to pay $75,000 for his contract, hitting no higher than .265. But the young man Daniel called "a brand-new Frank Peter Joseph Crosetti" got off to a torrid start in 1936, compiling a nine-game hitting streak in April that took him to a .414 average.[15]

Accompanying Daniel's article was a cartoon by Willard Mullin, the premier sports cartoonist of his era, that depicted Lazzeri, Crosetti, and DiMaggio marching with bats slung over their shoulders and singing, "Oh, the miners came in '49—Th' Wops in '51." Ten years after Lazzeri had joined the Yankees, the Italian stereotypes were alive and well. Six weeks after Daniel's article appeared, a story by Arthur Mann titled "The Three Musketeers of Swat" appeared in *Liberty Magazine*, a general-interest publication that was widely read from the 1920s through the 1940s. Describing how "a trio of sluggers, all from sunny Italy, have staged a sudden Roman holiday in baseball," he wrote: "The three Latins are part and parcel of the heaviest hitting Yankee team since the Ruth-Meusel-Gehrig slugging era. Even if this team fails by some miracle to win the 1936 pennant, they will have established one remarkable record—the biggest batch of Italian rooters outside of the Metropolitan Opera House on *Aida* night." Then, with an allusion to Italy's invasion of Ethiopia nine months earlier, Mann added: "If Mussolini were foolish enough to call Lazzeri, Crosetti, and DiMaggio to the colors today, he would get only the horselaugh and a Mulberry Street razzberry. Not even a Maffia, a Purple Gang, or a double-barreled vendetta could bomb the three Italians from the line-up of the New York Yankees now. The left-field fans from Little Italy, led by the guy with the Italian flag, wouldn't stand for it."[16]

In a July 1936 article titled "Viva Italia," Daniel also incorporated an allusion to Ethiopia in addressing what he termed the Italian "invasion" of baseball: "This surely is Italy's year. Italy has finally invaded baseball with a bang. And this invasion is a wholesome—a most welcome one." With regard to the Yankees' triumvirate, he wrote: "For a team to boast two sons of Italy, as did the Yankees with the establishment of Crosetti as a regular, was considered phenomenal or bizarre, according to the way you looked at it, and the way in which your psychology responded to the invasion of baseball by the sons of immigrants from Europe. But for a major league outfit to take the field day after day with three Italian players set something of a record."[17]

As many after him would do, Daniel, a major booster of the new Yankee rookie, gave primary credit to the arrival of DiMaggio for bringing Italian fans to the ballpark for the first time: "The exploits of Di Maggio [sic], in combination with those of Lazzeri and Crosetti, have intrigued Italians all over the country. They have established . . . a new school of fans, who heretofore evinced little or no interest in major league baseball."[18]

While there is no question that DiMaggio drew large numbers of Italian fans to the ballpark and would go on to become not only the greatest sports hero Italian Americans have ever had, but also a twentieth-century cultural icon, he was not the first to attract large numbers of Italian fans. That honor unquestionably belongs to Lazzeri, the player who also inspired the Italian American community to celebrate him with banquets. As Graham wrote, "As they had done when Lazzeri had first worn a Yankee uniform nine [sic] years before, Italian fans poured into the ball parks all over the circuit to see the new hero."[19]

For Daniel to say that Italians had "heretofore evinced little or no interest in major league baseball" seems disingenuous, given that he was considered to be one of the most knowledgeable baseball writers of his era and was covering the Yankees for the *New York Telegram* when Lazzeri was breaking in. His words extolling DiMaggio's impact are similar to what others wrote about Lazzeri's historic role in creating a new fan base, as cited in chapter 5 above. Fred Lieb: "Many New York fans of Italian ancestry had hardly heard of baseball until Tony Lazzeri joined the Yankees." Bill Slocum: "Tony is the fellow who first brought the banana peels, the lunch baskets, the salami sandwiches and the bottles of homemade red wine to the towering three deck stadium on the right bank. That is to say, he's the guy who first made the Italian population of greater New York City big league baseball and Yankee conscious."

Lazzeri's groundbreaking role as a magnet for new fans has more recently been confirmed by John Thorn, official historian of Major League Baseball: "Perhaps Lazzeri's greatest contribution to the game was bringing Italians in mass to every American League stadium. Because of Lazzeri, thousands of people of Italian descent were introduced to baseball for the first time, and they came back again and again."[20]

Just as he had been for Crosetti in 1932, Lazzeri was also a mentor to DiMaggio. In an otherwise undated story from 1936 found in the Lazzeri Scrapbooks, James M. Kahn wrote: "The part that Lazzeri has played in the development of Frankie Crosetti into one of the outstanding shortstops in baseball has already been firmly established. But he is repeating that service to the team which he has bolstered so well and so long in guiding Joe DiMaggio. Smoking a pipe and looking older, he now has the appearance, as well as the wisdom, of a shrewd veteran." Many years later, Harry Jupiter would quote DiMaggio as saying, "Tony took care of the kids from San Francisco." And Lefty Gomez, another Yankees teammate and San Francisco native, said of Lazzeri: "He taught us what it meant to be a Yankee."[21]

Gomez, affectionately known as "Goofy" for his playful sense of humor, was the source of a frequently retold story concerning Lazzeri's reputation as a smart ballplayer. Among the several versions that have appeared in print Graham's account may be the closest to the truth. In a game during DiMaggio's rookie season a ball was hit to Gomez with a man on first. Crosetti went to the bag to receive the throw, but Gomez instead threw it to Lazzeri, who was ten feet off the bag.

"'What the hell did you throw the ball to me for?' Lazzeri demanded. Gomez replied: 'I was reading in the paper the other day what a smart fellow you were and I was just curious to see what you would do in a spot like that.'" When the players returned to the dugout, Joe McCarthy asked Gomez why he had thrown the ball to Lazzeri. "I was a little confused," Gomez said. "When I looked around there were two Dagoes near the bag and I didn't know which one to throw it to." To which McCarthy said: "There was another one in center field. Why didn't you throw it to him?"[22]

Lazzeri's support for DiMaggio went well beyond giving him a ride to spring training and providing tips on how to deal with the writers. On May 19 the Yankees were playing the Indians in Cleveland. With the Yankees leading 7–4 after eight innings, DiMaggio led off the ninth with a single. When Gehrig hit a grounder to second, Roy Hughes tossed the ball to shortstop Bill Knickerbocker for the force. DiMaggio slid hard into second to break up the double play—exactly what a player was expected to do. But Knickerbocker took exception to the rookie's zeal and fired the ball into DiMaggio's ribs as he lay on the ground. That triggered an immediate response from Lazzeri, who "stormed from the Yankee dugout and charged like a bull at Knickerbocker. Tony was followed by a squadron of Yanks, while a platoon of Indians came racing across from their bench."[23] The umpires intervened before any punches were thrown and order was restored, but the message was clear: Don't mess with our prize rookie.

Following Lazzeri's historic performance on May 24, his rejuvenation was celebrated by *The Sporting News* in an editorial titled "Reincarnation of Murderers' Row." After noting that many believed this might be Lazzeri's last season in the Majors, the column continued: "Tony has seen the minors beckoning to him on previous occasions and has disregarded the summons, but never has he snubbed Father Time more emphatically than this season, when he has written new slugging marks into the record books that are destined to stand for a long time to come. And with DiMaggio, Gehrig, Crosetti and Dickey hitting far above the .300 mark, and liberally mixing extra-base hits in their total, Tony has plenty of company in that reincarnation of the old Murderers' Row that struck such terror into the hearts of opponents."[24]

The evocation of the Murderers' Row iconic squad was no blatant exaggeration. In 1936 the Yankees were no longer the close-but-no-cigar team they had been the previous three seasons, just good enough to finish second. They were now a juggernaut, running roughshod over their opponents just as their

1927 predecessors had done. They took over sole possession of first place on May 10 and stayed there the rest of the season, clinching the pennant on September 9, earlier than any previous AL team. While their record of 102–51 fell eight games short of the 110–44 record of 1927, they finished 19½ games ahead of the defending World Series champion Tigers. They set Major League records in runs scored, home runs, RBIs, and total bases. The starting lineup produced a batting average of .300, led by Dickey's career-high .362. Gehrig, who hit .354 with 49 homers (tying his career high) and 152 RBIs, won his second MVP award and extended his record string of consecutive games to 1,808. Four other starters (DiMaggio, Lazzeri, Dickey, and Selkirk) drove in more than 100 runs. Crosetti had his best offensive season, reaching career highs in, among other categories, runs scored, hits, homers, RBIs, and OPS.

DiMaggio more than lived up to his advance billing. In 138 games he batted .323, led the league in triples, and drove in 125 runs. (Lazzeri and DiMaggio were the only Yankees rookies with more than 100 RBIs until Hideki Matsui in 2003.) His 29 homers set a franchise rookie record that stood until Aaron Judge hit 52 in 2017. He also proved to be an all-around player with exceptional skill as a fielder and as a base runner. The rookie sensation garnered the most votes in the All-Star Game balloting, surpassing even Gehrig. (He started in right field and hit third but had a rough day, going 0 for 5 and mishandling two balls in the outfield in a 4–1 loss to the NL.) After starting the season in left field, he moved to right after Chapman was traded to the Senators on June 14 for Jake Powell, who took over in center. (In his six-plus seasons in New York Chapman hit .305 and led the AL in stolen bases three times, but, in the words of Frank Graham, "Ben was hot-headed, quarrelsome, and at times would sulk.")[25] When Powell struggled at the plate, Myril Hoag replaced him in center, but a collision with DiMaggio in late July put Hoag out of action for the remainder of the season. The rookie moved to center, which would be his permanent home. In the vast expanse of

Yankee Stadium center field gave the man, who would become known as the Yankee Clipper for his ability to gracefully track down long fly balls, plenty of room to show what he could do.

The pitching staff exceeded Babe Ruth's expectations by leading the league in wins, ERA, and innings pitched. Ruffing led the staff with twenty wins, followed by Pearson with nineteen. Johnny Murphy, who had become primarily a relief pitcher in 1935, appeared in twenty-seven games, only five as a starter, but he posted a 9–3 record and finished twelve games, with numerous performances that would now be recorded as saves. Gomez, a four-time twenty-game winner, won thirteen, but his 4.39 ERA was the worst of any of his full seasons.

After appearing in 123 and 130 games in the previous two seasons, Lazzeri, the rejuvenated aging veteran, played in 150 games, the most since 1927 and the third most of his career. He started in 149 of those games—two at shortstop—and finished 146. He drove in 109 runs, the most since 1932 and the fourth most of his career, and batted .287 with 14 homers. What makes his RBI production even more impressive is that whereas he hit in the fifth spot in 1935, in '36 he hit primarily in the seventh (55 games) and eighth spots (77 games). His on-base percentage of .397 was 36 points above his 1935 number—he drew a career-high 97 walks—and his OPS of .838 topped his 1935 figure by 60 points.

Lazzeri was not quite done setting records when the regular season ended. Facing the crosstown Giants in the World Series, the Yankees were mystified in Game One by Carl Hubbell, the NL MVP who posted a 26–6 record with a 2.31 ERA, in a 6–1 loss. But in Game Two, with President Roosevelt throwing out the ceremonial first pitch from a box seat at the Polo Grounds, their bats came alive in a big way as they humiliated five Giants pitchers who, wrote Jack Miley, "were in and out like a gang of drunks threshing through a revolving door."[26] The final score was 18–4, setting new marks for most runs in a World Series game by one team and the most total runs by both teams.

Lazzeri set a World Series record and equaled two others in the game. With the Yankees holding a 5–1 lead in the third inning, ten years and one week after his fateful World Series strikeout against Grover Cleveland Alexander, he came up with the bases loaded to face reliever Dick Coffman, the Giants' third pitcher of the inning. When Coffman threw him a slow curve, Lazzeri hit a liner into the fifth row of the right-field stands to push the lead to 9–1. Only one other player, Elmer Smith of Cleveland in 1920, had ever hit a grand slam in the World Series. Lazzeri's four RBIs in one inning also equaled Smith's record. Both Lazzeri and Dickey set a World Series single-game record by each driving in five runs, surpassing the previous record of four RBIs held by nine players, including Lazzeri.[27] (Lazzeri's fifth RBI came on a sacrifice fly in the seventh.) The AP reported that when Lazzeri went to the clubhouse after the game, he found a telegram waiting for him. It read: "Congratulations—Elmer Smith."[28]

The Yankees piled on by scoring nine more runs over the final four innings, including six in the ninth, in what John Drebinger called "the most decisive, humiliating defeat ever suffered by a contender in the thirty-one years of world series warfare." The game ended when DiMaggio, "twisting, turning and running like a deer, raced to the cinders beyond the bleacher line in distant center to make a marvelous catch of [Hank] Leiber's fly with his back half turned to the plate."[29] The rookie also tied a Series record by recording all three outs in the ninth.

With the Series tied at one game apiece, play moved to Yankee Stadium. In stark contrast to Game Two the third match was a pitchers' duel, with the Yankees coming out on top, 2–1, behind a strong outing by "Bump" Hadley. The Giants were counting on bouncing back in the next game with Hubbell on the mound; he had won his last sixteen decisions, his last loss coming on July 13. But the Yankees, behind a complete-game performance by Pearson, prevailed again, 5–2, before a single-game World Series record crowd of 66,669. The Giants came back with a ten-inning, 5–4 win in Game Five. When Lazzeri drove in Powell to tie the game in the sixth, "a huge Italian flag was hoisted in the bleachers. From time to time it appeared, swinging bravely in the golden sun, but along about the 10th, a few belligerent Giant fans declared sanctions against the swinger, and the flag vanished."[30] At the Polo Grounds the next day the Yankees clinched their fifth World Series by winning another slugfest, 13–5, with Rolfe, DiMaggio, Powell, and Lazzeri all contributing three hits. Powell, the mid-season acquisition, hit .455 for the Series and scored eight runs, while Lazzeri and Gehrig each drove in a Series-best seven runs.

As far back as 1931 Lazzeri's career was said to be in a downward spiral. Going into the 1936 season, the consensus was that he was burned out and nearing the end of the road. But like the mythical phoenix that springs back to life from its own ashes, the man so many had written off showed remarkable resilience and toughness. Recognition of his achievement came on February 7, 1937, at the fourteenth annual dinner of the New York chapter of the BBWAA. With more than eight hundred guests packed into the grand ballroom of the Commodore Hotel and speakers including Mayor Fiorello LaGuardia, Postmaster General James A. Farley, New York Supreme Court justice William T. Collins, and Babe Ruth, Lazzeri was presented with the "Player of the Year" award for "outstanding achievement and high contribution to baseball." Initiated in 1930, the award was not limited to New York players; the previous two winners were Dizzy Dean and Hank Greenberg. Also honored was future Hall of Famer Travis Jackson, recently retired shortstop and captain of the New York Giants, who was named the "Player of Most Meritorious Service."[31]

The fact that the New York baseball writers' selection to receive this award was the "quiet man" of the Yankees, who gave them so little copy to put into their stories, speaks volumes about the writers' respect for Lazzeri. On that occasion Frank Graham wrote the following about one of the players he most admired in his many years covering the Yankees for the *New York Sun*:

Seeing him there made you think of the many times you had been around with him since he came up with the Yankees eleven years ago.... And you thought that of all the ball players who have come up and stuck around for ten years or so Tony has changed less than almost any you could call to mind. Maybe this is because the mark of the busher never was on Lazzeri. He wasn't like some of these kids who come up out of the tank towns with their brakeman's haircuts and their mail order clothes. Tony is a big town guy. Born in San Francisco which is a big town in all its aspects.[32]

The Sporting News editorial column that appeared four days after the writers' dinner extolled the veteran's 1936 comeback. Noting that prior to the season there was "considerable doubt that Lazzeri could finish the campaign as a regular," the column proclaimed that he "not only came back with one of the best showings of his career, but inscribed his name in the record books with a flourish. . . . By his brilliant showing, Tony completely fooled many critics, and even should 1936 prove to be his farewell year as a regular, he has the satisfaction of knowing he celebrated the event in a blaze of glory"[33]

Of all the uncertainties regarding the details of Tony Lazzeri's life away from the baseball diamond, none is more mystifying than an event that occurred near the end of 1936. On December 8 Lazzeri filed suit in Redwood City, California (county seat for San Mateo County), for divorce from Maye on grounds of cruelty. Details are scarce, but according to one newspaper account, Lazzeri alleged that "his wife scolded and upbraided him before friends to his humiliation; told him she 'wished she had never married him' and wanted to get rid of him 'the quicker the better,' and on two occasions left their home in Millbrae, once going to Reno." He also claimed that she wrongly accused him of being unfaithful.[34] The suit asked that the court decide custody of their son and that Maye be restrained from withdrawing family funds in three San Francisco banks. Lazzeri also stated that she had threatened to sell joint real estate holdings in Marin and San Mateo Counties. According to an AP release, "Lazzeri said his wife 'nagged' and 'scolded' him which he said embarrassed him and undermined his health."[35]

But things changed quickly. On page 2 of an early edition on December 9, the *Daily News* reported the divorce filing in a caption below a photo of Tony and Maye, above which was the heading "Tony Says Love's Lost!" Then, in a later edition on the same date, the paper ran the same photo, again on page 2, but this time the heading read "Love Lost . . . Regained," with the caption explaining that the suit would be withdrawn and quoting Tony as having said the previous evening, "It's all a mistake."[36]

On December 9 Lazzeri did withdraw the suit after he and Maye met with attorneys and reconciled. He was quoted as saying, "It was just a misunderstanding. We've been married 14 years and we're going back home now and will stay married many times 14 years. Everything has been adjusted."[37] One of the attorneys present at the reconciliation meeting stated: "It was just a case of misunderstanding which arose, due partly to the fact that Lazzeri's occupation as a ball player kept him away from his home here so much. Filing of the divorce papers yesterday actually forced the couple to realize they couldn't get along without each other and without their son David, 5."[38] A week later a golf course photo confirming the Lazzeri reconciliation appeared in the *Oakland Tribune;* it showed Tony giving a putting tip to Maye while Yankees teammate Red Ruffing looked on.[39]

While there obviously were ongoing problems that preceded Maye's departure from home on two occasions and Lazzeri's decision to file for divorce, whatever the underlying causes may have been, they have been lost to history. My research turned up no further newspaper coverage of the matter beyond December 10. It's as if this brief drama that threatened to forever alter the lives of Lazzeri, his wife, and their son immediately disappeared into a black hole, leaving behind no evidence of the issues that led Lazzeri to seek a divorce, the emotional distress it inflicted on the couple and their son, or any lingering effects it may have had on the marriage. The absence of prolonged public gossip mongering must have been a blessing for Lazzeri, who was granted the privacy he treasured.

Even Lazzeri's grandson Matt, who was born several years after Tony died, was unable to shed much light on the relationship between his grandparents. "She had him on a pedestal, basically talked more about his playing days or their time in New York," he said of Maye. "I think she really enjoyed being part of that crowd. She always dressed well; I never saw her in casual attire. I believe she enjoyed their relative affluence and lifestyle and made sure they looked the part. She didn't talk about my grandfather much, certainly never really the things that I would've wanted to know—What kind of a man was he?, What kind of a husband was he?"[40]

12

Farewell to Pinstripes

C oming off their 1936 World Series win, several Yankees players were hoping for, and some demanding, significant pay
raises. Colonel Ruppert, however, was taking a hard line.
Gehrig, the reigning AL MVP, was reportedly looking for $40,000,
a significant jump from his $23,000 salary of 1936, but the Yan-
kees' initial offer was for $31,000. Ruppert was still angry at both
Gehrig and Gomez for going on Babe Ruth's Japan tour in 1934,
arguing that they were out of shape in 1935 and cost the Yanks
the pennant. Lefty Gomez, who had a poor season in 1936, was cut
from $20,000 to $13,500. Gehrig ultimately signed for $36,000.

Following his impressive 1936 performance, Lazzeri was asking for $16,000, seeking a return to the salary he had earned in
1930 and 1931, before a Depression-imposed cut of $4,000 in 1932
lowered the figure to $12,000, where it stayed for five years. On
February 8, while in New York to receive the Player of the Year
award at the BBWAA dinner, he signed his contract. According
to the *Daily News*, "Tony, being an especial favorite of Jake Ruppert's, attached his signature to the parchment in the Yank office
before the usual camera battery."[1]

While the amount of the contract was not publicly disclosed at
the time of the signing, Daniel reported that Lazzeri had indeed
received the $4,000 raise he had requested, but the amount con-
firmed by the Yankees' financial ledgers (housed in the Baseball
Hall of Fame Library) was $15,000. "Lazzeri was somewhat sur-

prised," wrote Daniel, "but others were not, for Ruppert had indicated sympathy with the Lazzeri cause. Lazzeri did a grand job last season and it had been taken for granted that he would get a good increase."[2]

Lazzeri had prepared himself well for the 1937 season, reporting to spring camp in excellent condition. Jack Smith reported that "those scribes who annually tapped out finis to the big-time career of Tony Lazzeri . . . can't believe their eyes. The reason is that for the last week Tony has been cavorting around here like a gazell [sic] on a diet of Mexican jumping beans."[3] Nevertheless, also in the Yankees camp was yet another youngster widely believed to be the presumptive replacement for the thirty-three-year-old veteran.

As early as 1930 the Yankees had been bringing in potential replacements for Lazzeri, such as Jimmie Reese, Jack Saltzgaver, and Don Heffner, but they all proved incapable of replacing him. The latest candidate was Joe "Flash" Gordon, a Los Angeles native who, like Lazzeri, was a product of the PCL. A shortstop in his one year with the Oakland Oaks, he went to the Newark Bears in 1937, where the Yankees converted him to second base, presumably with the expectation that he would step in for Lazzeri at some point.

As discussed above with regard to Lazzeri's rookie season, it was the norm for veterans to shun newcomers who might threaten to take their jobs. Lazzeri, instead, did whatever he could to help out the twenty-two-year-old Gordon. "He could have ignored the rookie and nobody would have censured him for it," wrote Harold C. Burr in 1939. "Gordon had rushed up through the Yankee farms to a fanfare of trumpets. In his old courageous heart Lazzeri knew that the arrival of Gordon doomed him and his fat World Series checks that might have kept coming in for years if Gordon had failed. But Tony saw to it that he didn't fail."[4]

Gordon did not fail. After spending two weeks in the Yankees camp, the slick-fielding infielder spent the 1937 season with Newark, hitting .280 with twenty-six home runs. Beginning in 1938, he was the Yankees' starting second baseman for seven years before spending the final four years of his career with the Indians. A nine-time All-Star, he was the AL MVP in 1942, set the AL record for home runs by a second baseman, and was elected to the Hall of Fame by the Veterans Committee in 2009.[5]

To virtually no one's surprise the Yankees' 1937 season proved to be more or less a carbon copy of 1936 as they once again coasted to the AL pennant, finishing thirteen games ahead of Detroit. They were never more than two games behind, then took sole possession of first place on May 24 and remained there for the rest of the season, finishing with a 102–52 record. On the very next day, however, a temporary shadow was cast over the Yankees' indomitable march to victory by one of the most dramatic events of the season. That day the Yankees faced the Tigers at Yankee Stadium. In the fourth inning Bump Hadley hit Tigers catcher and manager Mickey Cochrane square in the temple, fracturing his skull. For two days the life of one of the game's greatest catchers hung in the balance. He ultimately recovered, but his season, and his career as a player, were over.

DiMaggio, who had bulked up to 195 pounds over the offseason, surpassed Gehrig as the team's leading hitter. He batted .346, hit a league-leading 46 homers, and drove in a team-high 167 runs. Gehrig hit a team-best .351 with 37 homers and 158 RBIs, while Dickey contributed 29 homers and 133 RBIs. Overall New York led the league in homers, RBIs, and slugging percentage. The pitching staff was no less impressive, leading the AL with a 3.65 ERA. Gomez returned to form with a 21–11 record and led the league in ERA, shutouts, and strikeouts, while Red Ruffing was 20–7 and prize reliever Johnny Murphy won 13 while starting only 4 games but finishing 30.

For Lazzeri, however, the season was a humbling experience after his record-setting performance in 1936. Once again the drumbeat of criticism was heard, and not without reason. Even Frank Graham, who considered Lazzeri one of his all-time favorites, joined the chorus. After praising the play of Gehrig, Rolfe, and Crosetti, he wrote: "Only Lazzeri, among the infielders had slipped. It was Tony's twelfth campaign, and he was showing signs of wear."[6]

In fact it was one of Lazzeri's worst seasons. In the ten games between May 7 and May 18 he went 4 for 37, dropping his average from .370 to .253, with no home runs or RBIs. "I can't get a hit to save my life," he said at the time. "I know what I am doing and I can't stop it. I am not striding right and I can't wait for the ball to come to me. I have to reach for it. Naturally, when I do that, I am off balance and can't get any power into my swing." When one writer asked him why he didn't correct the problem since he seemed to know what was wrong, he shrugged and replied, "You'll have to answer that one."[7]

Lazzeri never got his average back to .300 for the remainder of the season. He sat out for twenty-four days following a hand injury on August 24, when his batting average stood at .238, limiting him to 126 games, his third-lowest total as a Yankee. His batting average (.244) and OPS (.747) were the lowest of his entire fourteen-year career, and while he still showed his home run power (14), his 70 RBIs were the second fewest of his twelve years with the Yankees, and his 109 hits were the fewest. Near the end of the season Newspaper Enterprise Association writer Richard McCann offered a blunt assessment: "[Lazzeri] is just about done as a regular player. He has been slow, unsteady, and brittle this year."[8]

In one of the brighter moments of his season Lazzeri displayed his baseball shrewdness in the April 26 game against Philadelphia by initiating an unlikely triple play. With runners on first and second in the eighth inning, Chubby Dean hit a low liner right at Lazzeri, who chose to trap the ball instead of catching it on the fly. He flipped the ball to Crosetti to force Bob Johnson, and Crosetti threw to first to erase Dean. Then as Wally Moses, who had hesitated when he thought Lazzeri would catch the ball on the fly, headed to third, Gehrig fired the ball to Rolfe for the tag to complete the triple play. (Some accounts said that Lazzeri trapped the ball, others that he dropped the ball, but either way all agreed that he did so intentionally to set up the triple play.)

Lazzeri had stumbled occasionally in recent years, but each time it appeared that Father Time had caught up with him, he managed to turn back the clock, at least for a while. But given his overall disappointing season, the thirty-three-year-old veteran finally had to face the reality of his situation, leading to this story in the *Daily News*: "After reading his own obituary for the past three years, Tony Lazzeri today wrote his own death notice with the statement, 'If I am not a major league manager next year, I will not stay in baseball. I think I am good for another two or three seasons, but I don't want to play any more and I won't.'" It is not surprising that Lazzeri admitted he was hoping to be hired as a manager, but he made it clear he would not accept a Minor League position. "I've saved my money," he said, "and rather than return to the minors in any capacity I'll stay home with my family." Noting that "there are few shrewder baseball men anywhere," the article concluded that the Yanks would like to keep him in their chain and would probably offer him a chance to manage one of their farm teams.[9]

Having announced his retirement, Lazzeri decided to have some fun on the field by resorting to an unusual, and somewhat risky, prank. In the eighth inning of the opener of a double-header at home against the A's on September 29, Lazzeri managed to pocket the game ball and slip a ball that he had doctored to make it soft to pitcher Kemp Wicker. When Wicker delivered the pitch, A's cleanup hitter Bob Johnson took a mighty cut, but the mushy ball went nowhere. The game was meaningless; the Yanks had clinched the pennant, and the A's were languishing in seventh pace, 48½ games behind. But when the umpires discovered that Lazzeri was the culprit, they announced that since he had violated a rule that prohibited tampering with the ball, they would report the incident to league president Will Harridge. The violation carried a possible $500 fine, but I found no evidence that Harridge followed up on the report.[10]

The World Series was a rematch with the Giants, who finished the season with a 95–57 record, edging out the Cubs by three games. Game One matched the teams' two aces, Gomez and Hubbell. Just as he had done in the 1936 Series opener, Hubbell handcuffed the Yankees, at least through the first five innings. But the Yankees exploded for seven runs in the sixth, followed by a Lazzeri homer in the eighth, for an 8–1 win. (For hitting the first homer in the Series, Lazzeri won a set of car tires.) The heavily favored Yanks won the first three games by a combined score of 21–3 before Hubbell came back to win the fourth game, 7–3. But the Yankees wrapped up the title in Game Five, 4–2. It was their fifth World Series title in eleven years, a span in which they won twenty of twenty-three games, including sweeps in 1927, 1928, and 1932. Only Lazzeri and Gehrig played in all of those games.

In his sixth and final World Series with the Yankees, for one brief moment Lazzeri once more provided a demonstration of the greatness that had once been his norm. He led all hitters in average (.400), on-base percentage (.526), and OPS (1.260) and had at least one hit in each game. In the deciding game, with the score tied at 2–2 in the fifth, he hit a triple, then scored the winning run on a single by Gomez. "A surprise in the Series was the magnificent playing of Lazzeri," wrote Graham, "who, for at least those five days, was the Lazzeri of old."[11] Even more emphatic was United Press (UP) correspondent George Kirksey: "'Poosh 'em up Tony' is at his best around second base and at the plate when the blue chips are on the line and the ball game's on the fire, and he stood out today, one of the most glamorous and valuable players of all time."[12]

Seven years later an unidentified UP writer added a footnote to that final game of the 1937 Series. The last out came on a ground ball to Lou Gehrig at first. As Gehrig fielded the ball, Gomez came off the mound to cover first base. Gehrig could have made the putout himself, but instead tossed the ball to Gomez, who stepped on the bag to end the game and the Series. Gehrig "remembered that Gomez had thrown his heart out on the mound and driven in the winning run" and thus had earned the right to keep the game ball. But "Lefty did some thinking of his own. He thought of Tony Lazzeri—thought of how Tony had been the center and the heart of the Yankee team—of how Tony had been the fielding and hitting star of the series. Tony was going. Lefty knew that, and Lefty was staying. So Lefty Gomez didn't keep that ball though he wanted it badly. He tossed it to Tony Lazzeri."[13]

Once Lazzeri announced his plan to retire and his desire to manage, the criticism of his on-field performance morphed into widespread affirmation of his qualifications to lead a Major League club. Given his long-standing reputation as one of the smartest players in baseball, it was widely anticipated that he would indeed land a managerial job. "Regret over the departure of Lazzeri," wrote Graham, "was tempered by a belief that he was on his way to a managerial job in either the National League or the American League in the near future."[14]

In his "Daniel's Dope" column in the *New York World-Telegram*, Dan Daniel wrote: "There is the impression that Lazzeri would make an able manager in the major leagues. Tony is perhaps the craftiest, the quickest thinking ballplayer in the majors. He is a scrapper and a hustler, and we are sure that any club which he managed would reflect those qualities. Even when Babe Ruth was the brilliant standout of the club, Lazzeri shone with the brilliance of defensive genius and offensive timeliness."[15]

The rumor mill that had churned out so many trade possibilities in preceding years now turned its focus to speculating on which club would sign Lazzeri as its manager. Among the teams listed as possibilities were the Browns, Indians, and Boston Bees. The day after Lazzeri's retirement announcement appeared, a story by Lew Zeidler suggested that Lazzeri was already assured of being hired as manager of the Indians: "Otherwise, why did he speak when he was still in the employ of the Yankees? Baseball men have long given Tony credit for being smart—one of the game's smartest, in fact, and that includes managers as well."[16]

On October 15, in the midst of the speculation about Lazzeri's future and while he was on a train returning to San Francisco, the Yankees announced that the twelve-year veteran had been given his unconditional release. The news was communicated to Lazzeri in a letter from Colonel Ruppert that began with the salutation "Dear Tony" and read in part: "We have received word from a reliable source that you have a chance to sign with a major league club either as coach or assistant manager. With this in mind the New York club is hereby granting you your unconditional release. While we are taking this step with keen regret, we are doing it in keeping with the promise we made to you some time ago, in appreciation of your long and faithful service."[17]

The story made sports-page headlines across the country, and in at least two cases was front-page news. *The Sporting News* began its coverage with the conclusive statement that Lazzeri was "undoubtedly on his way to the managership of some major league club."[18] According to Hy Hurwitz of the *Boston Globe*, the Yankees' announcement "was regarded in baseball circles as the removal of the final barrier to Lazzeri's appointment as manager of the Boston Bees."[19]

It turned out that Lazzeri's chance to sign as a coach or assistant manager had come from Cubs owner Phil Wrigley, who asked Ruppert to release Lazzeri so that the Cubs could pursue him. In fact when Lazzeri reached San Francisco on October 17, he revealed that he had stopped in Chicago to discuss a deal, but he refused to identify the club or the nature of the discussion, leaving open the speculation that he might be in line for a managerial post. "I have a deal on," he told Prescott Sullivan of the *San Francisco Examiner*, "but I have to keep it a secret. All I can say right now is that it's a job of some kind." Sullivan reported that a telegram was awaiting Lazzeri when he arrived home, "demanding that he return to Chicago immediately to consummate the deal." But Lazzeri stuffed the message in his pocket, saying, "Next week will be time enough. I need a little vacation."[20]

In spite of Lazzeri's refusal to identify the kind of job he had been approached about, based on the proximity of both Cleveland and St. Louis to Chicago, where Lazzeri met with his prospective employer, Sullivan felt comfortable enough to begin his story with this declaration: "Tony Lazzeri, batting star and fielding sensation of the 1937 world series, will manage either the Cleveland Indians or the St. Louis Browns next year."[21] (There had been rumors in 1935 that the Indians had offered the manager's job to Lazzeri but that Ruppert had refused to release him.)

There was plenty of mystery surrounding Wrigley's interest in Lazzeri, even in Chicago. According to Irving Vaughn, "The guesses on the real reason Wrigley desires to pay Tony's freight charges from San Francisco to here and return have included everything but the bat boy's job. Despite Wrigley's insistence there is no present intention of firing [current manager] Grimm, Lazzeri has been pictured as the next manager." In any case the fact that Lazzeri had not rushed back to Chicago suggested to Vaughn that he had not been promised the top job by the Cubs. Otherwise "Tony would have set a transcontinental record." Instead he was delaying his return "because he still has hopes in connection with the St. Louis Browns and the Boston Bees management."[22]

Even NL president Ford Frick publicly commented on Lazzeri's qualifications to manage. According to an AP story, "Frick boosted Lazzeri for the Chicago Cubs managerial spot today when he told newsmen 'he would make the Cubs a good man'" and called him "a smart baseball man, a fine fellow and, I believe, a good leader."[23]

After a ten-day hiatus, during which the managerial positions for which Lazzeri had been rumored to be a candidate had been filled, he did return to Chicago. He and Wrigley met on October 28, when Lazzeri signed a contract for an undisclosed amount—estimated to be $12,000–$13,000—to serve as coach and utility infielder in 1938. (Following his outstanding performance in the World Series, Lazzeri admitted he was reconsidering his decision to retire from playing.) "This is just what I wanted," he said following the signing. "It will add a lot to my baseball future and gives me a start toward reaching my goal, a managing job."[24] Whether he and Wrigley discussed the possibility of his becoming the manager at some point in the future is unknown.

As for Wrigley's motivation for signing his new player-coach, he offered this rationale: "What I'm really trying to do is to capture some of that Yankee spirit I admire so much. It seems to me that for a long time Lazzeri has typified that spirit, and I'm sure he can impart it to our players."[25]

But the drama wasn't quite over yet. Just how close Lazzeri might have been to reaching his goal of managing was a matter of some uncertainty and even controversy. One front-page headline in *The Sporting News* summed it up: "Lazzeri Puts Cubs in 3-Way Managerial Mix-Up," followed by this subhead: "Grimm-Hartnett Factions Uneasy." Gabby Hartnett, the Cubs' thirty-six-year-old All-Star catcher who finished second in the NL MVP vote in 1937 and was generally considered to be a de facto assistant manager, was favored by those who thought he would be a better manager than Grimm, who would begin his seventh year on the job in 1938. Now Lazzeri's presence as a high-profile coach muddied the waters. The story noted that signing a coach is usually "covered by a couple of lines in the public prints, but Tony was welcomed like a conquering hero. It must have made the veteran feel like he might be stepping into something far more complicated than was apparent on the surface. . . . Instead of the two parties made up of the pro-Grimms and pro-Hartnetts, there will be a three-cornered struggle. The new entry will be the Lazzeri-for-manager clique."[26]

In mid-November a UP story suggested that given Wrigley's disappointment over the Cubs' failure to win the 1937 pennant, the hiring of Lazzeri was "interpreted generally as a warning to Grimm that the Cubs had better step lively in 1938 or have coach Lazzeri directing their destinies—even before the season ends."[27]

As if to underscore the lingering confusion over Lazzeri's job, a tongue-in-cheek complaint from a reader appeared in the column of *Chicago Tribune* sports editor Arch Ward: "It has been

24 hours since any Chicago newspaper has carried an exclusive story on Tony Lazzeri's status with the Cubs."[28]

The issue carried over into the new year, with the AP reporting that "there has been much conjecture about how far [Lazzeri's] powers will extend as the reported third managerial brain of the Cubs." Meanwhile, "the nearby Millbrae golf course is his training ground," where his daily routine consisted of 18–27 holes of golf.[29] One can only wonder what Lazzeri thought of all the media coverage that his signing with the Cubs had generated.

The initial response of many to Lazzeri's announcement of his desire to manage was not *whether* he was qualified or whether he *might* be hired as a manager, but rather which team *would* hire him. Given this widespread assumption, together with the many reminders of Lazzeri's reputation as someone who had an astute baseball mind and the ringing endorsements of his qualifications, the question must be: Why was he *not* hired? Perhaps teams were reluctant to hire someone with no managerial experience, but that didn't prevent earlier stars such as Ty Cobb, Nap Lajoie, Rogers Hornsby, Frankie Frisch, and Joe Cronin from being hired in spite of having no previous experience. Might there have been an unspoken reluctance to hire someone afflicted with epilepsy? Or did the same institutional ethnic bias that had made some teams reluctant to sign Lazzeri as a player prevent them from hiring him as a manager? Had he been hired, Lazzeri would have been the first full-time Major League manager of Italian descent. (Oscar Melillo would serve as acting manager of the St. Louis Browns for the final nine games of the 1938 season, but no Italian American would be hired as a full-time manager until 1951, when the Cubs appointed Chicago native Phil Cavarretta.) In any case why Tony Lazzeri did not get a chance to do the job that so many baseball people agreed he was qualified to do remains as one more unresolved mystery of his life.

Whatever the future held for Lazzeri following the 1937 season, his twelve-year career as a Yankee had come to an end. He had gotten off to a historic start in his first three seasons; then, following his injury-plagued 1928 season, he came back with his best year in 1929. After that he struggled at times, especially in significant parts of 1930 and 1931, and the cause of his sudden decline at the age of twenty-seven remains unclear. Recall that in 1931 the *Brooklyn Times Union* had flatly proclaimed that "Tony Lazzeri, once a dangerous right-hand hitter, is through at 27."[30] But Lazzeri's ride into the sunset lasted longer than many had predicted. The forecast of his demise became something of a "loop" that kept repeating itself year after year beginning in 1930. Yet he kept finding ways to bounce back, especially in 1932, 1936, and the 1937 World Series, and he often showed signs of brilliance that brought back memories of his prime years. Through it all he retained his great popularity with the fans and his role as the man the Yankees looked to for leadership.

Near the end of 1937 White Sox manager Jimmy Dykes summed up what Lazzeri meant to the Yankees. He predicted that New York would not win its third consecutive World Series in 1938, but not because the pitching would fail or because DiMaggio wouldn't hit: "They won't win because Lazzeri's gone. He was the brains of the ball club. Whenever some pitcher got into a jam, whenever Catcher Bill Dickey was undecided what to call for, or whenever the outfielders needed directions on where to play for a certain hitter—they went to Lazzeri. He was the dynamo that ran that club. The fans did not know this, but we ball players did."[31]

13

Twilight Trail

A fter Lazzeri had played for the Cubs, Dodgers, and Giants, all within the span of fourteen months, and had recently been signed to manage the Toronto Maple Leafs of the International League, in June 1939 *Time* magazine ran a recap of the career of "the craftiest, quickest-thinking ball player in the major leagues." He was "the mastermind of the Yankee infield" who had helped his team win six pennants and five World Series and "next to Babe Ruth, the most popular player ever to wear a Yankee uniform."[1] The article was called "Twilight Trail," a fitting title to encapsulate the final phase of Lazzeri's time in the big leagues. He was making the difficult transition from his twelve years with the Yankees, trying to find ways to satisfy his desire to continue to play the game he loved, and laying the groundwork for the managerial position he hoped to have when his playing days ended. It proved to be a period of rapid changes that more often than not led to disappointment and frustration but not surrender.

One benefit of being a Cubs employee was that Lazzeri didn't have to make the annual cross-country trek to St. Petersburg for spring training in 1938. Instead he only had to make the short flight from San Francisco to Los Angeles, then from there take the boat to Santa Catalina Island, where the Cubs had been training since 1921, soon after William Wrigley, Phil's father and principal owner of the club, had purchased the entire island.

When the Cubs' train from Chicago arrived in Los Angeles on February 24, Lazzeri was waiting at the station. The next day a photo appeared in the papers showing manager Charlie Grimm standing between Lazzeri and Gabby Hartnett, who were shaking hands, with all three smiling. It had the appearance of a photo op designed to dismiss any speculation that there might be friction within the Cubs' new brain trust trio between the manager and either or both of the two men often identified as his possible replacement. (Like Lazzeri, Hartnett had made it known that he would like to manage one day.) However, the caption below a photo in the *Oakland Tribune* read: "Baseball gossip predicts a war for the job held by Grimm, with Tony getting it or leaving the Cubs in mid-Summer."[2] In addition, when Cubs shortstop Billy Jurges was asked where Lazzeri fit into the picture, he replied: "I don't know, and apparently no one else out there knows. It's a strange setup." Then after pointing out that if anything were to happen to Grimm, Hartnett was in line to replace him, Jurges added: "He's very popular in Chicago and the fans undoubtedly would resist any managerial change that didn't include Gabby."[3]

When the first Cubs arrived on the island, they were met by a large crowd; schools and businesses were closed for the day. Leading a caravan to the team's hotel was Phil Wrigley himself, dressed in cowboy garb and sitting on his $10,000 silver saddle. (The younger Wrigley had inherited both the team and the island from his father in 1932.)

The day after the welcoming ceremony, an AP release proclaimed that the mystery behind Lazzeri's position with the Cubs was lifted with the announcement that "Lazzeri will serve as one of the principal members of Manager Charlie Grimm's newly created board of strategy, organized to bring the 1938 National League championship to Chicago."[4] The other members of the board were Hartnett, now officially designated as a coach, and the two other Cubs coaches, John "Red" Corriden and Roy Johnson. Since the release included no clarification of what Lazzeri's spe-

cific role within the newly created board would be, it is unclear
to what extent, if any, the mystery had been lifted.

The speculation regarding Lazzeri's role, as well as that of
Hartnett, continued into April, prompting Wrigley to make an
"emphatic declaration" that neither was in line to succeed Grimm.
He was quoted in a UP report as saying that "Lazzeri is a coach and
a utility infielder working under Grimm like the rest of the players." He also declared that he "never would select another manager from the ranks" (as he had with Grimm in 1932) so as to avoid
once again "going through several trying years of developing a
manager."[5] That resolution would prove to have a short shelf life.

With all the media speculation as to whether Lazzeri was in
fact a manager-in-waiting, it would be reasonable to assume that
there might have been some tension between him and Hartnett,
the presumptive heir to Grimm's throne, and perhaps between
him and Grimm, on whose head sat the crown. But as competitive
as Lazzeri was on the field and as much as he may have wanted
to be a manager, there's a reason why, throughout his career, he
was one of the best liked players in the game, by opponents as
well as teammates.

Warren Brown, who covered Chicago sports for many years,
wrote a history of the Cubs in 1948, and received the J. G. Taylor
Spink Award in 1973, refuted the notion of any ill will between
Lazzeri and either Hartnett or Grimm: "All were certain that
his presence would lead to complications. All were wrong. From
the first, Lazzeri, who sees much and says little, hit it off with
Grimm, and hit it off with Hartnett, who had been designated as
a coach as well as player, when the 1938 season began."[6] Brown
may have gotten it right, but if so, it seems odd that Grimm,
in his 1968 autobiography, refers to Lazzeri only once and then
somewhat dismissively: "With the exception of [Dizzy] Dean and
Tony Lazzeri, whom we picked up from the Yankees, this was
just about the same team from 1937. Tony didn't play much."[7]

By mid-July, as the Cubs were languishing in third place, rumors
regarding Grimm's likely departure intensified, with Lazzeri's

name still appearing as a possible replacement. On July 20, the day after a seven-game winning streak had been snapped and with the Cubs' record at 45–36, the suspense ended when Wrigley broke his vow not to promote from within by naming Hartnett as the new manager. Even at that point in the season Lazzeri's status within the organization remained more or less a mystery, and Lazzeri himself refused to answer repeated questions about the state of the Cubs. Hartnett did announce that the "board of strategy," now consisting of himself, Lazzeri, and the other two coaches, would remain unchanged.

Brown quoted Lazzeri as saying, after Hartnett was named to replace Grimm, "All I've got to say about this is that Gabby ought to have been manager long ago. All I hope is that he'll find some place for me to get into the games every day. He's my friend and he's going to be a great manager."[8]

In addition to the uncertainty regarding Lazzeri's position as a coach, there was also skepticism about his ability to contribute on the field, not surprising given his 1937 numbers. But he did see a good amount of playing time at the start of the season. He appeared in eleven of the team's first thirteen games, ten as a starter, filling in for Stan Hack at third and then Jurges at short, when both were out with injuries. In those games Lazzeri batted .375, with four homers and twelve RBIs.

Looking to generate more offense from his light-hitting lineup, on May 11 Grimm put Lazzeri, again subbing for Jurges, into the cleanup spot. He went 2 for 4 that day, then helped snap a three-game losing streak the next day by going 4 for 4 with five RBIs in a 9–5 win over the Dodgers. He continued to start at short, and hit in the cleanup spot, through May 17. In that stretch of five games he hit .478 (11 for 23), with one homer and seven RBIs. At that point his season average stood at .356, with a .472 on-base percentage and a .616 slugging average.

Nevertheless, on May 18 Jurges, who had appeared in ten games and was hitting .152 with no homers and five RBIs, returned to the starting lineup. Meanwhile, in spite of his hot bat and the Cubs' modest offense, Lazzeri, who led the Cubs in average and home runs, was primarily relegated to a pinch-hitting role from that point on; he started in only four more games. His hope that Hartnett would play him on a regular basis went unfulfilled. Appearing in fifty-four games, twenty-three as a starter, he hit .267 with five homers and twenty-three RBIs. In the words of *Chicago Tribune* writer Irving Vaughn, "The ex-Yankee who helped the Cubs at the start of the season . . . gradually melted into the status of a forgotten man."[9]

Lazzeri may have become a forgotten man in Chicago, but he was still beloved in New York. In the Sunday comics section of the *Daily News* two days before the Cubs made their first visit to New York to face the Giants, Lazzeri was the hero in a Huskies cereal ad. It was common practice at the time to run advertisements in the form of comic strips featuring famous celebrities and athletes alongside classic strips such as *L'il Abner* and *Dick Tracy*. In the ad Lazzeri is visiting the zoo, dressed in a suit and tie, when a black leopard that has escaped its cage is about to attack a young boy. Lazzeri saves the boy's life by picking up an iron pipe and slugging the leopard just in time. Tony then advises the boy to eat healthy foods and get plenty of rest and assures him that he eats Huskies every day.[10]

In that same issue the *Daily News* ran an AP story about Lazzeri's surprising performance with the Cubs. "For a ball player whose active playing days were supposedly counted out by old Father Time, Signor Lazzeri is doing a bang up job by proving to the Cubs he still is a mighty handy man to have around. . . . Always known as a great 'money player,' at his best when the going was hardest, Tony has filled in at second base, shortstop and third base and has played brilliantly."[11]

Following Hartnett's appointment, it took a while for the players to adjust to their new leader, who was more of a disciplinarian than "Jolly Cholly" Grimm. But on August 30 the Cubs moved into second place for the first time since June 30, even though their record under Hartnett stood at a modest 22–19 and they were 6½ games behind the Pirates. From that point on they won nineteen of their next twenty-five games to bring them within 1½ games of first place on the eve of a three-game home series against the Pirates, who had slipped to 12–10 in September.

In the first game of the series Hartnett chose to start Dizzy Dean, who had not pitched since September 18. Prior to the season Wrigley had paid $185,000 and three players to get Dean from the Cardinals. But the man who had been one of the best of his era had lost his fastball, if not his fan appeal, and now had to rely on guile and control. To that point he had started only nine games but had managed to post a 6–1 record. Now, in his biggest game of the year, before 42,338 fans, he held the Pirates to one run in 82/3 innings in a 2–1 win to close the gap to half a game.

The next day, September 28, it took four pitchers to get the Cubs through the top of the eighth, trailing by a score of 5–3. In the bottom of the inning, with men on first and second and no one out, Hartnett sent Lazzeri up to pinch-hit with orders to bunt. In the most crucial game of the season, once again Lazzeri lived up to his reputation as a clutch hitter. After failing to get the bunt down in two tries, he lined a double to right to narrow the lead to one run. Babe Herman then singled to score Jurges, but Joe Marty, pinch-running for Lazzeri, was thrown out at the plate and the score remained tied. By now darkness was creeping in and the umpires were prepared to call the game after the ninth inning, setting the scene for one of the most dramatic moments in Cubs history.

After the Pirates went quietly in the top of the ninth, the first two Cubs were retired, bringing Hartnett to the plate to face Pirates reliever Mace Brown. Hartnett watched—assuming he could see them—two strikes go by, both curveballs by most accounts. Brown then tried to sneak a third strike by Hartnett, but the catcher-manager connected, and the ball soared through the darkening sky, unseen by many fans, until it landed in the left-center-field bleachers. What came to be known as the "homer in the gloamin'" had put the Cubs into first place to stay. Edward Burns wrote that "the mob started to gather around Gabby before he reached first base. By the time he reached second he couldn't have been recognized in the mass of Cub players, frenzied fans and excited ushers except for that red face, which shone out even in the gray shadows."[12] The Cubs beat a demoralized Pirates crew the next day, 10–1, and went on to win the pennant by two games.

Having won their fourth NL title in ten years, the Cubs met the Yankees—who again dominated the AL, winning the pennant by 9½ games—in a rematch of the 1932 World Series, which the Yankees swept. As Yogi Berra might have said, the 1938 Series was a case of déjà vu all over again. The Cubs' dramatic season came to a predictable end with New York taking four straight, limiting the Cubs to nine runs. The star of the Series was Joe Gordon, Lazzeri's replacement at second base, who hit .400. (In the regular season he had a modest .255 average but hit twenty-five homers and drove in ninety-seven runs.) As for Lazzeri, this would be his seventh and final Series, and, as he had for much of the regular season, he got little playing time. He pinch-hit in the final two games, going hitless with one strikeout—a far cry from his heroics in the 1937 Series. It would also prove to be the last World Series for both Colonel Ruppert, who would die on January 13, 1939, and Lou Gehrig, who would retire on June 21, 1939, at age thirty-six after being diagnosed with amyotrophic lateral sclerosis (ALS), the debilitating disease that would later bear his name.

Lazzeri made his biggest splash in Chicago when he announced he was leaving the Cubs. On October 25 the *San Francisco Examiner* reported that Lazzeri had confided to friends that he had asked for his release at the end of the World Series and that Wrigley had agreed to grant it. The next day the headline on the first page of the *Chicago Tribune* sports section read: "Lazzeri Says He's Through with Cubs." Wrigley confirmed that he had agreed to provide the release when Lazzeri told him he wanted to look for a better job but said that Lazzeri had yet to make a formal request.

Vaughn suggested in his story that "Lazzeri may be taking his release simply to get out of what was for him an uncomfortable situation. To avoid a possible charge that he was chiseling to get the job [as manager], the Italian athlete leaned backward. He kept to himself most of the time."[13]

Predictably Lazzeri had little to say publicly about his experience with the Cubs. But he was cited in one story as saying that while the wages and work were pleasant enough, he would have liked to play baseball instead of talk it: "I've got a lot of baseball left in me and I'd like to continue playing. I think I could have helped out the Cubs on the field." His hope now was to land a job as a utility player or as a player-manager.[14]

If he did not do as much as he would have liked to help the Cubs on the field as a player, Lazzeri did come away with the satisfaction of knowing he had helped develop one of his young teammates. Clay Bryant, a twenty-six-year-old right-hander who was in his fourth year with the Cubs in 1938, had won a total of eleven games in his first three seasons. In 1938 he posted a 19–11 record with a 3.10 ERA and was considered to be the most improved pitcher in the NL. He credited Lazzeri for his dramatic improvement: "Lazzeri changed my grip on the ball. I always gripped the ball across the seams. I still do but Lazzeri got me to move my grip a little further around on it. That helped my control a lot."[15]

For someone so competitive and used to playing regularly, it must have been frustrating for Lazzeri to spend the majority of the season on the bench, especially given his productivity early in the season. As for his position as a coach and as a member of the "board of strategy," it never was clear exactly what role he played or to what extent, if any, he was involved in decision making. His stated hope when he accepted the job was that it would give him a start toward reaching his goal of becoming a manager. Did that happen? What, if anything, did he gain? The fact that he requested his release at the end of the season suggests that he wasn't anxious to repeat the experience—at least not in Chicago.

If, as was the case in 1938, Lazzeri had hopes of landing a managerial position in the offseason, he was disappointed again in 1939. Reportedly he did, however, receive offers from several clubs either to play, coach, or both. It was expected that he would accept a $10,000 offer from the Cleveland Indians to serve as a player-coach under Ossie Vitt, who had managed him in Salt Lake City in his record-setting 1925 season. Instead on December 10, five days after receiving his formal release from the Cubs and four days after his thirty-fifth birthday, Lazzeri signed with the Brooklyn Dodgers to play second base at a salary estimated to be higher than the $12,500 he had reportedly received from the Cubs. There his double-play partner would be thirty-three-year-old player-manager Leo Durocher, a one-time Yankees teammate. "It won't be the fastest double play combination up there," wrote Walter Judge, "but it will be the smartest." Acknowledging that "Lazzeri's legs aren't what they used to be," Judge added that "Lazzeri remained a good fielder with the Yankees because of his uncanny ability to play the batters and get the jump on the ball." He quoted Lazzeri as saying that "it was only with the understanding that I would play regularly that I agreed to join the Dodgers."[16]

It seems curious that any big league club would sign a thirty-five-year-old veteran who had appeared in only fifty-four games the previous season with a guarantee that he would play regularly. It was generally believed that Lazzeri was no longer an everyday second baseman, but the proud veteran was not ready to agree. But just as had happened when Lazzeri was signed by the Cubs, some wondered if there was another motive behind his acquisition. Once again his hiring raised questions about potential internal strife, especially since the Dodgers staff already included two coaches, Wade Killefer and Charlie Dressen, who were former managers and therefore potential replacements should Durocher fail. Lazzeri was perceived by some as a third potential replacement, but he insisted that his priority was to play second base and that he had no interest in coaching.

In a statement that contradicted Lazzeri's understanding that he had been assured he would play regularly, Larry MacPhail, the Dodgers' general manager, quickly sought to quell the concerns about Lazzeri's role with Brooklyn, claiming that no commitments had been made: "Sure, he'll play second base if he wins the job. But my main idea in offering a proposition is that I'm sure he can help us as an extra infielder and as a pinch hitter." To further clarify, MacPhail added: "He isn't a candidate to take Leo Durocher's job—and neither is anyone else in the Dodger organization."[17]

Under MacPhail, who was in his first year as GM, and the newly appointed Durocher, both ambitious and flamboyant characters, the Dodgers were looking to move up after spending six seasons in the second division of the NL and finishing seventh in 1938. How would Lazzeri fit into that picture? As MacPhail had said, Tony had to win the job as second baseman. His primary competition in spring training came from twenty-six-year-old Pete Coscarart, a good-field, no-hit infielder who had appeared in thirty-two games for Brooklyn in 1938, twenty-two as a starter, with a paltry .152 average, no homers and six RBIs. But even in the early days of spring training he was being tabbed as the first-string second baseman, and the handwriting was on the wall regarding Lazzeri's hope, perhaps even expectation, of being an everyday player. By late February Durocher was announcing that "Coscarart will be our regular second baseman IF he can hit .250" and that the Dodgers were looking for another utility infielder, "someone who's a hitter and a hustler." As for Lazzeri, the lippy skipper pronounced him to be "too slow," adding that "he's alright for replacement at second and third base, though."[18]

It was during spring training that Lazzeri, perhaps frustrated by his uncertain situation with the Dodgers, engineered what may have been his most elaborate prank, as recounted by Pete Reiser, then a promising prospect in the Dodgers' camp at Lakeland, Florida. One day Lazzeri surprised Reiser by inviting him to go along on a ride to St. Petersburg, where the Yankees trained.

Once in the car, Reiser noticed a large suitcase in the back seat of the car. "Tony was pretty quiet," he recalled, "like he had something on his mind." When they arrived at the Yankees' camp, there was no one around except for an elderly gentleman who greeted Lazzeri warmly and asked him what he was doing there. According to Reiser, Tony answered, "The Yankees brought me back," a reply that delighted the old man, who said he knew the Yankees had made a mistake in letting him go.

Lazzeri, carrying the suitcase, and Reiser entered the locker room. Once inside, the former Yankees' star locked the door and opened the suitcase, which contained "a couple of hammers and a load of these big railroad spikes." The two of them proceeded to nail the Yankees' spikes to the floor. The rookie admitted he was scared: "These weren't just spiked shoes I was nailing to the floor—these belonged to Joe DiMaggio, Lou Gehrig, Bill Dickey, Joe McCarthy." When they finished that task, Lazzeri took a pair of scissors and began cutting up parts of the Yankees' uniforms, "snipping at sleeves and trouser legs." When they left, the old man said, "I'll tell them you were here," to which Lazzeri replied, "I think they'll know."[19]

As the season got under way, it was obvious that Lazzeri would be riding the bench. But on April 23, in the Dodgers' fifth game, he got a chance to show what he could do when Coscarart was spiked in the foot and had to come out of the game. Lazzeri pinch-hit in the seventh for the injured second baseman and promptly hit his first homer of the season, then singled in the ninth in a 5–4, twelve-inning loss to the Phillies. He started at second in the next nine games until Coscarart returned on May 7, then started at third in the next two games.

Then just as the Dodgers were about to leave New York for a series in Boston that began on May 12, Lazzeri was stricken with inflamed tonsillitis and confined to bed. On May 13 he received a telegram informing him that he was unconditionally released by Leo Durocher.[20] A stunned Lazzeri told the AP: "It was a surprise to me. I thought I was doing well and expected to join the club in Chicago. I don't know what I'm going to do now."[21] In fact Lazzeri had been doing well, at least at the plate. On May 8, after appearing in thirteen of the Dodgers' first sixteen games, eleven as a starter, his average stood at .306 with three home runs, six RBIs, and an excellent on-base percentage of .479. The next day, in what proved to be his final game, he went 0 for 3, dropping his average to .282. He did, however, make six errors.

Being released must have felt to Lazzeri like salt in the wound of being relegated, once again, to the role of a bench player as he had been in Chicago. For the man who for twelve years had been a key player for the most dominant franchise in baseball and who was confident he still had plenty to contribute on a day-to-day basis, it was unquestionably difficult to accept the reality that he was now considered a utility infielder whose primary role was to wait patiently on the bench until one of the starters was injured or needed an occasional day off.

Lazzeri's disappointment was lessened somewhat the day after he was informed of his release—termed his "baseball obituary" by the AP—when he received a phone call from Bill Terry, manager of the Giants, offering him a job as their third baseman. Lazzeri accepted the offer, becoming the tenth player to that date to wear the uniform of all three New York teams. Still unable to play because of his tonsillitis, one week after the call from Terry he boarded the Giants' train as they headed to St. Louis on their first western swing. But when the team left for Chicago on May 18, he stayed behind to have his abscessed tonsil removed at St. John's Hospital. He rejoined the team in Pittsburgh on May 22 and made his debut five days later.

According to Grantland Rice, Lazzeri's signing by the last-place Giants was not surprising: "With the Giants stumbling and needing help at third base and with Lazzeri on the market, it was a cinch that Bill Terry would grab him."[22] Third base was a musical-chairs position for the Giants in 1939, with five players, in addition to Lazzeri, and all younger than he, making between eleven and seventy starts at the position. Lazzeri started at third in all thirteen games the Giants played between May 27 and June 7, compiling a .295 average with one home run and eight RBIs. (His two-run homer in the bottom of the seventh inning against the Cardinals on June 3 was a game-winner.)

Terry had hired Lazzeri in the hopes that he could provide some power at third base, but with the exception of the one homer, all of his hits were singles. Whether it was due to his lack of power, his inconsistent fielding (including four errors in thirty-six chances), or a combination of the two is not clear, but following a 7–1 loss to the Cubs on June 7, in which he made two errors, for the second time in less than a month, Lazzeri was given his outright release. According to Hy Turkin, Terry was livid following his team's four errors and all-around sloppy play: "Poor Bill was so rent up with wrath he used old Tony Lazzeri as a blow-off valve. He approached Poosh 'Em Up after the game, looked him smack in the eye and yelled: 'You're fired!'"[23]

Less than a week passed before Lazzeri was once more offered a job, only this time it wasn't a Major League team that came calling. On June 11, 1939, he signed a two-year contract with the Toronto Maple Leafs of the eight-team AA International League as their player-manager, replacing Jack Burns, who remained with the team as their first baseman. At the time Toronto, which had recently reorganized and had no Major League affiliation, was in last place, as it had been all season, 18½ games out of first. Lazzeri, who had said when he left the Yankees in 1937 that he would be interested in managing only in the Majors, must have realized, after going through two postseasons with no offers, that proving himself with Toronto might provide his best chance for ultimately landing a Major League position. Among Lazzeri's opposing managers were three former Major League skippers: Rogers Hornsby (Baltimore Orioles), Burleigh Grimes (Montreal Royals), and Steve O'Neill (Buffalo Bisons).

The "Twilight Trail" article in *Time* magazine, mentioned, above, pointed out that Lazzeri signed his contract with the Maple Leafs on the same day that his 1926 World Series nemesis, Grover Cleveland Alexander, "along with ten other living Immortals, was installed in Baseball's Hall of Fame in Cooperstown."[24]

Toronto had been a part of the International League since 1912, after having been in the Eastern League since 1896. From 1901 to 1903 and again in 1905 and 1906, the team was managed by future Yankees GM Ed Barrow, the man who brought Lazzeri to New York. Two of Toronto's earliest stars were future Hall of Famers Nap Lajoie and Wee Willie Keeler. Soon after Lazzeri signed with Toronto, a sports column in the *Ottawa Citizen* noted his popularity: "To a man, Brooklyn Dodgers were tickled when Tony Lazzeri caught on with Toronto Maple Leafs. During his brief term with the Brooklyns, Lazzeri was a prime favorite with every member of the team."[25] (The Dodgers were affiliated with the Montreal Royals in the International League.)

Lazzeri's managerial career got off to a good start on June 19 when Toronto beat the first-place Rochester Red Wings by a score of 6–2. The next day he made his playing debut, striking out as a pinch-hitter in the seventh, as the Leafs won, 8–7, in fifteen innings. The apparently rejuvenated Leafs went on to win seven of their first ten games under their new leader. "The magic of Tony Lazzeri has brought a change in the Toronto Leafs, along with a reawakening of interest in the fans," began a *Sporting News* story following an early five-game winning streak. "He made an instant hit with the fans when he took over the coaching duties at third base, giving that position new life and action."[26]

During his first road trip to Rochester, Lazzeri spoke about the adjustments he had to make in his new role as manager. He said the team members were hustling and he was more than satisfied with their play, but he was having a hard time learning how to eat before night games. "Some of the boys say eat at 2 o'clock, some say at 4," he said. For the most part he was eating sandwiches, but one day his wife did cook a hot meal for him. "It was swell," he said, "but when I got out to [the] park I was so stuffed I could hardly move." He also admitted that he had a lot to learn about the game he had been playing most of his life: "This is the first managerial job I ever had, and I'm starting to learn baseball all over again, just like a green rookie. It's one thing to go out and play yourself, have someone tell you what to do in a tough situation, and quite another when you have to do the telling. Especially when a game may hinge on your decision."[27]

On July 4 Lazzeri went to New York to be part of Lou Gehrig Appreciation Day at Yankee Stadium. The ceremony had been arranged, in spite of Gehrig's protests, to honor the "Iron Horse" who on May 2 had taken himself out of the lineup after 2,130 consecutive games due to his affliction with ALS, the incurable disease that would take his life less than two years later at the age of thirty-seven. Lazzeri, standing to the left of Babe Ruth, was one of several members of the 1927 Murderers' Row lineup that appeared on the field. The team marched to the center-field flag pole, where the 1927 World Series flag was raised. Gehrig was presented with several gifts, including an eighteen-inch trophy from his current teammates. As the ceremony was coming to an end, Gehrig, overcome by emotion and reluctant to speak, was finally convinced by manager Joe McCarthy to approach the microphone. In one of the most moving moments in baseball history, with his head bowed, Gehrig uttered the famous lines: "For two weeks you've been reading about a bad break. Yet today I consider myself the luckiest man on the face of the earth. . . . I may have been given a bad break, but I've got an awful lot to live for." In his front-page story in the *New York Times*, John Drebinger called it "as amazing a valedictory as ever came from a ball player."

For a while there was some optimism that under Lazzeri's leadership the Leafs might be able to escape the cellar, where they had been lodged all season. And they did sneak into seventh place briefly in mid-July, following a three-game sweep of Newark, but a doubleheader loss on July 16 dropped them back to last place.

Toward the end of the season Lazzeri found himself in a sad duel with Grimes—the Montreal manager and, for a brief time in 1934, a Yankees teammate—to determine which of the two, both in their first year in the International League and neither with a chance for the playoffs, could stay out of the cellar. The prize went to Grimes as Montreal (64–88) finished a half game ahead of Toronto (63–90), whose record after Lazzeri took over was 44–52.

Lazzeri appeared in thirty-nine games, twenty of them in the field at second base, with a modest .227 average and one home run. He also was one of fourteen Toronto pitchers to see action that season. On August 20 he entered the game in the second inning after Montreal had scored seven runs. In five innings he gave up eight hits and three walks, with the major damage coming in the sixth, when Montreal scored four runs for a final score of 13–4.

"Toronto was mired before Tony came along, and all his efforts to haul it out have been futile," wrote one columnist. "Even so Tony is popular with Maple Leaf fans and from all appearances will stay on another year to see what he really can do. 'Tis well that Tony is firmly entrenched at Toronto, for no doubt he has grown tired of being bandied about."[28] On September 12 Toronto president Don Ross announced that Lazzeri would return as manager in 1940.

Back home in California, Lazzeri once again played golf more or less on a daily basis at the Millbrae Country Club. In December he, along with Ty Cobb and other major leaguers, played in Lazzeri's annual tournament that paired professional ballplayers with Millbrae club members. Together with his club partner, Lazzeri, who shot a gross score of 76, won the tournament by defeating Cubs infielder Dick "Rowdy Richard" Bartell and his partner in a playoff.

In January 1940 Lazzeri was elected as a director of the Association of Professional Ball Players of America, whose president at the time was Walter Johnson. Other members of the board of directors were Gabby Hartnett, Joe Cronin, Eddie Collins, Jimmy Dykes, Lou Gehrig, Mickey Cochrane, Lefty O'Doul, and legendary umpire Bill Klem. (With the exception of Dykes, all would end up in the Hall of Fame.) The association was established in Los Angeles in 1924, "when twelve former players gathered and determined there was a need to assist the less fortunate members of the baseball profession." By 2020 the association, headquartered in Scottsdale, Arizona, had grown to over 101,000 members, with a mission "to furnish financial assistance to the sick or indigent ballplayer or member of the baseball family when he becomes of an age where he is no longer able to provide for himself and has no other source of income."[29]

14

Final Years in Uniform

n 1940, just before leaving for their second year in Toronto, Tony and Maye left their home in Millbrae and moved back to San Francisco, where they bought a brand new home on Rossmoor Drive in the Lakeside district. They purchased the two-story, nine-room home on February 28, only four days after it was first open to the public for inspection. A project of the Stoneson Brothers, major builders in the San Francisco area, Lakeside was conceived as a small, quiet neighborhood of tree-lined streets complete with a small commercial area.[1] Under the title "For the Man of Means," the plan for the development was spelled out in the October 1936 issue of *California Homes* magazine. "If you are a San Francisco executive or professional man, you'll like Lakeside. Close to your executive offices . . . close to your favorite golf course and bridge club; close to your heart in the architecture of your needs."[2] Given Lazzeri's passion for golf, it was probably not coincidental that their new home was located only four miles from the Olympic Club, one of the most exclusive country clubs in America at the time. It is not known exactly when Lazzeri began playing at the club, but it certainly would have been before he was admitted as a member on October 8, 1941.

It is hard to imagine a more obvious sign of Lazzeri's assimilation into mainstream American culture than to be accepted as a member of such a prestigious and selective organization. Founded in 1860, the Olympic is considered to be the oldest athletic club in the United States. Among its nineteenth-century members were Mark Twain, William Randolph Hearst, and Leland Stanford, as well as athletes such as "Gentleman Jim" Corbett, winner of the world heavyweight title in 1892. In the 1920s the club moved to its current site along the western edge of the city south of Golden Gate Park, where it built two eighteen-hole golf courses and a clubhouse. Five U.S. Open championships were held at the club between 1955 and 2012.

Lazzeri's admission to such a club in San Francisco, however, did not mirror a universal shift in attitude with regard to ethnic minorities. Had he lived elsewhere, it might have been a different story. A decade later both Yogi Berra and Dom DiMaggio, at the time two of the most recognized and esteemed Major League ballplayers, were blackballed when they applied to country clubs in New Jersey and Massachusetts respectively. "In about '50, '51, they wouldn't let me into a country club in New Jersey," Berra told me. "They didn't like Italians then. I went to an Italian club; I got in there real quick."[3] DiMaggio, a seven-time All-Star who had retired from baseball in 1953 and become a successful businessman, was blackballed by two members of the club to which he applied. "I was a jock, an Italian, and Catholic," he said. "The club was embarrassed, so they asked me to reapply, and I was let in."[4]

The fact that the Lazzeris had purchased a new home in 1932 and then another upscale residence in 1940, together with Tony's admission to the Olympic Club, indicates that they had not only survived the Depression years, but had also thrived. Clearly their prosperity was not just the result of Tony's significant earnings in baseball, but also of their wise investments. In addition to their home, they also had various real estate holdings. Following their move to Millbrae in 1932, they purchased and operated an apartment building on El Camino Real in downtown Millbrae.[5] In addition, when Tony filed for divorce in 1936, he referred to jointly held real estate in both San Mateo and Marin Counties, as well as funds in three San Francisco banks. (The purchase of the San Francisco home four years after Tony filed for divorce also suggests renewed stability in their marriage.) All of these assets make Colonel Ruppert's statement (cited in chapter 8) that Lazzeri's uncharacteristically poor performance in 1931 was the result of his distress over a major loss in the stock market crash seem even less credible.

In 1940 Toronto became an affiliate of Connie Mack's A's, due at least in part to Mack's respect for Lazzeri's keen baseball insight. In hopes of at least climbing out of the cellar, the Maple Leafs did some serious housecleaning in the offseason, with very few starters remaining from the 1939 squad. Lazzeri was generally pleased with his pitching, which one preseason forecaster even called exceptional, and his main concern was to add more power to his lineup. He also hired "Sad Sam" Jones, a Yankees teammate in 1926, as a player-coach. No one was forecasting a pennant contender, and possibly not even a first-division finish, but there were certainly expectations of improvement over the previous season.

One of the newcomers to the Leafs was twenty-four-year-old second baseman Dario Lodigiani, who, after having played regularly at second and third for Mack in 1938 and 1939, was sent to Toronto. He recalled what it was like to play in Philadelphia: "Playing for Mr. Mack was like playing for your father. If you made a mistake, he would never say anything at the time, but he'd write it down in his notebook. Then the next day he'd call you over and let you know about it in a quiet way." The fans, however, were less congenial: "If you played in front of those Philadelphia fans, the toughest fans in the world, you could play anywhere. They had these cups filled with ice. They'd suck the lemonade out of [the ice], and if you made a boot, whoom!, it would come down on you. One day I made an error late in the game, and somebody took off his shoe and threw it at me. I went over and picked it up; it was a brand-new Florsheim, size 8½, and I thought to myself, 'Throw the other one down and I've got a pair.'"[6]

Like Lazzeri, Lodigiani was a San Francisco native of Italian descent. He grew up near the DiMaggio family and played youth baseball with both Joe and Dom. When he was playing for the White Sox, his friendship with his fellow San Franciscan Major Leaguers got him in trouble:

> One time we were in Chicago and here come the Yankees with Crosetti and DiMaggio, and I went to talk to them. In those days, when Judge Landis was commissioner of baseball, he had a rule: no fraternization. You couldn't talk to players on the other team. That day Judge Landis was sitting in the front row, and he signaled me to come over. I went over and he said, "Did you read that bulletin about no fraternizing? The next time I see you talking to those fellows, it's going to cost you some money." I told him they were friends at home, and he said, "I don't care where they're from; you don't talk to them at the ballpark."

In 143 games with Toronto, Lodigiani hit .281 with seven homers. About Lazzeri as a manager, he said: "He was pretty sharp. He didn't holler at anybody, but he was a really cagey guy." When the team was on the road, he and Lazzeri were roommates for a specific reason: "We roomed together because he was an epileptic. My mother was kind of an epileptic, so I knew what to do if he had a spell. His wife Maye was the one who asked me, and I said, 'Sure.'"

In an interview with Paul Votano, Lodigiani recounted the one epileptic seizure that he witnessed. It occurred while he, Lazzeri, and a few players were walking to their hotel after seeing a movie. "I'll never forget it," Lodigiani said. "We brought him under the cover to an entrance to a shoe store. The attack was over in a matter of minutes. That's the only time I remember seeing him like that."[7]

Soon after the Major and Minor Leagues began play, a reminder of Lazzeri's impact as a Yankee appeared in a UP story that ran in newspapers across the country regarding the poor attendance at Yankee Stadium. "The customers are staying away in droves. This year's dull, drab Yanks have apparently lost their 'sock appeal'— and, consequently and subsequently, their crowd appeal. There is no Babe Ruth, Lou Gehrig or Tony Lazzeri around to drag the customers in. They are going to the race track and elsewhere instead—Ebbets Field, for instance, where they can see the colorful Dodgers play."[8]

As for the Maple Leafs, they once again got off to a good start, beating the Yankees' Newark affiliate, the Bears, 5–4, on a two-out, ninth-inning home run in the season opener. Early in the season Lazzeri expressed his optimistic outlook for his reconfigured club: "I'm not going to have to apologize for this club any time this season. We're greatly improved, have some classy pitching and good defense. We have power, too."[9]

But things didn't go as well as hoped. The Leafs again spent much of the time in the cellar, though they did climb up to sixth place early in July, only to fall back to the bottom of the heap within a week. The affiliation with Connie Mack didn't seem to offer much help. Already in early June columnist Jimmy Powers acknowledged that "poor Tony Lazzeri is having a tough time at Toronto, but so far the 'wolves' have let him alone on account of he ain't got no ball players."[10] By mid-July the much-hyped pitching staff had, as one writer put it, "blown up right in the good signor's face."[11]

By this time there were murmurs that Lazzeri was unlikely to return in 1941. When the Leafs were hopelessly buried in last place in late August, twelve games behind seventh-place Syracuse, one paper proclaimed: "Poor old Tony Lazzeri is on the griddle up there and they are frying him plenty."[12] The team for which Lazzeri had said he would not have to apologize lost 101 games in 1940, 11 more than in 1939, finishing 39½ games out of first place. The pitching staff fell well below expectations, and not one of the regulars hit as high as .290. Nor did the power that Lazzeri had hoped for ever materialize, as the team hit a total of fifty-three home runs, compared to seventy-eight by the first-place Rochester Red Wings.

On November 7, two months after the season ended, the Maple Leafs issued this statement: "In view of the uncertainty of Toronto continuing in the International League in 1941, Mr. Tony Lazzeri's contract has not been renewed. Mr. Lazzeri severed his connection with the Toronto Ball Club with absolute good-will and under an arrangement which was entirely satisfactory to all parties concerned." The club further announced that it had neither hired a new manager nor approached the Harbor Commission for a renewal of its lease on Maple Leaf Stadium.[13] However, Toronto's uncertain situation apparently was resolved quickly. On November 25 Russell "Lena" Blackburne, a scout for the A's and former White Sox manager who had played for the Maple Leafs in the past and managed the team in 1932, was appointed as the Leafs' new manager.

On the day after Toronto announced its new hire, columnist Doug Vaughan offered the following assessment of Lazzeri's difficult situation with the Maple Leafs. Given his "quick agile mind that could see and interpret everything on the field at a moment's notice, [Lazzeri] figured to be a good manager. But if he was[,] the owners and fans of the Toronto Leafs couldn't see it. . . . He discovered that managing a minor league club was a man sized job, more difficult than a similar assignment in the majors because you don't have the assistants to take care of some of the detail work."[14]

Having moved from Major League ballplayer to Minor League manager, Lazzeri came full circle by returning to his Minor League roots as a player. On December 4, 1940, two days before his thirty-seventh birthday, it was announced that he would play second base for his hometown San Francisco Seals in 1941.[15] This was the PCL franchise that had been the stepping stone to the big leagues for many other San Francisco natives, including Ping Bodie; Babe Pinelli; Frank Crosetti; and Vince, Joe, and Dom DiMaggio. The Seals, managed since 1935 by Lefty O'Doul, Lazzeri's teammate and fellow prankster with the Salt Lake City Bees in 1924 and 1925 and two-time NL batting champion, were hoping that in addition to providing solid offense, Lazzeri would help develop Froilan "Nanny" Fernandez, a promising young shortstop.

Inevitably there were questions about Lazzeri's durability, not only because of his age, but also because he had appeared in only thirteen games with Toronto in 1940, getting three hits for a .176 average. But as he did each offseason, he attempted to maintain his stamina and strengthen his legs by playing daily rounds of golf. In addition to pursuing his passion for golf, he also organized a couple of benefit baseball games pitting Tony Lazzeri's All-Stars—a collection of local Major and Minor Leaguers— against San Francisco–area amateur teams, with the proceeds going to local charities.

The "agile ancient," as one writer dubbed Lazzeri, performed well at the Seals' spring training camp in Boyes Hot Springs, California. On March 28 in a preseason game against the Philadelphia A's at Seals Stadium, he had three hits, scored two runs, and handled nine chances at second flawlessly. But in the seventh inning, as he ran to second with a double, he pulled a ligament in his left leg and was sidelined for several days, raising again the question of durability. After missing several games at the start of the season, he got off to an excellent start; at the end of April, after appearing in ten games, he stood ninth in the PCL with a .379 average.

That, however, was a pace the thirty-seven-year-old veteran was unlikely to sustain over the long PCL season. In the second week of June, when an injury to another player necessitated shifting Lazzeri from third base to second, Abe Kemp pointed out that "Tony's legs have been a constant source of trouble to him"; then he added: "Lazzeri will give the best that he can, for he is that kind of a ballplayer."[16]

Lazzeri did play in 102 of the Seals' 176 games, the seventh most of anyone on the roster. His batting average was a modest .248, but he was third on the team in walks, giving him a solid .351 on-base percentage. His three home runs were negligible, but other than shortstop Nanny Fernandez with nineteen, no other Seals player hit more than five. Overall it was a disappointing season for the Seals, who finished in a tie with the Oakland Oaks for fifth place with a record of 85–91.

That season Lazzeri lost his mother. On September 23 Giulia Lazzeri died at her Missouri Street home of a heart attack at age seventy-nine, survived by her husband, Agostino, and John Barosso, her son from her first marriage.

On November 7 the Seals announced that Lazzeri, at his own request, had been given his unconditional release. It was the sixth such notification he had received in five years, beginning with the Yankees' farewell announcement on October 15, 1937. Approaching his thirty-eighth birthday, once again Lazzeri came to the end of a season not knowing what his future in baseball might be, or if he even had one. Lazzeri said that he had no immediate plans, but it was clear what his hope was: "I'd like to get a manager's job, and I may go back to the National Association meeting next month to see if I can line up something."[17] Lazzeri did attend the Minor League meeting in Jacksonville, Florida, where, on December 3, he was hired by Frank Lawrence, owner of the Portsmouth (Virginia) Cubs of the Piedmont League, as the club's player-manager for 1942. Tony Lazzeri was again part of the Chicago Cubs' organization, this time as a manager.

In early March 1942 Lazzeri and the family packed up the car and once again made the cross-country drive, this time to their new baseball home; Frank Lawrence had rented for them a small house located a few blocks from the ballpark. Situated in southeast Virginia, Portsmouth was a port city of about fifty thousand, across the Elizabeth River from Norfolk, site of the Norfolk Naval Shipyard. After living in cities like San Francisco, New York, Chicago, and Toronto, Lazzeri must have felt like he was returning to his Minor League days in places like Peoria and Lincoln.

Of course there were new concerns in 1942 regarding baseball because of the U.S. entry into World War II following the attack on Pearl Harbor. Given Portsmouth's location near the Norfolk Naval Shipyard, there was concern that it might be a target of enemy planes. Since the Cubs played many of their games at night, the implementation of blackout rules would have an impact on their schedule. On March 21 Lawrence was quoted as saying he had not been informed by the government of any plans to forbid night baseball in Portsmouth and Norfolk. Lawrence also said that he was planning a March 26 welcome party for Lazzeri and was expecting about fifteen hundred guests, "the biggest crowd we've ever had in our auditorium."[18]

In April Lazzeri spoke with George Wright of the *Richmond Times Dispatch* regarding the potential impact of the war on baseball. There was, in fact, widespread concern as to whether Major League baseball should continue during the war, but President Franklin Roosevelt, in his "Green Light Letter" to Commissioner Landis in January 1942, endorsed the continuation of the game, citing its importance as a needed morale booster when people on the home front would be working longer hours than ever before. Lazzeri was of the opinion that while Major Leaguers would be drafted, many of the big stars had dependents and other responsibilities that would keep them out of the service. While many of the younger players would enter the military, a combination of old timers and new players would maintain the quality of play. His predictions proved to be relatively accurate for the 1942 season, but thereafter, with more than five hundred Major Leaguers serving in the military, the quality of big league play was significantly lowered for the duration of the war.[19]

Lazzeri was also of the opinion that "minor league owners are going to be hard put to find players, what with the draft and other complications," a prediction that proved to be right on the money. While most of the higher-level Minor Leagues survived the war, the total number dropped from forty-one in 1941 to twelve by 1945 due to the lack of young players. Lazzeri also expressed surprise at the intensity of preparation for war in Portsmouth and Norfolk: "I didn't even realize we were at war until I hit Portsmouth. Out on the Coast the preparations are not so nearly out in the open. At least I didn't see so much defense work." At the end of his article Wright offered this physical description of Lazzeri: "There are grey streaks in the once coal-black hair. His skin is ruddy from many hours under the broiling sun and his eyes are sharp, just sharp enough to look through you when he focuses on you."

In 1942 Portsmouth was in its seventh year as a member of the Class B Piedmont League, locally known as the Tobacco Circuit, which had existed since 1920 with teams in Virginia and North Carolina. In 1941 the Cubs had finished a distant second to the Durham Bulls with a 75–65 record. Among the five other new managers in the league in 1942 was Lazzeri's former Yankees teammate Ben Chapman, who led the Richmond Colts.

In their season opener on April 23 the Cubs lost to their cross-river rivals, the Norfolk Tars, 6–1, as Lazzeri, starting at second base and hitting in the cleanup spot, went 0 for 4. After losing four of their first five games, the Cubs picked up the pace, winning eleven of sixteen to get to within 1½ games of first by mid-May. By the start of June, with Lazzeri hitting over .300, the Cubs were still in the race, two games out of first. At that time Lazzeri refused to say that he had the best team in the league, but he did say that "we're the team to beat to win the pennant. And that is saying a lot because I think our league is very well balanced."[20]

Lazzeri's Cubs proved him right by continuing to win. By July 4 they were in first place with a 43–24 record, three games ahead of Greensboro. They led the league in batting average—with five of the top ten hitters—and runs, but they were only fifth in homers. Lazzeri was hitting .271, with one home run. In a July 7 doubleheader with Chapman's Richmond Colts, Lazzeri had a little fun with his former teammate. With Chapman on the mound, Lazzeri came to the plate in the second inning of the opener and motioned for the Richmond outfielders to come in. Chapman then proceeded to walk him on four pitches.

The Cubs started slipping after July 4 and eventually lost their lead, falling behind future Hall of Famer Heinie Manush's Greensboro Red Sox. The two teams then stayed neck and neck until the last days of the season. The Cubs pulled into a half-game lead on September 3 but ultimately lost the pennant to Greensboro by the slightest edge in a season in which the teams did not play the same number of games. Playing four more games than their closest rival, Portsmouth finished with a record of 80–55, compared to Greensboro's 78–53, totals that gave the Red Sox the edge by two percentage points, .595 to .593. The Cubs' record was the best in their seven-year existence in the league, and Lazzeri was voted manager of the all-league team.

In the first round of the four-team postseason Shaughnessy playoffs, the Cubs defeated Chapman's Colts in seven games. During the game in which the Colts were eliminated, Chapman lived up to his reputation as an umpire baiter and hothead when, during an argument over a call at first base, he punched umpire I. H. Case in the face when Case ejected him from the game. Piedmont League president Ralph Daughton, who was at the game, immediately suspended Chapman for thirty days and fined him $100. (Chapman was subsequently banished from baseball for one year but came back to manage Richmond in 1944.) Daughton also commended Lazzeri, who played the peacemaker by separating the two men. Portsmouth then lost to Greensboro in the finals, four games to two. Playing in ninety-eight games, Lazzeri hit .242 with two homers (RBI totals are not available). The highest average on the team was .299, and homers were hard to come by, with the team hitting a grand total of twenty.

When Lazzeri drove back to California at the end of the season, he took along his Portsmouth catcher, Roy Partee, the team's leading hitter. Along the way they made a stop in Salt Lake City, where, wrote columnist Les Goates (who had covered Lazzeri in his record-setting season of 1925 with the Bees), "his name has been a household word in this sportive hamlet ever since." Goates also noted the change in Lazzeri's appearance: "Slightly gray around the temple, with hair-line receded considerably, Lazzeri nevertheless appeared to be the same agile, lean and healthy athlete as of yore." As for Partee: "Due to Tony's tutelage and expert business acumen, Roy will get his chance next season with the

Boston Red Sox." In fact Partee would play in ninety-six games with the Sox in 1943 and go on to a five-year big league career.[21]

On December 26 Frank Lawrence announced that Lazzeri would return as Portsmouth manager in 1943. However, there was uncertainty about the makeup, perhaps even the existence, of the Piedmont League due to wartime travel restrictions. Lawrence himself expressed a desire to see a total restructuring. Soon after announcing Lazzeri's reappointment, he said: "I'm strongly in favor of disbanding the Piedmont league, and reorganizing the old Virginia league—but under a new name."[22] Meanwhile, Lazzeri, the former boilermaker, was spending the offseason contributing to the war effort by working in a San Francisco shipyard.

On February 5 the AP issued a story indicating that Lazzeri had notified Lawrence that his playing days were over and he would not be returning to Portsmouth.[23] One report indicated that he had physical ailments that had kept him out of the Portsmouth lineup for part of 1942. To what extent, if any, his decision was influenced by the uncertain status of the Piedmont League is unknown. In the end the Piedmont League survived, but it fielded only six teams in 1943.

After withdrawing from the Portsmouth job, Lazzeri continued to pursue managerial positions. He reportedly was being considered for the position with the Utica Braves, a new entry in the Class A Eastern League. Utica chose instead to hire long-time Major League catcher Wally Schang as its manager, reportedly because it would not meet Lazzeri's asking price. But Lazzeri ultimately did end up in the Eastern League, the same league to which he had refused to report in June 1924, when the Salt Lake City Bees wanted to option him to New Haven. On April 5 it was announced that he had been named player-manager of the Wilkes-Barre Barons, an affiliate of the Cleveland Indians. Sports columnist Chic Feldman applauded the move by the Barons: "He has background, personality and a tremendous following which dates back to his stardom days in the Yankee Stadium. Together these factors add up to a strong box office influence which will be as essential in the coming, trying year as ration coupons in the shop of Benny the Butcher."[24]

Lazzeri agreed to the deal in a phone call from Mike McNally, the Barons' general manager who had had a ten-year Major League career as an infielder, including four seasons with the Yankees between 1921 and 1924. McNally indicated that he had spoken with Portsmouth owner Frank Lawrence, who told him that Lazzeri "is a great buy at any price. They made plenty of money there with just a fair club. Tony, Lawrence said, was alone responsible for it."[25]

The new manager, now often described in the press as "the soft-spoken Italian" and occasionally as "colorful," arrived in Wilkes-Barre on April 12, just in time for the start of spring training. He was greeted at the train station by a contingent of Barons executives and players, civic leaders, and fans, and three days later he was given the key to the city by Mayor Charles N. Loveland. Instead of training in Sumter, South Carolina, as they had in 1942, the Barons were forced by limits on wartime travel to set up camp in Wilkes-Barre, a necessity that made for some chilly conditions. Lazzeri's twenty-five-man squad consisted of some Cleveland farm hands and untested youngsters. At a time when wartime issues caused many minor loops to disband, the Eastern League faced the double complications of travel restrictions and slim rosters. The eight-team league was spread over four states: Pennsylvania, New York, Connecticut, and Massachusetts. Most of the travel was done by bus since several of the cities had no direct rail lines available.

The anticipated box office appeal of Lazzeri was realized when 3,041 paying customers showed up at Artillery Park for the Barons' 2–0 win on opening day, with the new manager in the starting lineup at second base. That turnout prompted a hometown paper to proclaim: "Wilkes-Barre still is a great baseball town," noting that the crowd nearly equaled the entire attendance at the three other opening games in the league.[26] At the end of May the Barons were in second place, 3½ games behind the Scranton Red Sox. Lazzeri, who was starting regularly at second and hitting sixth, put together a ten-game hitting streak in early June as Wilkes-Barre held on to second place, but by the end of the month the Barons had fallen to eight games behind Scranton, only one game ahead of the third-place Elmira Pioneers.

Then in a doubleheader sweep on July 4 against the Binghamton Triplets at home, Lazzeri had his best day at the plate in a long time. Playing third and hitting fifth, he went 2 for 3 with a double in the opener, then hit two homers in three at bats and drove in three runs in the nightcap. In the four-game series, all won by the Barons, he was 8 for 12 with seventeen total bases. On July 14, however, the Barons lost both a doubleheader to the Hartford Bees and their manager. In the third inning of the second game, as twilight was setting in, Lazzeri was hit in the back of the head by Hartford pitcher John Dagenhard. He was taken to the hospital for X-rays and released, but he would be out of action for several days. He resumed managing on July 20, still out of uniform due to lingering headaches, and did not return to the lineup until July 23. It was the first serious beaning of his career.

At the end of July the Barons remained in second place with a record of 48–37, trailing Scranton by 10½ games. Then, after losing twenty of their next thirty-six games, they found themselves in sixth place at 64–57. But following a streak in which they "made the heads of Wyoming Valley fans spin with a 'where they will stop nobody knows' brand of baseball," they managed to grab the final playoff spot by finishing fourth.[27] Their record of 77–61 left them one game out of third and 1½ games out of second but ten games behind Scranton. Lazzeri, who played sparingly after being hit in the head on July 14, hit .271 with three homers in fifty-eight games.

For the second consecutive season Lazzeri found himself in a postseason playoff. The Eastern League's Governor's Cup playoffs, which involved the top four teams, began on September 14, with a best-of-five format in the first-round games and a best-of-seven in the finals. The Barons and Pioneers split the first two games in Elmira, then did the same in Wilkes-Barre to force a fifth and deciding game in Elmira. The Barons' season came to an end on September 19 in a tough loss. After they scored in the top of the ninth to tie the game at 1–1, the Pioneers pushed across a run in the bottom of the inning to wrap up the series.

Gene Woodling, the Barons' twenty-year-old center fielder who led the league with a .344 average, made his Major League debut three days later with the Cleveland Indians, hitting .320 in eight games. After two years in the military, he went on to a seventeen-year career, including seven seasons (1949–55) as a key player for the Yankee teams that won five consecutive World Series titles. Regarding his season with Wilkes-Barre, Woodling said: "I couldn't have played for a better guy than Lazzeri. Great handling young people. You were family; that's the best way I can put it. He and his wife were very good to us. You just couldn't play for better people."[28]

Times Leader sports editor F. X. (Effie) Welsh also had high praise for Lazzeri's role in leading the Barons. In spite of a team "comprised of inferior material on the whole . . . Tony performed splendidly throughout the campaign and held the respect of every player on his team."[29] A letter to the editor from "An Old Time Fan" who claimed to be one of the "oldest boosters of the Barons" stated: "Never have I seen a baseball player or manager who has rated so high with the fans of the Wyoming Valley. His mere appearance always inspired confidence and how the fans, old and young, would yell whenever he played or went in as a pinch hitter." The fan's final sentence reflected the continuing uncertainty of Minor League baseball as the war raged on: "If the Barons play next season I believe it would be a grave mistake not to have Tony Lazzeri as their pilot."[30]

However, the Wilkes-Barre franchise chose to do exactly what the "Old Time Fan" hoped they wouldn't. On January 11, 1944, almost four months after the season had ended, newspapers across the country carried the news that Mike McNally was asking Lazzeri to resign. Apparently the news came as a surprise. "I won't resign. Let them fire me," Lazzeri was quoted as saying. "Why, a year ago they practically begged me to take the job. They represented it as having a future because of the major league tie-up."[31] A UP report indicated that Lazzeri said he had no inkling of the action until he received the notice from McNally: "If they had wanted to be nice about it, they could have informed me sooner. Now the winter meetings are over. All the 1944 jobs have been filled."[32] McNally countered by saying that he had informed Lazzeri the previous fall that, given the uncertainty of conditions in 1944, "it would be all right by the local club if Tony cared to look for something better," a statement that seems a far cry from telling Lazzeri they weren't planning on bringing him back.[33]

On February 9 McNally announced that the Barons had hired Jack Sanford, a thirty-four-year-old Minor Leaguer, as player-manager. As Lazzeri had predicted, it was indeed too late for him to find a job in baseball for the 1944 season.

After twenty-two years in uniform Tony Lazzeri's career in professional baseball had come to an end. The game had largely defined his life from the time he was a youngster on the Jackson Playground diamond. He had married and had a son, but we know relatively little of that side of his life. His public persona was all about baseball and, to a much lesser extent, golf. But his baseball experience from 1938 on was far different from the years when he was playing in the media capital of America, starring for the game's most successful franchise and celebrating five World Series titles. Yet even after the glory years with the Yankees ended and when, both as a player and a manager, he often faced difficult and disappointing times in his final five years, while he may have been disappointed from time to time in the way he was treated by management, he never turned sour on the game itself. Rather than retiring after enduring three seasons (1938–40) in which he had played and coached or managed for four different teams with mixed results, he continued to pursue his lifelong passion, even when it meant adjusting to the Minor League routine, with its long bus rides and a level of baseball well below that to which he was accustomed. He never lost the work ethic he had acquired as a fifteen-year-old manual laborer in a boiler factory.

Given his penchant for privacy, it is unlikely that Lazzeri missed being in the big league spotlight. But what about his professional pride? How does someone who had been one of the best players of his generation, and whose temperament was ill-suited to life on the bench, adjust to a role as a part-time player? Moreover, rather than serve as a stepping stone to the Major League managerial position he hoped for, his last two years managing in the Minors proved to be not a transitional stage but the end of the line. In addition to everything else he endured, not to be forgotten is his daily struggle with epilepsy, the private affliction that he concealed from the public throughout his career. To what extent his disorder impinged upon his baseball career or his daily life will never be known, but to ignore its existence would be a great disservice to his memory. It was a challenging part of his life that he would not allow to limit him. But whatever disappointment, possibly even bitterness, he may have felt in those final years in uniform, Tony Lazzeri never lost his competitive fire or the tenacity he displayed as a young fighter, whether the opponent was the other guy in the ring, the opposing team on the diamond, or his own illness.

15

Life after Baseball

part from brief mentions in stories concerning other ball-players or occasional reminiscences of some of his past exploits on the diamond, Lazzeri essentially disappeared from the newspapers in 1944 following the announcement of his successor at Wilkes-Barre. There were, inevitably, occasional reminders of the strikeout by Grover Cleveland Alexander in Game Seven of the 1926 World Series. One in particular served as a sad illustration of the dramatically different paths their lives had taken over the intervening years. A little more than five years after Alexander had been part of the first induction ceremony at the Hall of Fame on June 12, 1939, a UP release with an East St. Louis dateline revealed that local police and members of the American Legion were collecting funds for the former great, "who was found wandering the streets in pajamas last night." He told police he was penniless and had walked away from a hospital where he was a patient.[1] Alexander's longtime struggle with epilepsy and alcohol finally came to an end when he died on November 4, 1950.

Now that Lazzeri was out of baseball and no longer in the spotlight, he had to find new ways to fill his time. One way was to pursue even more vigorously his second-favorite passion: golf. And he certainly had an inviting place to play and hang out once he had been admitted as a member of the Olympic Club in October 1941. But golf was not merely a diversion for him. He brought the same competitive spirit that he had displayed on the diamond to the fairways and greens. Recognized as one of the best golfers among professional ballplayers, he routinely shot in the mid 70s and lower 80s. On June 10, 1944, Lazzeri defeated W. C. Lynch, 3 and 2, to reach the deciding match in the Olympic Club Director's Cup tournament, but he lost the final round to W. P. Scott, 3 and 2.[2]

Following Lazzeri's death in 1946, the following tribute appeared in the *Olympian Magazine*: "Upon retiring from the national pastime, Lazzeri joined the Olympic Club in order to keep in shape by playing golf and he was one of the real stars of golfdom at the Olympic Club at Lakeside, where he made himself just as popular with his links associates as he had been on the diamond with his fellow players and the millions of fans who applauded his sensational fielding and his timely hitting."[3]

But as much as Lazzeri loved golf, it was not enough to fully occupy him, and fairly soon after he was notified in 1944 that he was not returning to Wilkes-Barre, he took on a new occupation. In July he and co-owner Joseph Gaddini applied for a license to sell alcoholic beverages at the Melody Lane, a cocktail lounge located in the fashionable Nob Hill neighborhood of San Francisco. By mid-July his name appeared on the tavern's marquee. The following ad, complete with a photo of Lazzeri, appeared in the 1945 and 1946 San Francisco Seals programs: "Fans, You will always enjoy a good evening with Poosh 'Em Up Tony Lazzeri and Joe Gaddini at their much improved Melody Lane, 729 Bush Street. Cocktails and Entertainment with Bob Campbell's Ten Fingered Band." As the ad suggests, unlike many sports celebrities who own or co-own restaurants or taverns, Lazzeri invested his time as well as his money in the new venture. He enjoyed sharing his stories and reliving his baseball memories with patrons.

In September 1945, nineteen years after Lazzeri's 1926 World Series strikeout, the celebrated journalist and author Bob Considine, whose "On the Line" column appeared in major newspapers across the country, spoke with Lazzeri at the Melody Lane.

A relatively effusive Lazzeri expressed the frustration that must have eaten at him all those years:

> "Funny thing," he said, "but nobody seems to remember much about my ball playing, except that strikeout. There isn't a night goes by but what some guy leans across the bar, or comes up behind me, at a table in this joint, and brings up the old question. Never a night.
>
> "Nobody ever remembers that two years later, under the same circumstances, the same Alexander, same Lazzeri, same bases filled, I cleaned the sacks with a double. I never can get anybody to remember the 1937 series, either. We were playing the Giants, you know, and I came up with the bases filled. Terry brought in Dick Coffman to pitch to me and I put one in the stands in right center at the Polo Grounds. I got a wire that night from Elmer Smith, the old Cleveland outfielder who's the only other guy who ever did that in a series. Still got it. . . . But nobody wants to see it, I guess. All they want to talk about is that dam' time I struck out."[4]

Asked who he thought was the best Yankees pitcher while he was with the team, Lazzeri named Herb Pennock. "You always knew where he was going to put the ball," he said. As for the toughest pitcher he faced, he had a surprising answer: George Earnshaw, a winner of twenty-one or more games for the A's in three consecutive years beginning in 1929. "That fellow never got enough credit," he said. "He was tougher to hit than Bob [Lefty] Grove." Not surprising was his choice for his own career highlight: the day in 1936 when he hit two grand slams and drove in eleven runs against the Athletics. He also expressed his appreciation for having been a Yankee. "Around New York I used to hear that expression, 'Once a Dodger, always a Dodger.' But how about 'Once a Yankee, always a Yankee?' There never was anything better than that. You never get over it."[5]

In addition to his work at the Melody Lane, Lazzeri also spent time visiting wounded war veterans in local hospitals. *San Fran-*

cisco Examiner sports editor Curley Grieve, who sometimes went along, recounted how Lazzeri would entertain the veterans with funny stories, including the one about replacing Babe Ruth's eye wash with water. Nor did he hesitate to recount his historic World Series strikeout. "In hospital tours with [this] writer during the war," Grieve wrote, "the modest and unabashed Lazzeri proved tremendously popular when he provided the war wounded with a pitch by pitch account of his darkest moment."[6] Years later Bob Broeg described Lazzeri as "a generous host to WWII Marines who frequented his bar in San Francisco."[7]

Notwithstanding the frustration he expressed to Considine over the lingering effects of the infamous strikeout, Lazzeri never lost his passion for the game. Tapping his skull, he told Considine: "You know, I'm as much in baseball today as ever. I mean in here."[8] He proved it the following summer by returning to his old role as a mentor, as he had been to Crosetti, DiMaggio, and other San Franciscans. In late May 1946 the *San Francisco Examiner* announced plans for a free baseball school to be held during the first three weeks of July for boys from late grammar school through senior high school. (The clinic was part of a nationwide program sponsored by Hearst Newspapers.) The big draw of the school was its teaching staff, consisting of three former Major League infielders, all San Francisco natives: Lazzeri; Ossie Vitt, third baseman for the Tigers and Red Sox (1912–21) and manager of the Indians (1938–40); and Willie Kamm, third baseman for the White Sox and Indians (1923–35). The *Examiner* pronounced the program "far and away the biggest thing ever done for kid ballplayers in this town" and "the greatest baseball school ever conducted on the Pacific coast."[9]

The school, which was endorsed by the MLB commissioner and the presidents of the American and National Leagues, would operate Monday through Friday, morning and afternoon, (except for July 4), and take place at playgrounds throughout the city, including Jackson Playground, where Lazzeri had first learned the game. At the conclusion of the school, all-star teams in the 16–18 age group from each playground would be selected to take part in a tournament. The top two players selected by the school's teaching staff would be awarded a trip to New York to be part of a U.S. all-star team representing Hearst newspapers nationwide, and it would face an all-star team from metropolitan New York in the Hearst National Diamond Pennant Series at the Polo Grounds on August 15. (The following year the event would be renamed the Hearst Sandlot Classic.)

On July 1 one thousand of the twelve hundred kids who had enrolled for the opening session showed up at Recreation Park, including one girl, fifteen-year-old Doris Wheeler. (A streetcar strike hindered attendance.) On Sunday, July 7, the *Examiner*, which provided extensive coverage of the school, published a photo of Lazzeri showing nine-year-old Joseph Bonetti how to grip the bat. Both are smiling broadly. The caption noted that the bespectacled youngster resembled Dom DiMaggio—then in his third season as the Red Sox center fielder—but added that Bonetti's favorite player was Joe DiMaggio.

More than three thousand youngsters participated in the three-week program. The tournament following the end of the daily sessions concluded on July 28, with the team representing Jackson Playground defeating the Big Rec Playground of Golden Gate Park, 22–0. The next day the three-man "faculty" of Lazzeri, Vitt, and Kamm announced the "Big Nine" of the tourney, which included four members of the Jackson Playground team. Then at a dinner at Seals Stadium honoring the "Big Nine" on July 30, the jury announced the two players selected to play in the Hearst tournament in New York: Dimitrios "Jimmy" Baxes, second baseman for Jackson Playground, and Jim Mangan, catcher for Big Rec Playground. For Baxes and Mangan, as well as for all the players selected to play for the U.S. all-star team, the event was more than one game at the Polo Grounds. They saw a Yankees–Red Sox game, attended a Broadway play, paid a visit to West Point, and were guests of the mayor of New York.

The game at the Polo Grounds on August 15 drew a crowd of 15,269 who saw the New York team win, 8–7, in eleven innings. The home plate umpire was future Hall of Famer Bill Klem. Baxes, with whom Lazzeri had spent a lot of time improving his hitting and fielding during the *Examiner* school, proved to be a good choice to represent San Francisco. He was the unanimous choice as the MVP of the game, for which he was awarded the Lou Gehrig Memorial trophy by Gehrig's widow, Eleanor. Baxes was also one of nine players in the game who went on to play in the Majors.

Tony Lazzeri never got to enjoy the news that his young protégé had been selected as MVP at the Polo Grounds, where he himself had played. He died suddenly a week before the game. Immediately following the end of the tournament that concluded the baseball clinic, Tony spent a week with Maye, David, Maye's sister June, and June's husband, Louis Servente, at a resort along the Russian River, located about sixty miles northwest of San Francisco. Tony then returned alone to the city to resume work at the Melody Lane. At 10:30 a.m. on Tuesday, August 6, Tony called an employee at the tavern to say he would be at work in an hour, but he never appeared. When employees were unable to reach him by phone that day and the next, they contacted Maye on August 7. She and Louis immediately returned to San Francisco. When they entered the house on Rossmoor Drive at around 4:00 p.m., they discovered Tony's lifeless body on the first flight of stairs.

Newspaper accounts differed in their representation of the details regarding the circumstances and cause of Lazzeri's death. Some, including a report by the AP that appeared in both the *Los Angeles Times* and the *New York Times* on August 8, surprisingly reported that the body was found at the Lazzeri home in Millbrae, whereas the Lazzeris had been living in the house on Rossmoor Drive in San Francisco since 1940.[10] The most egregious error regarding the place where Lazzeri died came from a surprising source. It appeared years later in *A Farewell to Heroes*, a 1981 book by Frank Graham Jr., the son of the noted sportswriter and editor who for many years covered the career of Lazzeri, one of his favorite players. The younger Graham wrote that his father "grieved when Tony Lazzeri, age forty-two, died alone in the night in a cheap hotel room."[11]

Since his body was found near the foot of a staircase, there was speculation that Lazzeri might have had an epileptic seizure and struck his head while falling down the stairs. Others listed the apparent cause of death as a heart attack. Some speculated that a seizure may have triggered a heart attack. Even at the time of Lazzeri's induction into the Hall of Fame in 1991, the situation was not clear to some. Art Rosenblum of the *San Francisco Chronicle* asked, "Was it epilepsy, a heart attack or both?"[12]

Some sources reported that the coroner's office estimated that Lazzeri had been dead for about twenty-four hours when the body was found, while others cited the time as thirty-six hours. According to the *San Francisco Examiner*, the last contact with Lazzeri had occurred at 10:30 a.m. on Tuesday, August 6, when he made the call to the Melody Lane.[13] Either of those time frames would suggest that Lazzeri died not long after making that call. Maye was reported as saying that Tony had appeared to be in good health, though he did complain of being extremely tired on several occasions.

The death certificate, issued on August 9 following an autopsy, listed the cause as "coronary arteriosclerosis, acute passive congestion of viscera, compatible with acute cardiac failure." After reading the report, Dr. Chad Carlson of the Medical College of Wisconsin concluded the following:

> The death certificate notes findings "compatible with" acute cardiac failure, but a definitive cause of death is not clearly indicated. Passive congestion of the viscera (internal organs) is fairly non-specific and no mention is made of evidence for ischemia or damage to the heart suggesting an acute heart attack. It is possible that his epilepsy contributed to his death directly in the form of sudden unexplained death in epilepsy or more indirectly by

putting strain on his heart during or following a seizure. There is an entity called "sudden unexplained death in epilepsy" [SUDEP], which takes the life of people with epilepsy for no clear reason. We only find the cause of death to be SUDEP when we can't find another cause. It also is possible that his death was not secondary to his history of epilepsy.[14]

News of Lazzeri's death at the age of forty-two shocked the baseball world. Several telegrams to Maye from former associates are preserved in the Lazzeri Scrapbooks. Ed Barrow, the man responsible for bringing Lazzeri to the Yankees, wrote: "Sincere sympathy to you from the Barrow family on Tony's death. We all loved him." From Eleanor Gehrig: "Please know how deeply I feel with you and David." Among others who wrote were Frank and Norma Crosetti, Bill Dickey, and Cesare Rinetti, the Salt Lake City restaurateur who was close to Tony and Maye. Jimmy Baxes and Jim Mangan, the two baseball school standouts chosen to represent San Francisco in the Hearst game, were in Wyoming, on their way to New York, when they learned of Lazzeri's death. Walter Judge wrote: "The boys asked this writer through the *Examiner* to convey their condolences to the widow and son of a man they had come to know and admire. 'He taught me more about how to play the position than I knew existed,' said Baxes."[15] In his obituary of Lazzeri, Curley Grieve noted that Tony "spent the final month of his life in the service of youngsters in his native city."[16]

On Saturday, August 10, three hundred people attended a service at the Carew and English Mortuary conducted by the Rev. John A. Collins of St. Paul's Episcopal Church in San Francisco, after which the body was taken to El Cerrito, California, for private burial at the Sunset Mausoleum. Four of the pallbearers were baseball friends, including Lazzeri's two fellow instructors in the baseball school, Ossie Vitt and Willie Kamm, as well as Gus Suhr and Taylor Douthit. The others were Curley Grieve and family friend Hector Facciola.[17] (Grieve was named sports editor of the *San Francisco Examiner* in 1931, a position he held until his death in 1966. Highly esteemed for his character as well as his work, he received numerous writing and editing awards and was credited with playing a major role in bringing the New York Giants to San Francisco. There is, I suppose, a hint of irony in having Grieve serve as a pallbearer for the man who was once so reticent with sportswriters, but given his prominent position in San Francisco, it is also an indication of Lazzeri's stature in the community.)

In his interview with Considine (discussed above), Lazzeri said: "The game was good to me; it's given a lot of great memories and I'd like to see my kid be good enough to have a major league career." David Anthony Lazzeri was fourteen when his father died. Known as Tony Jr., the younger Lazzeri did play sandlot ball, but his best sport was basketball. At Santa Clara University he played against future Celtics Hall of Famer Bill Russell, whose University of San Francisco team won back-to-back NCAA titles in 1955 and 1956. After serving in the air force during the Korean War, he had a long career as a marketing manager with Texaco in California, Oregon, and Washington. He and his wife, Marilyn (Johnson), were married in 1955 and became the parents of three sons, Matt, Michael, and Peter. In an interview with the *Seattle Times* David recalled meeting Ruth, Gehrig, and DiMaggio on visits to Yankee Stadium as a child and caddying for his father at the Olympic Club. And like his father, he became an avid golfer.[18] David passed away in 2013 at the age of eighty-one.

16

Legacy

As great a player as ever lived.

—RED SMITH

Tony Lazzeri began his career with the Yankees bearing the distinction, and burden, of having hit more home runs in a single season than anyone in the history of the Minor or Major Leagues. Given the failure of previous PCL sluggers, there was widespread skepticism of his chances for success in the big leagues. To some extent the doubts were confirmed when he hit "only" eighteen homers in his rookie season. And that would prove to be his single-season high, which he would match three more times.

However, in 1926 eighteen homers were enough to put the twenty-two-year-old rookie in third place in the AL and tied for fifth in the Majors. His 117 RBIs trailed only Ruth in the AL and Jim Bottomley in the NL. More important, in his twelve years with the Yankees he proved to be one of the elite power hitters in the game. From 1926 to 1937 only six players—Gehrig, Ruth, Jimmie Foxx, Al Simmons, Earl Averill, and Goose Goslin—hit more homers in the AL. And only five—Gehrig, Simmons, Foxx, Ruth, and Goslin—drove in more runs than Lazzeri, who averaged 96 RBIs per year. Four times he was in the top nine in the AL in both slugging average and OPS. Over that same period Lazzeri's offensive Wins above Replacement (WAR) total of 48.3 trailed only those of Gehrig, Ruth, Foxx, Charlie Gehringer, Simmons, and Goslin.[1] What is truly noteworthy is that, with the exception of Gehringer (a second baseman) and Averill (an outfielder), every other player on those lists, all Hall of Famers, were first basemen or outfielders—typical positions for power hitters. At that time 165-pound second basemen like Lazzeri were not expected to hit the ball over the fence or drive in a hundred runs. The term "slugging second baseman" was an obvious oxymoron. (Rogers Hornsby, widely acknowledged as the best right-handed hitter of all time, was in a league of his own as a second baseman. From 1915 through 1937 he hit over .400 three times, compiled a lifetime average of .358, and led the NL in homers twice and in RBIs three times.)

Lazzeri also set batting records that neither Ruth nor Gehrig could match. In addition to holding the AL record for most RBIs in a game with eleven, he holds the Major League record of fifteen RBIs in consecutive games. He was the first Major Leaguer to hit two grand slams in one game; he held the record for most home runs in three consecutive games (six) until 2002 and for homers in four consecutive games (seven) until 1974. He is also the only Major Leaguer to complete a natural cycle with a grand slam.

With the exception of 1937, his final and poorest season with the Yankees, Lazzeri's slugging average, on-base percentage, and OPS were all above the league average, usually by a significant margin. For his career he batted .292, with 178 home runs and 1,194 RBIs. He posted a .380 on-base percentage, a .467 slugging average, and an .846 OPS. Seven times he drove in more than 100 runs and five times hit .300 or above. In seven World Series, including two at bats for the Cubs in 1938, he hit .262, with 4 home runs and 19 RBIs.

Impressive as they may be, the raw numbers of Lazzeri's statistics don't tell the whole story of his value to the Yankees. It was not just how many hits he got so much as when he got them. He was often acknowledged as one of the best clutch hitters of his time. In Lazzeri's rookie season, for example, Fred Lieb wrote:

"'Push 'em up Tony' saved his hits for moments when they were needed most. No member of the Yanks, not even Ruth, has broken up as many close games this year as the California Italian."[2]

As accomplished as he was on offense, Lazzeri was far from being a one-dimensional ballplayer. An excellent base runner, he was in the top ten in steals in the Majors three times and in the AL five times, with a total of 148 stolen bases in his career. The Power-Speed statistic, developed by Bill James, measures the combined impact of home runs and stolen bases. Lazzeri led the AL in that category in 1927 and 1933, finished second to Ruth in 1926, and seven other times finished in the top eight.

Also not to be overlooked in evaluating Lazzeri's value to the Yankees is the fact that he played a key position on defense, and initially he played it very well. Beginning in his Minor League days and continuing into the first several years with the Yankees, Lazzeri's defense received almost as much praise as did his hitting. Observers were particularly impressed by his strong, accurate arm and his versatility. According to an unsigned 1929 article from the *New York Telegram* found in the Lazzeri Scrapbooks, "Lazzeri is accepted as the greatest second baseman in the American League and would play 154 games at that position if he were never needed elsewhere, but he is also a great shortstop, an excellent third baseman, and a capable outfielder." Miller Huggins, Lazzeri's manager from 1926 to 1929, and the man who taught him how to play the position, said: "I've seen a few better second basemen, but not many. He has a phenomenal pair of hands, a great throwing arm and he covers acres of ground."[3]

But as time went on, especially in and after 1931, there were recurring comments indicating that Lazzeri was an "ageing" ballplayer who was slowing down, had limited range, and was having difficulty in turning the double play. Prior to the start of the 1936 season, Joe McCarthy noted that "the veteran begins to weaken at the mid-point of the season."[4] (Oddly enough, his second and third highest number of double plays came in 1936 and 1935 respectively, suggesting that his decline was not uniform across the seasons.) Lazzeri committed thirty-one errors as a rookie, second most in the AL—perhaps not surprising since he was still learning the position after playing primarily at short in the Minor Leagues—and he led the league in errors in 1929, 1933, and 1936. Clearly he was highly regarded for his defense in his early years, as he had been while in the Minors, but overall, advanced analytics have not favored Lazzeri. In 1927 he ranked second in the Majors in defensive WAR, but that was the only time in his career he finished in the top ten. But to put things into perspective, the analytical measurement of defense for players from earlier eras is less reliable than that of offense since there is less defensive play-by-play data available. For example, variables such as defensive positioning and routes to the ball that can now be tracked electronically are not available for the pre-computer eras. All of this means that the portrait of the defensive value of a player such as Lazzeri is less detailed and comprehensive than his offensive portrait.

"Today it sometimes seems that statistics are bigger than the game or the players, in the eyes of the 'Media,' at least."[5] Those words, written by Red Smith in 1979, now seem prescient in light of the ever-increasing use of advanced analytics as a means of quantifying a player's strengths and weaknesses. However, whether we rely on traditional statistical measures or the more complex data now available, numbers alone cannot provide a full appreciation of Tony Lazzeri's contributions to his team. For example, however we may evaluate the numerical data on Joe DiMaggio, we cannot dismiss the "eye test" of his contemporary and rival, Ted Williams, who watched him play for years and considered him to be the greatest player he ever saw. The same is true of the opinions of those players, executives, and writers who saw Lazzeri play.

Red Smith and Arthur Daley, both Pulitzer Prize winners, were two of the most esteemed sports columnists of their era. Two days after Lazzeri's death, they offered their assessments of his career and impact. Smith, who, having been cautioned by his editor at the *New York Herald-Tribune* against "godding up" athletes, was not prone to hyperbole, captured the irony of Lazzeri's legacy: "It was Lazzeri's misfortune that although he was as great a player as ever lived, the most vivid memory he left in most minds concerned the day he failed." Lazzeri "was the man who made the crowds"—a reference to the new fans who flocked to see him play—"and who made them roar." Recalling the time the New York writers chose Lazzeri as the "Player of the Year" in 1936, Smith succinctly summed up all the qualities that he brought to the game: "They could just as well have made it 'Player of the Years,' for in all his time with the Yankees there was no one whose hitting and fielding and hustle and fire and brilliantly swift thinking meant more to any team."[6]

The same day that Smith's column appeared, Daley wrote in his column that Lazzeri "was a truly great performer, a tremendous long-ball hitter, a money player almost without equal and one of the smartest athletes ever to patrol the diamond. . . . He left a mark on baseball that never will be forgotten, even if part of his memory will contain one of his rare failures."[7]

For Shirley Povich of the *Washington Post*, the passing of Lazzeri "recalls the unhappy lot of the great Yankee second baseman who left the big leagues famed more for one failure than for all the heroics he compiled in his 14 years in the majors." Lazzeri was "the first of the Italian stars with the Yankees. Crosetti, DiMaggio, Rizzuto and Russo came along later." With regard to the player with whom Lazzeri was most commonly compared, Povich concluded: "If Charlie Gehringer was the best second baseman of his time, then Lazzeri surely ranked as the second best, even tossing his hitting out of consideration."[8]

Dick Bartell, an eighteen-year Major League infielder, called Lazzeri "the most respected player on the Yankees."[9] Angelo "Tony" Giuliani, a catcher for the St. Louis Browns who played against Lazzeri in 1936 and 1937 and later worked as a scout for many years, told me: "Tony Lazzeri was a great infielder [who] knew all the odds and ends of the game of baseball. He had a great natural talent."[10] Frank Crosetti said of his longtime double-play partner: "He not only was a great ballplayer, he was a great man. He was a leader. He was like a manager on the field."[11]

As noted in chapter 12, White Sox manager Jimmy Dykes understood that Lazzeri, even at the end of his career, brought valuable intangible assets to the Yankees: "He was the brains of the ball club. Whenever some pitcher got into a jam, whenever Catcher Bill Dickey was undecided what to call for, or whenever the outfielders needed directions on where to play for a certain hitter—they went to Lazzeri. He was the dynamo that ran that club."[12]

Perhaps no one was better qualified to assess Lazzeri's stature in the game than Ed Barrow, the Yankees' GM who signed him when so many others shied away. In his 1951 autobiography Barrow called Lazzeri "one of the greatest ballplayers I have ever known." But he also made what would prove to be an unfortunately accurate prediction: "The contrariness of human nature may ultimately fix Lazzeri's most conspicuous place in baseball as the fellow whom Grover Cleveland Alexander struck out . . . but his rightful place in baseball history should be as one of the greatest Yankees of them all. Bridging the span between the first team to win a championship for the Yankees and the great teams that were to follow . . . he made his influence felt on the field and off. The help he gave in making Frankie Crosetti and Joe DiMaggio outstanding Yankees can never be overestimated."[13]

It is telling that the testimonies provided by Lazzeri's contemporaries address not only his skill and achievements as a ballplayer, but also his character and personality, praising him for the passion with which he played the game, his exceptional baseball smarts, and his role as a leader and mentor. The writers took note of Lazzeri's reserved nature from his first days in spring training, labeling him as reticent, laconic, and even taciturn, descriptions that suggest a solemn, perhaps even sullen, persona. But Lazzeri was neither sullen nor aloof. He kept the Yankees' clubhouse loose with his playful pranks and was no less popular with his teammates than he was with the fans. Yankees pitcher "Sad Sam" Jones, a teammate in 1926, described Lazzeri as "a very witty guy, full of fun. Quiet, but always up to something. A real nice guy."[14] He was also well liked by the writers, even if he wasn't as forthcoming as they might have wished. Recall that Paul Gallico noted his "gentleness" and "a warmth that was appealing and endearing," and Frank Graham described him as "sensitive, thoughtful, shy."[15]

In the years following Lazzeri's death he was the recipient of various accolades and awards. In 1961 the San Francisco Recreation and Park Commission voted to name the diamond at Jackson Playground in his honor. He was inducted into the National Italian American Sports Hall of Fame soon after its founding in 1977, and in 1989 he was inducted into the Bay Area Sports Hall of Fame. In a 1969 poll of fans to select the "Greatest Yankee Team," Lazzeri was selected as the top second baseman. The other top vote getters who played with Lazzeri were Ruth (right field), Gehrig (first base), Rolfe (third base), Dickey (catcher), and Ruffing (right-handed pitcher).[16] Lazzeri's statistics still put him at or near the top of the list of all-time Yankees second basemen as of the end of the 2019 season. He was first in hits, triples, RBIs, and on-base percentage and second in eight other offensive categories. In his 2001 book, *Few and Chosen: Defining Yankee Greatness across the Eras*, Yankees Hall of Fame pitcher Whitey Ford selected the top five players at each position. Lazzeri was his number one choice at second, ahead of Joe Gordon, the man who succeeded him.[17]

The most significant and enduring tribute came in July 1991, when Lazzeri was inducted into the Baseball Hall of Fame following his election by the Veterans Committee on February 26. His candidacy was in the committee's hands because he had not been elected by the BBWAA when he was on the writers' ballot from 1945 through 1962. Like many others of his era, Lazzeri had the misfortune of appearing on the ballot at a time when there was still a long list of worthy candidates who played at an earlier time and had not yet been elected. Consequently in his first ten years on the ballot, the highest percentage of votes he received was 17.4, with 75 percent required for election. By 1955 enough of the earlier candidates had been inducted so that Lazzeri's total spiked to 26.3 percent, still well below the threshold. His highest vote came the next year, when he received 33.2 percent. In 1958, a year in which no candidates were elected by the writers, Lazzeri was seventh in the voting at 30.1 percent. The six players ahead of him were all subsequently elected, but it is curious that the seven players with fewer votes were later elected, four of them by the Veterans Committee, prior to Lazzeri's selection in 1991. He fell off the ballot after 1962, his last year of eligibility.[18]

Two factors that may have counted against Lazzeri were the relative brevity of his career at fourteen years and the fact that he was overshadowed by three iconic teammates: Ruth, Gehrig, and DiMaggio. According to Bill Deane, the foremost expert on Hall of Fame voting: "Dying young did not help; other things being equal, voters are more apt to choose a living candidate."[19] Since five of his Yankees teammates—Ruth, Gehrig, Pennock, Dickey, and DiMaggio—had been elected by the BBWAA before Lazzeri's eligibility ran out and Ed Barrow was elected by the Veterans Committee in 1953, voters may have been reluctant to add yet another Yankee from that era.

Lazzeri's induction into the Bay Area Sports Hall of Fame in 1989 sparked interest in promoting his candidacy for the Baseball Hall of Fame. Harry Jupiter reported that when Joe DiMaggio was told of Lazzeri's selection to the local Hall of Fame, he said: "That's nice, and it's high time. He ought to be in the big Hall of Fame, the one in Cooperstown. Tony was great, one of the best I ever saw." In the same story Jupiter quoted Crosetti as saying: "Check the records, look at the numbers. I've never understood why Tony isn't in the Hall of Fame."[20] Dante Benedetti, a San Francisco restaurateur and longtime baseball coach at the University of San Francisco, organized a petition drive that reportedly gathered seven hundred signatures.[21] Kevin Johnson, a Seattle resident and friend of Lazzeri's son, David, sent to the

Hall of Fame a packet of materials that included a comparison between Lazzeri's statistics and those of second basemen in the Hall of Fame, a summary of Lazzeri's career, and letters of support from Mark Koenig and "Babe" Dahlgren.[22] (Dahlgren was a teammate of Lazzeri in 1937 and the man who replaced Lou Gehrig at first base when the Iron Man's streak of 2,130 consecutive games ended on May 2, 1939.) Without citing a source, Dwight Chapin wrote that Johnson also "buttonholed former Lazzeri rivals like Charlie Gehringer and Bobby Doerr, who in turn lobbied committee members like Ted Williams."[23]

The eighteen-member Veterans Committee, chaired by Charles Segar, former president of the BBWAA, consisted of executives, writers, broadcasters, and former players and managers. Up for their consideration were two separate ballots of fifteen candidates prepared by a screening committee, one consisting of former Major Leaguers and the other of managers, executives, umpires, and Negro League stars. Only one candidate could be elected from each list. Bill Veeck, the maverick owner whose promotional innovations (like exploding scoreboards and midget at bat) were loved by fans but abhorred by fellow owners, was the surprise pick from the second list, while Lazzeri was only the second player in four years to receive the 75 percent vote required for induction. (Among the other candidates were two second basemen, Joe Gordon and Nellie Fox, both of whom would later be elected.) After fifty-two years, no longer would Lazzeri's name appear in the Hall of Fame only on someone else's plaque.

As is often the case with Veterans Committee selections, there were varying opinions on the choice of Lazzeri. For example, two prominent *Washington Post* columnists from different eras expressed diametrically opposed opinions. Thomas Boswell, whose career at the *Post* began in 1969 and who never saw Lazzeri play, casually dismissed him, with no explanation, as "a marginal old timers committee pick."[24] But Povich, a member of the selection committee who had been at the *Post* since 1922 and saw Lazzeri play throughout his career, lamented "the unconscionable tardiness" of Lazzeri's election.[25] Bill Madden called Lazzeri's selection "long overdue" but also "a bit of a surprise, inasmuch as the Veterans Committee seemingly has gone out of its way to reject former Yankees."[26] As secretary-treasurer of the BBWAA from 1966 to 1988, Jack Lang was in charge of counting the Hall of Fame votes and calling players to tell them they had been elected. Following Lazzeri's election, he said: "I've been one of the guys pushing him for years. I can't believe some of the guys they put [into the Hall] while they overlooked Tony all these years. He is definitely not in the class of the have-nots. He should have been in a long time ago."[27]

Aside from Lazzeri's intangible contributions to his team, here is how his statistics rank relative to the eight other Hall of Fame second basemen who debuted after 1895 and ended their careers by 1950: Nap Lajoie, Eddie Collins, Johnny Evers, Rogers Hornsby, Frankie Frisch, Charlie Gehringer, Billy Herman, and Joe Gordon. Lazzeri was fourth in home runs and sixth in RBIs. Since totals in both categories are cumulative, they are somewhat dependent upon the number of a player's times at bat. To put Lazzeri's productivity in perspective, while he ranked seventh in at bats relative to his fellow Hall of Famers, he was third in at bats per home run and second in at bats per RBI, confirming his reputation as a clutch hitter. He was third in slugging average and seventh in batting average. And among all twenty Hall of Fame second basemen as of 2019, he ranked fourth in slugging average, seventh in RBIs and on-base percentage, ninth in home runs, and tenth in batting average.

In Cooperstown on Sunday July 21, 1991, MLB commissioner Fay Vincent stood at the podium and read the inscription on Lazzeri's plaque. He then introduced Maye Lazzeri, now eighty-five years old, who had come from San Francisco, accompanied by her son and daughter-in-law, to make the acceptance speech:

> I think this is about the proudest moment in my life, and I want to thank my son, Tony Lazzeri Jr., and his wife, Marilyn, for coming here with me to receive this beautiful award and meet all these

wonderful men, with just two women along [laughter], and they are really something, each one. And I want to thank them for being my husband's friends and I want to thank all of my husband's friends and fans [who] for over the years have shown him so much respect and love and have never forgotten to remember him. And I want to thank all of you and this beautiful, beautiful area. Everybody in the world should see it. Thank you.[28]

Maye, who never remarried, passed away three years later, on April 18, 1994, almost forty-eight years after Tony died.

Marilyn Lazzeri recalled that she and her husband sat at the same table as Pee Wee Reese and Willie McCovey at an event the evening before the induction ceremony: "We were treated really well. People were so nice to my Tony. All these ballplayers would come up to him and tell him what they thought about his dad. Ted Williams sat with us, and we had a nice conversation. On the way to the ceremony I got into a car with Yogi Berra, so that was my big thrill."[29]

History would prove to be less kind to Lazzeri than were his contemporaries. While greatly appreciated and lauded by those who played with and against him and the writers who saw him, today he is primarily remembered for the wrong reason. His batting records, his reputation as the respected leader of the great Yankees teams that won five World Series in twelve years, as one of the most popular players of his era, and as one of the smartest men in baseball—all that has been buried under the weight of one at bat. That one swing and miss in October 1926 not only became an albatross that haunted Lazzeri until his death almost twenty years later, but it also came to serve as the unfair signature of a great career. Ever since 1939 visitors to the Hall of Fame have been reminded of the strikeout by the note on Grover Cleveland Alexander's plaque, which now hangs less than the distance from the pitching rubber to home plate from Lazzeri's own plaque. People have forgotten about his sixty homers in 1925 and his grand slam in the 1936 World Series. They have forgotten that in one game in 1936 he became the first player to hit two grand slams and set a still-standing AL record with 11 RBIs. And, of course, they never knew that he achieved all that he did while struggling with epilepsy.

Of all the positive elements of Lazzeri's career that have been largely forgotten over the years, none is sadder than the fact that, in his years with the Yankees, he was, as noted by several sources in this book, exceeded in popularity only by Babe Ruth, the single most revered figure in the history of American sports. Not even Lou Gehrig matched Lazzeri's fan appeal. In his biography of Gehrig, Jonathan Eig noted that "for all his accomplishments, his movie-star looks, and his gentlemanly manner, fans, somehow, had never shown overwhelming enthusiasm for him."[30]

When Lazzeri was acquired by the Giants in 1939, Grantland Rice noted that he "was full of surprises in his career, one of which was his tremendous appeal to the crowds."[31] Perhaps Rice found Lazzeri's popularity surprising because he was quiet and lacked the colorful nature of Babe Ruth. But no less surprising at that time was that someone of Lazzeri's lineage could achieve such stardom in America's national pastime.

Like most children of immigrants, Lazzeri lived a dual existence. At home he was immersed in the Old World culture of his parents, but on the playgrounds and in school he was exposed to a very different way of life by teachers, by more assimilated playmates, and by textbooks that depicted a distinctly American way of life. At that time baseball was such a significant cultural institution that it became a metaphor for the melting pot, a living textbook to help newcomers assimilate. In 1923 Frederick Lieb, president of the BBWAA, wrote that other than the schoolhouse, "there has been no greater agency in bringing our races together than our national game, baseball."[32]

John Thorn, who came to America as an immigrant child born to Holocaust survivors and went on to become the official historian of Major League Baseball, knew what it was like to feel different:

"As an immigrant boy myself, I wished for nothing more fervently than to be one of the gang. Baseball eased the transition, permitting me to be that contradiction in terms describing each member of an American minority: the same but different. As a game emphasizing individual accomplishment within the context of unified effort, baseball offered a model of how one might become part of the team . . . how an outsider might be an American."[33]

Even though Lazzeri was not an immigrant, he too knew what it was like to be considered an outsider, a state of mind that in his case was likely exacerbated by his being an epileptic. Although he became an elite ballplayer and an important part of the Yankees' success, the frequent references by writers to his Italian heritage as a "wop" and "dago" served to remind readers that he was somewhat different from his teammates. (Lazzeri may have been admitted to the exclusive Olympic Club in the relatively cosmopolitan city of San Francisco in 1941, but in light of the discrimination that Yogi Berra and Dom DiMaggio encountered in the 1950s by being blackballed, it is highly unlikely that he would have been admitted to an East Coast country club.)

Lazzeri was the same but different. It was the same desire, expressed by Thorn, "to be one of the gang" that motivated Francesco Pezzolo (Ping Bodie) and many other early Italian ballplayers to play under assumed names. But in spite of the frequent media reminders of Lazzeri's heritage as part of an ethnic group that engendered enough public suspicion and hostility to foster stringent anti-immigration laws in 1921 and 1924, this son of immigrants—through his skill on the diamond, together with his modest demeanor, strong work ethic, and quiet leadership—managed to become one of the biggest stars and most popular players in the nation's favorite sport.

In addition, as a star who was cheered and admired by countless assimilated Americans, Lazzeri not only convinced large numbers of first- and second-generation Italian Americans to become fans, but he also became their idol, a symbol of their own hopes of feeling at home in a new land that was not always welcoming.

His success offered them hope that they too might have a shot at the American Dream. In the words of Pulitzer Prize winner Ira Berkow, Lazzeri infused pride "in a community whose immigration to America was still a relatively new thing, and whose striving for assimilation, like that of other immigrant groups, was subject to discrimination and racial stereotyping."[34]

Ultimately baseball provided Lazzeri not only with a means of learning how an outsider might become an American, but also the opportunity to make a new life for himself away from the iron mill that he entered at the age of fifteen. In the process he became an unprecedented figure in baseball as the first major star of Italian descent. His is a classic American success story but one that had an impact far beyond the five World Series rings he won and all the records he set. John Thorn wrote of Lazzeri's historical significance: "Looking back at the fullness of his career, it's clear that Tony Lazzeri was so much more than the stats that won for him a plaque in Baseball's Hall of Fame. He built a baseball bridge that others—both future players and ardent fans—walked across to the American game."[35]

Lazzeri was the one who made the connection, both on and off the field. He was the one who inspired a generation of previously skeptical and uninterested immigrants to connect with baseball and the one who was idolized and celebrated by Italian communities. He provided them with a model of success in America and a reason to take pride in their heritage. It is difficult, I believe, to overestimate Lazzeri's impact, as one of the most esteemed and popular players in America's national pastime, in countering negative perceptions of Italians. As the antithesis of all the stereotypes that had been lodged in the public consciousness for many decades, he helped change the way they were perceived by others. It may well be that at a time of unprecedented nationwide media coverage of baseball, he did more than anyone before him to enhance the public perception of Italian Americans. Given his modest, unassuming nature, that was clearly not a role he sought, but he proved to be the right person at the right time to fill it.

He also set an example for young ballplayers to emulate. Sports columnist Harry Jupiter wrote of Lazzeri's role in building the bridge from the West Coast to the big leagues for those that followed him: "Tony Lazzeri, more than any other player, eased the path for the remarkable flow of spectacularly talented baseball players from San Francisco and the Bay Area to Yankee Stadium." Lefty Gomez, one of those talented players who followed Lazzeri to Yankee Stadium, was quoted by Jupiter as saying: "He was the guy who taught us what it meant to be a big leaguer. He taught us what it meant to be a Yankee. What was expected of us, and how we had to behave."[36] Lazzeri was also the link between two generations of Yankees' dynasties: the Murderers' Row team of the mid-twenties and the squad that won four consecutive World Series from 1936 to 1939, including two after Lazzeri left the team. Even at the end of his time in pinstripes, when he was not the player he once had been, Lazzeri remained the linchpin that held those teams together, the one his teammates looked to for guidance and stability.

When Tony Lazzeri made his debut in the third decade of the twentieth century, only fifteen players clearly identifiable as of Italian heritage had ever appeared in the big leagues. By the third decade of the twenty-first century, thirteen Italian Americans had been inducted into the Baseball Hall of Fame as players or managers. Many others had been selected as recipients of MVP and Cy Young Awards. Still others had moved into front office positions as general managers and owners, and in 1989 A. Bartlett Giamatti, once the president of Yale University, was elected as commissioner of Major League Baseball.

In light of the integral part that Italian Americans have played in the game for so long, it may now be difficult to comprehend the singular impact an Italian baseball hero like Lazzeri could have had almost a century ago. But to the extent that any one person can be said to have opened the door—not only for Joe DiMaggio, but also for all those who followed, either as fans who embraced America's game for the first time or as players and other participants who helped shape the game—that distinction belongs to Tony Lazzeri.

Notes

Preface

1. Reina Berner (director of the Epilepsy Institute of New York), quoted in Ira Berkow, "Lazzeri Meets Alexander Again," *New York Daily News*, March 4, 1991, C5.

2. Quoted in Harry T. Brundidge, "Believe It or Not," *The Sporting News*, December 11, 1930, 7.

1. Growing Up in San Francisco

1. Cinel, *From Italy to San Francisco*, 18–21.

2. Giuila's first son, whose name was anglicized as John, is listed in both the 1930 and 1940 U.S. Census reports as living with her and Agostino and is identified as Agostino's stepson. He died in 1968 and is buried alongside Agostino and Giulia in the Italian cemetery in Colma, California. Brundidge ("Believe It or Not," 7) mistakenly identified Lazzeri's stepbrother as Johnny Brocusa rather than Barosso.

3. Matt Lazzeri, email to the author, July 14, 2018.

4. Marilyn Lazzeri, telephone interview with author, July 16, 2018.

5. I found no information in the San Francisco city directories regarding the family's residence prior to 1907.

6. Thomas Carey, email to the author, December 3, 2019.

7. Harry T. Brundidge, "Believe It or Not," *The Sporting News*, December 11, 1930, 7.

8. *San Francisco Examiner*, April 10, 1986, 72. Since 144 Missouri is the address of the upper flat and we know from city directories and census reports that the Lazzeri family, probably from the time they purchased the house in 1911, lived in the first-floor flat (no. 142) and rented the upper, it may be that the family was renting the upstairs flat prior to purchasing the house.

9. Lazzeri file in Baseball Hall of Fame Library. In 1997 the Jackson Playground clubhouse was named in honor of Lou Spadia.

10. *Washington Post*, March 26, 1926, 17.

11. Brundidge, "Believe It or Not," 7. In a phone call to the San Francisco Public Schools office, I was told that elementary school records are available only for students born in 1911 and later.

12. Quoted in Brundidge, "Believe It or Not," 7.

13. Quoted in Brundidge, "Believe It or Not," 7.

14. Quoted in Brundidge, "Believe It or Not," 7.

15. Established in 1869, the company is referred to in city directories as both Main Street Iron Works and Main Iron Works. Brundidge mistakenly identified the factory as Maine Iron Works.

16. Quoted in Brundidge, "Believe It or Not," 7.

17. Dobbins and Twichell, *Nuggets on the Diamond*, ix.

18. Dario Lodigiani, interview with author, October 2, 2000.

19. Dario Lodigiani, interview with author, October 2, 2000.

20. Dom DiMaggio, interview with author, July 7, 2002.

21. Lazzeri Scrapbooks. As noted in the preface, "Lazzeri Scrapbooks" will refer to clippings compiled by Agostino Lazzeri.

22. Lazzeri Scrapbooks.

23. Quoted in Brundidge, "Friday the Thirteenth, Lucky for Joe Cronin," *The Sporting News*, December 31, 1931, 8.

24. Linn, *The Great Rivalry*, 124.

25. Quoted in Harry Jupiter, "Lazzeri the Great," *San Francisco Examiner*, February 19, 1989, 5–6.

26. Quoted in Brundidge, "Believe It or Not," 7.

2. The Agony and the Ecstasy

1. Mackey, *Barbary Baseball*, 1.

2. *Salt Lake Telegram*, July 23, 1922, 13.

3. *San Francisco Examiner*, March 16, 1922, 33.

4. *Salt Lake Telegram*, March 24, 1923, 4.

5. Quoted in Harry T. Brundidge, "Believe It or Not," *The Sporting News*, December 11, 1930, 7.

6. "Sfist Memoirs: A Baseball Love Story," March 30, 2012. https://sfist .com/2012/03/30/sfist_memoirs_a_baseball_love_story/ (accessed November 20, 2018).

7. Quoted in Harry Jupiter, "Lazzeri the Great," *San Francisco Examiner*, February 19, 1989, 7.

8. *Salt Lake Telegram*, May 20, 1923, 6; June 10, 1923, 12.

9. Poisall, July 1923 column from unidentified newspaper; in Lazzeri Scrapbooks.

10. *Peoria Journal Transcript*, July 16, 1923; in Lazzeri Scrapbooks.

11. Both quotations from unidentified papers in Lazzeri Scrapbooks.

12. *Decatur Herald*, August 10, 1923, 12.

13. *Moline Daily Dispatch*, September 10, 1923, 14.

14. *Salt Lake Telegram*, December 28, 1923, 6.

15. *Salt Lake Telegram*, March 15, 1924, 4.

16. *Oakland Tribune*, April 4, 1924, 34.

17. *Salt Lake Telegram*, May 4, 1924, 14.

18. *Salt Lake Telegram*, June 29, 1924, 12.

19. Quoted in *Lincoln Star*, July 10, 1924, 8. Prior to being named the Links in 1917, the Lincoln entry in the Western League had been called the Ducklings, Treeplanters, Railsplitters, and Tigers. In 1924 they were often called the Solons in game stories.

20. *Lincoln Star*, July 20, 1924, 7.

21. *Lincoln State Journal*, August 13, 1924, 3.

22. *Lincoln State Journal*, August 14, 1924, 6.

23. *Lincoln State Journal*, August 14, 1924, 6.

24. For more on the subject, see Connell and Gardaphé, *Anti-Italianism*.

25. *Reports of the Immigration Commission*, 209.

26. *New York Times*, March 16, 1891, 4. On April 12, 2019, New Orleans mayor LaToya Cantrell issued a formal apology to the families of the eleven immigrants killed in the 1891 lynching.

27. *Indiana (PA) Gazette*, October 13, 1925, 3.

28. *Lincoln Star*, December 23, 1925, 10.

29. *The Sporting News*, January 14, 1926, 3.

30. *New York Tribune*, May 12, 1918.

31. Reynolds, "The Frisco Kid," 22.

32. *Lincoln State Journal*, August 15, 1925, 4.

33. *Lincoln Star*, August 22, 1925, 12.

3. "The Greatest Thing I've Ever Seen"

1. *Salt Lake Telegram*, June 30, 1924.

2. *Los Angeles Times*, July 25, 1926.

3. Quoted in Kimball, "Bringing Fame to Zion," 43.

4. *Los Angeles Times*, April 24, 1925, 37.

5. *Ogden Standard-Examiner*, April 24, 1925, 13.

6. *San Francisco Examiner*, May 25, 1925, 26.

7. *San Francisco Examiner*, June 27, 1925, 30.

8. *San Francisco Examiner*, June 28, 1925, 88.

9. *San Francisco Examiner*, June 29, 1925, 24.

10. *San Francisco Examiner*, June 29, 1925, 27.

11. Unidentified newspaper in Lazzeri Scrapbooks, June 29, 1925.

12. *Los Angeles Times*, July 5, 1925.

13. *New York Daily News*, July 14, 1925.

14. Mackey, *Barbary Baseball*, 95.

15. Levitt, *Ed Barrow*, 225.

16. Barrow, *My Fifty Years in Baseball*, 145–46.

17. Barrow, *My Fifty Years in Baseball*, 146–47.

18. Stout and Johnson, *Yankees Century*, 116.

19. Montville, *The Big Bam*, 227.

20. Alexander, *Breaking the Slump*, 192.

21. *New York Daily News*, August 2, 1925, 7.

22. Uniform Agreement for the Assignment of a Player's Contract to or by a Major League Club; photocopy courtesy of Adam Cohen.

23. *Los Angeles Times*, September 13, 1925, 13.

24. *Los Angeles Times*, October 19, 1925, B1.

25. *Los Angeles Times*, August 29, 1956, 31.

26. Quoted in Sillito, "'Our Tone,'" 351.

27. *The Sporting News*, June 29, 1974; *Sacramento Bee*, October 19, 1925; quoted in Notarianni, "Italianità in Utah," 352.

28. Only five other players have hit 50 or more homers in the history of the PCL: Ike Boone, 55 (1929); Gus Suhr, 51 (1929); Gene Lillard, 56 (1935); Steve Bilko, 55 (1956) and 56 (1957); Bill McNulty, 55 (1974); Gorman Thomas, 51 (1974); Ron Kittle, 50 (1982).

29. *Los Angeles Times*, August 9, 1925, 17.

30. Sillito, "'Our Tone,'" 348.

31. *Salt Lake Tribune*, May 24, 1925, 21. Exactly what did Rinetti mean when he urged Lazzeri to "Poosh Um Up"? Derks apparently took it to mean "hit it over the fence" since his dialect headlines routinely refer to Lazzeri homers.

32. "Bees Star Hits the Big Time," *Salt Lake Tribune*, October 3, 1993, C2.

33. *Salt Lake Tribune*, May 25, 1925, 8.

34. *Salt Lake Tribune*, October 3, 1925, 12; October 12, 1925, 8; October 19, 1925, 9.

35. Notarianni, "Italianità in Utah," 323–24.

36. Sillito, "'Our Tone,'" 357.

37. Maye Lazzeri, quoted in Sillito, "'Our Tone,'" 356.

38. Sillito, "'Our Tone,'" 349.

39. Herman Franks, telephone interview with author, June 19, 2001.

40. *Los Angeles Times*, August 29, 1956, 31.

41. *The Sporting News*, November 5, 1925, 5.

42. *Seattle Daily Times*, November 23, 1925, 20.

4. New Challenges

1. Bloodgood, "Players You Ought to Know," 318.

2. Bartell, *Rowdy Richard*, 33.

3. Gumina, *Italians of San Francisco*, 11.

4. Sacco and Vanzetti were electrocuted on August 23, 1927. Fifty years later, on July 19, 1977, Massachusetts governor Michael Dukakis effectively exonerated Sacco and Vanzetti by issuing a proclamation declaring that "any stigma and disgrace should be forever removed from the names of Nicola Sacco and Bartolomeo Vanzetti, from the names of their families and descendants." Among other reasons, he stated that their arrest and conviction was largely due to "prejudice against foreigners and dissidents at the time." *Boston Globe*, July 19, 1977, 1, 3.

5. Frank Graham, *The New York Yankees*, 114–15.

6. *New York Sun*, March 4, 1926. Two of Lazzeri's three ejections came at the hand of Bill McGowan. Recognized as one of the best at calling balls and strikes, McGowan could be confrontational; he was twice suspended by the AL for temperamental outbursts.

7. *New York American*, February 11, 1926, 19, 21.

8. Huggins, the Yankees manager since 1918, was not a disciplinarian, making his punishment of Ruth all the more surprising. But his decision was backed by both GM Ed Barrow and owner Jacob Ruppert, forcing Ruth to not only accept Huggins's sanctions, but also to apologize to the diminutive manager. Small in stature—his listed height of 5 feet 5 inches may have been generous—and gruff by nature, Huggins initially had trouble commanding the respect of his players, but in time he would become beloved.

9. Frank Graham, *The New York Yankees*, 114.

10. Ford Frick, *New York Evening Journal*; undated entry in the Lazzeri Scrapbooks.

11. Westbrook Pegler, "Yankees Pretty Fair Ball Players, but Not Ball Team," *Chicago Tribune*, March 14, 1926, A1.

12. *The Sporting News*, March 11, 1926, 1.

13. *The Sporting News*, April 15, 1926, 6.

14. *The Sporting News*, April 8, 1926, 2.

15. *Los Angeles Times*, June 20, 1926, A2.

16. *New York Times*, April 2, 1926, 16; April 3, 1926, 24.

17. *Brooklyn Daily Eagle*, April 17, 1926, 2; June 16, 1926, 26.

18. *New York Daily News*, May 8, 1926, 29.

19. *San Mateo (CA) Times*, October 14, 1936, 8.

20. *The Sporting News*, May 6, 1926, 1.

21. *New York Times*, May 19, 1926, 20.

22. *New York Daily News*, May 19, 1926, 36.

23. *New York Daily News*, April 1, 1926, 22.

24. Ford Frick, *New York Evening Journal*; undated entry in the Lazzeri Scrapbooks.

25. In a poll of members of SABR (Society for American Baseball Research) conducted between 1983 and 1985, Lazzeri was voted the AL Retroactive Rookie of the Year Award. See the summary article by Lyle Spatz in *The Baseball Research Journal* 17 (1988); http://research.sabr.org/journals/sabr-picks-1900–1948-rookies -of-the-year (accessed March 26, 2019).

26. Quoted in *Los Angeles Times*, October 8, 1926, B1.

27. Frank Graham, *The New York Yankees*, 118.

28. *Washington Evening Star*, September 15, 1926, 48.

29. Quoted in Graham, otherwise undated 1926 story in the *New York Sun*; in Lazzeri Scrapbooks.

30. Billy Collins, syndicated column, July 2, 1926; in Lazzeri Scrapbooks.

31. Frank Graham, *The New York Yankees*, 115.

32. *The Sporting News*, September 30, 1.

33. Phil Rizzuto, interview with author, June 12, 1993.

34. Barrow, *My Fifty Years in Baseball*, 145.

35. *Los Angeles Times*, October 8, 1926, B1.

36. Frank Graham, *The New York Yankees*, 115, 118.

37. *New York Times*, August 9, 1946, 29.

38. Appel, *Pinstripe Empire*, 145.

39. *Los Angeles Times*, July 25, 1926, A4.

40. Gallico, "Reign of Terror," 251.

41. Lane, "A Great Natural Ball Player Is Tony Lazzeri," 305.

42. Frank Graham, "Tony Lazzeri Was Like This," 57.

43. Quoted in *Montgomery Alabama Journal*, January 25, 1943, 8.

44. *New York Times*, March 5, 1928, 33.

45. Frank Graham, "Tony Lazzeri Was Like This."

46. *The Sporting News*, August 14, 1946, 14.

47. Lieb, *Baseball As I Have Known It*, 202.

48. Leavy, *The Big Fella*, 372.

49. *Brooklyn Daily Eagle*, August 2, 1927, A3. On August 6 (page 5) the *Eagle* reported that the previous day Lazzeri and Roberti, who had won his bout by a knockout, had met in the office of Humbert Fugazy, a prominent boxing promoter. According to Roberti, Lazzeri promised to "push him along on the heavyweight trail."

50. Poisall, "The Sport Trail," July 1923; in Lazzeri Scrapbooks.

51. Dr. Chad Carlson, interview with author, November 19, 2018. All quotations from Dr. Carlson are from this source.

52. Barrow, *My Fifty Years in Baseball*, 147.

53. Quoted in Dave Newhouse, "Yankee Hermit: Mark Koenig and His Memories," *The Sporting News*, July 5, 1980, 11.

54. Marilyn Lazzeri, telephone interview with author, September 22, 2018.

55. Berkow, "Lazzeri Meets Alexander Again," *New York Times*, March 4, 1991, C5. Also see Devinsky, "Cognitive and Behavioral Effects of Antiepileptic Drugs," pp. S46–S65, abstract: "All antiepileptic drugs (AEDs) have the potential for adverse effects on cognition and behavior. Most of the major AEDs, administered in therapeutic doses, cause little or no cognitive or behavioral impairment in group studies. Greater adverse effects have been found for phenobarbital (PB)."

56. *New York Times*, October 11, 1926, 26. The *Times* ran a summary of each broadcast the following day.

57. *San Francisco Examiner*, October 11, 1926, 9.

58. *St. Louis Post-Dispatch*, July 18, 1991, 8D.

59. In 1952, two years after Alexander died, Warner Brothers released *The Winning Team*, a biopic starring Ronald Reagan as the Hall of Famer. Reflecting the taboo associated with the illness, epilepsy is never mentioned by name.

Instead Alexander's neurological disorder is diagnosed as double vision. Further stretching the truth, the film portrayed the Lazzeri strikeout as the final out of the Series.

60. *New York Daily News*, October 17, 1926, 31.

61. Miller Huggins, quoted in Kimball, "Bringing Fame to Zion," 41.

62. *New York Times*, October 11, 1926.

63. *New York Daily News*, October 11, 1926, 2.

64. *San Francisco Examiner*, October 11, 1926, 32.

65. Clipping in Tony Lazzeri file in the Baseball Hall of Fame Library.

66. *Boston Globe*, October 11, 1926, 7.

67. *Washington Post*, August 9, 1946, 12.

68. *Los Angeles Times*, November 28, 1926, C29.

69. *Santa Ana (CA) Register*, October 26, 1926, 13.

5. The Reign of Terror

1. *New York Post*, March 30, 1927.

2. *New York Daily News*, March 21, 1927, 30.

3. *New York Times*, March 26, 1927, 14.

4. Quoted in *The Sporting News*, August 9, 1961, 37.

5. In his breezy, and occasionally inaccurate, history of 1927, Bill Bryson characterizes Vidmer's writing as "unreliable" (*One Summer*, 352).

6. *Chicago Tribune*, April 13, 1927, 23.

7. *New York Herald Tribune*, May 2, 1927; quoted in Fleming, *Murderers' Row*, 127.

8. Quoted in Fleming, *Murderers' Row*, 140; originally reported by Pat Robinson, *New York Telegram*, May 11, 1927.

9. Gallico, "Reign of Terror," 238.

10. *New York Daily News*, September 3, 1927, 20.

11. Gallico, "Reign of Terror," 249.

12. In a 1985 interview with Norman Macht, Carmen Hill, the Pirates' starting pitcher in the game, said that Gooch "did something that no catcher should ever do." He got down on one knee and signaled for Miljus to throw an overhand curve. Instead, according to Hill, Miljus threw "a sweeping sidearm, almost underhand pitch that rose as it came in." Gooch, who was down on one knee, "couldn't get up quick enough to do anything but knock that ball down, just far enough away for Combs to score the winning run." Macht, *They Played the Game*, 118–19.

13. Gallico, "Reign of Terror," 249.

14. Bartell, *Rowdy Richard*, 16–17.

15. Quoted in Macht, *They Played the Game*, 117.

16. Gallico, "Reign of Terror," 247.

17. *Pittsburgh Press*, May 12, 1927, 34.

18. *New York Times*, June 11, 1927, 13.

19. An otherwise undated article from June 1927 in Lazzeri Scrapbooks.

20. Frank Graham, *New York Sun*, July 12, 1927; quoted in Fleming, *Murderers' Row*, 265–66.

21. *Arizona Republic*, August 4, 1927, 7.

22. Lane, "A Great Natural Ball Player Is Tony Lazzeri," 305.

23. Lane: "Poosh-Em-Out' Tony Lazzeri and His Colorful Record," 501, and "A Great Natural Ball Player Is Tony Lazzeri," 305.

24. *The Sporting News*, June 16, 1927, 4; *Dayton (OH) Herald*, June 9, 1927, 20.

25. *New York Daily News*, October 9, 1927, 2.

26. "How the Yanks' Four Straight Gave Baseball a Good Name," *Literary Digest*, October 22, 1927, 64; quoted in Steinberg and Spatz, *The Colonel and Hug*, 297n53.

27. *New York Daily News*, June 9, 1927, 32.

28. *New York Daily News*, July 6, 1927, 32.

29. Pinelli, *Mr. Ump*, 73. In 1933 Pinelli became the first Italian American Major League umpire. At the end of his twenty-two-year career and in his final appearance as a home plate umpire, he called Don Larsen's perfect game in the fifth game of the 1956 World Series.

30. Angelo Giuliani, interview with author, June 8, 2001.

31. Lane, "A Great Natural Ball Player Is Tony Lazzeri," 305.

32. Lieb, "Baseball—The Nation's Melting Pot," 393; *The Sporting News*, December 6, 1923, 4.

33. White, *Creating the National Pastime*, 247.

34. For a discussion of the lack of Italian American Major Leaguers, see chapter 3 of Baldassaro, *Beyond DiMaggio*.

35. *New York Daily News*, October 9, 1927, 64.

36. Quoted in Vellon, "Italian Americans and Race during the Era of Mass Migration," 215.

37. Creamer, *Babe*, 16.

38. Lieb, *Baseball As I Have Known It*, 311.

39. *San Bernardino Sun*, October 8, 1937, 21.

40. *Brooklyn Daily Eagle*, June 16, 1926, 26.

41. *Time*, June 26, 1939, 48.

42. *Boston Globe*, June 22, 1927, 15.

43. *Boston Globe*, June 22, 1927, 20.

44. *New York Times*, June 23, 1927, 19.

45. *New York Sun*, August 25, 1927.

46. Quoted in Frank Graham, *The New York Yankees*, 119.

47. *United America*, June 18, 1927; in Lazzeri Scrapbooks.

48. *New York Daily News*, September 9, 1927, 53.

49. *New York Times*, September 9, 1927, 20.

50. *New York Sun*, 1931; in Lazzeri Scrapbooks.

51. Daniel and Gallico quoted in Holtzman, *No Cheering in the Press Box*, 2, 71.

52. Frank Graham, *The New York Yankees*, 118.

6. Playing through the Pain

1. *New York Times*, October 11, 1927, 33.

2. *Mt. Carmel (PA) Daily News*, October 18, 1927, 4.

3. *Oakland Tribune*, October 19, 1927, 16; October 22, 1927, 12.

4. Jose Malamillo, "White Sox Park and the Formation of a Nonwhite Spatial Imaginary," December 28, 2014. https://josemalamillo.wordpress.com/2014/12/28/white-sox-park-and-the-formation-of-a-nonwhite-spatial-imaginary/ (accessed April, 27, 2019).

5. *Los Angeles Times*, October 24, 1927, 11.

6. *San Francisco Examiner*, October 29, 1927, 20; October 30, 1927, 36.

7. *New York Times*, January 9, 1928, 35.

8. *Los Angeles Times*, February 19, 1928, 13.

9. Steinberg, *Urban Shocker*, 218–20.

10. *New York Daily News*, March 5, 1928, 29.

11. *New York Daily News*, March 6, 1928, 4.

12. Barrow, *My Fifty Years in Baseball*, 146.

13. After seventeen years as a player, Durocher managed the Dodgers, Giants, Cubs, and Astros over a twenty-four-year span between 1939 and 1973. His scrappy, aggressive approach to the game, as well as his off-field exuberance, carried over into his managerial career. In 1947 he was suspended for the entire season by Commissioner Albert B. "Happy" Chandler for associating with known gamblers. He won three pennants and one World Series and was inducted into the Hall of Fame as a manager in 1994.

14. *New York Daily News*, April 26, 1928, 39.

15. *Philadelphia Inquirer*, May 27, 1928, 45–46.

16. *Los Angeles Times*, July 1, 1928, 18.

17. "Leaves From a Fan's Scrapbook," *The Sporting News*, October 20, 1932, 6.

18. *San Francisco Examiner*, July 13, 1928; *Minneapolis Star*, July 13, 1928. The *Brooklyn Standard Union* reported on August 1 that the injury occurred "in a recent series in St. Louis" in a collision with Lou [*sic*] Blue. But two days later it reported that it had happened "about three weeks ago" in a collision with Bill Sweeney of the Tigers at Yankee Stadium. Charlie Gentile writes that the injury occurred "in St. Louis in early July" (*The 1928 New York Yankees*, 169), with no further clarification. But Lazzeri himself was quoted in a story in the *New York Times* on August 30 as saying that he "injured the shoulder sliding back to first during that Detroit game" (on July 11). That occurrence is confirmed by the inning-by-inning account of the game in retrosheet.com. http://www.retrosheet.com.

19. *New York Times*, August 18, 1928, 14.

20. *New York Times*, August 27, 1928, 20.

21. Lazzeri quoted in *New York Times*, August 30, 1928, 15. Among other Major Leaguers treated by Dr. Van Ronk were future Hall of Famers Dizzy Dean, Lou Gehrig, Charlie Gehringer, Lefty Grove, and Jimmie Foxx.

22. *New York Daily News*, September 2, 1928, 32.

23. Bill Dickey oral history interview, April 27, 1987. https://collection .baseballhall.org/PASTIME/bill-dickey-oral-history-interview-1987-april-27–0

24. Hoyt in Fleming, *Murderers' Row*, 12.

25. *New York Times*, April 23, 1930, 37.

26. *Los Angeles Times*, September 6, 1928, 9.

27. *Pittsburgh Press*, September 26, 1928, 30.

28. *Arizona Daily Star*, September 9, 1928, 10.

29. *New York Daily News*, September 9, 1928, 2.

30. The Yankees arrived in St. Louis for a series with the Browns on September 15, the day of Shocker's funeral. Six of his teammates—Hoyt, Gehrig, Combs, Gene Robertson, Mike Gazella, and Myles Thomas—served as pallbearers. Steinberg, *Urban Shocker*, 245n2.

31. *Philadelphia Inquirer*, September 10, 1928, 13.

32. *Los Angeles Times*, September 10, 1928, 10.

33. *New York Daily News*, September 10, 1928, 28.

34. Macht, *Connie Mack*, 501.

35. *St. Louis Post-Dispatch*, October 1, 1928, 13.

36. *New York Daily News*, October 21, 1928, 51. According to Leigh Montville, in one of the radio broadcasts supporting Smith, Ruth introduced Lazzeri, then asked him: "Tell us, Tony, who are the wops going to vote for?" Montville, *The Big Bam*, 280.

37. *St. Louis Post-Dispatch*, October 8, 1928, 31.

38. Quoted in *Reading (PA) Times*, October 18, 1928, 16.

39. *New York Daily News*, October 10, 1928, 45.

40. *New York Daily News*, October 10, 1928, 42.

41. Quoted in *Pittsburgh Press*, October 10, 1928, 28.

42. Undated clipping in the Lazzeri Scrapbooks.

43. *Pittsburgh Press*, January 6, 1929, 41.

7. Peak Performance

1. *Brooklyn Standard Union*, October 19, 1928, 30.

2. *New York Times*, October 20, 1928, 13.

3. *San Bernardino County (CA) Sun*, October 22, 1928, 7.

4. *Pittsburgh Press*, January 18, 1929, 45.

5. *Pittsburgh Press*, January 18, 1929, 45.

6. *Brooklyn Citizen*, January 13, 1929, 14.

7. *Brooklyn Standard Union*, January 14, 1929, 16.

8. *New York Times*, February 8, 1929, 25.

9. *New York Daily News*, February 27, 1929, 87. Apparently seeking to broaden his ethnic vocabulary, that spring Hunt described Lazzeri as "the spaghetti tamer" (March 1, 51) and "the illustrious spaghetti trainer" (March 9, 28).

10. *New York Times*, March 1, 1929, 26.

11. *New York Daily News*, April 8, 1929, 29.

12. *New York Times*, April 13, 1929, 17.

13. Quoted in Frank Graham, *The New York Yankees*, 151–52.

14. Quoted in Frank Graham, *The New York Yankees*, 152.

15. *New York Daily News*, March 24, 1929, 32.

16. *New York Times*, April 16, 1929, 38.

17. Quoted in *Brooklyn Daily Times*, October 7, 1929, 33.

18. Deane, *Award Voting*, 8–9.

19. Quoted in *New York Times*, September 26, 1929, 22.

20. Quoted in *Brooklyn Daily Eagle*, January 6, 1929, 36.

21. *Daily News*, October 11, 1929, 57.

8. A Major League Mystery

1. *New York Daily News*, October 19, 1929, 30; October 20, 1929, 83.

2. *Los Angeles Times*, October 20, 1929, 91. On October 31, even with Jimmie Foxx and Al Simmons in their lineup, the Pirrone All-Stars lost to the Royal Giants by the score of 10–3. *Los Angeles Times*, November 1, 1929, 14.

3. William McCullough, *Brooklyn Daily Times*, December 22, 1930, 12. When Italian-born Polli arrived at spring training, Hunt introduced him as "this earnest-visaged spaghetti worshiper" and "ravioli wrecker" and described him as having a "prominent rudder or breather" and "small, beady black eyes under brushlike brows." *New York Daily News*, March 1, 1930, 53.

4. *San Francisco Examiner*, February 9, 1930, 9.

5. *New York Times*, February 20, 1930, 33.

6. *New York Daily News*, February 22, 1930, 21.

7. *New York Daily News*, February 22, 1930, 34.

8. Mack and Shawkey quoted in *St. Louis Star and Times*, March 24, 1930, 18.

9. *Brooklyn Daily Eagle*, May 11, 1930, 35.

10. *Brooklyn Times Union*, May 11, 1930, 15.

11. *New York Times*, October 15, 1930, 30.

12. Frank Graham, *The New York Yankees*, 167.

13. *Washington Sunday Star*, August 24, 1930, 15.

14. *The Sporting News*, January 15, 1931, 5.

15. *The Sporting News*, March 26, 1931, 3.

16. *Chicago Tribune*, September 30, 1932, 19.

17. *New York Times*, October 15, 1930, 30.

18. Barrow, *My Fifty Years in Baseball*, 154.

19. Frank Graham, *The New York Yankees*, 181–82.

20. *San Francisco Examiner*, January 17, 1931, 17.

21. *New York Times*, March 22, 1931, S2.

22. *New York Times*, April 3, 1931, 32.

23. *New York Daily News*, April 15, 1931, 50. Of the eight *Daily News* writers polled to predict the AL pennant winner, three (including Hunt and Gallico) picked the Yankees, three picked the A's, and two chose the Senators. The unanimous choice to finish last was the Red Sox.

24. *New York Daily News*, March 20, 1931, 74.

25. *Salt Lake Tribune*, June 7, 1931, 21.

26. Paul Gallico explained why "if the articles signed by ballplayers are in reality prepared by professional newspapermen, they are such unspeakable blather. In the first place, the newspaperman is not willing to waste his bon mots, his flights of rhetoric and his genius upon an article signed by another who will collect five times the money that the writer is paid, and in the second, the real artist-ghost tries to put himself into the mind of the athletically skilled but intellectually numb ball player when he prepares his piece and writes accordingly." *New York Daily News*, September 26, 1932, 36.

27. *San Francisco Examiner*, June 11, 1931, 28.

28. *New York Times*, July 14, 1931, 33.

29. *Brooklyn Times Union*, July 7, 1931, 15.

30. *Sioux Falls (SD) Argus-Leader*, December 30, 1931, 14.

31. Quoted in *New York Telegram*, September 7, 1932; in Lazzeri Hall of Fame file.

32. *Chicago Tribune*, September 30, 1932, 19.

33. "Leaves from a Fan's Scrapbook," *The Sporting News*, October 20, 1932, 6.

34. Alexander, *Breaking the Slump*, 16: "Tony Lazzeri lost everything when a San Francisco bank went under"; Eig, *Luckiest Man*, 148: "Lazzeri had his savings wiped out when his bank in San Francisco collapsed."

35. Marilyn Lazzeri, telephone interview with author, August 13, 2019.

36. Matt Lazzeri, interview with author, September 3, 2018, and email to author, June 24, 2019.

37. Frank Graham, *The New York Yankees*, 141.

38. Alexander, *Breaking the Slump*, 51.

39. Barrow, *My Fifty Years in Baseball*, 147.

40. Dr. Chad Carlson, email to author, August 12, 2019.

41. Dr. Chad Carlson, email to author, September 4, 2019.

42. *Brooklyn Daily Eagle*, September 11, 1932, 40.

43. *New York Times*, September 27, 1931, S2.

9. The Big Revival

1. *Brooklyn Daily Eagle*, January 8, 1932, 26.

2. *San Francisco Examiner*, December 10, 1931, 24; *New York Daily News*, February 22, 1932, 32.

3. *The Sporting News*, December 10, 1931, 2.

4. *Baltimore Evening Sun*, December 23, 1931, 30.

5. *Brooklyn Daily Eagle*, January 8, 1932, 26. An Italian racing cyclist, Franco Georgetti won a gold medal in the team pursuit at the 1920 Summer Olympics and between 1926 and 1935 was an eight-time winner of the Six Days of New York, an indoor cycling event held in the velodrome of Madison Square Garden.

6. *Brooklyn Daily Eagle*, January 19, 1932, 23.

7. *Washington Post*, June 9, 1932, 18.

8. *Chicago Tribune*, September 20, 1932, 19.

9. *New York Daily News*, December 23, 1931, 34.

10. *Brooklyn Daily Eagle*, January 15, 1932, 22.

11. *San Francisco Examiner*, January 20, 1932, 20.

12. *San Francisco Examiner*, February 16, 1932, 17.

13. *Brooklyn Times Union*, February 28, 1932, 18.

14. *New York Daily News*, March 17, 1932, 50.

15. *New York Daily News*, March 13, 1932, 32.

16. Frank Crosetti, telephone interview with author, September 4, 1998. Unless otherwise indicated, all quotations by Crosetti are from this interview.

17. *Brooklyn Daily Eagle*, September 15, 1925, 25.

18. Quoted in Ford, *Few and Chosen*, 37.

19. *New York Daily News*, July 2, 1932, 24.

20. *New York Daily News*, June 4, 1932, 29.

21. In July Jurges was shot in his hotel room near Wrigley Field by an irate woman with whom he had recently ended a relationship.

22. *The Sporting News*, September 15, 1932, 3.

23. Quoted in Macht, *They Played the Game*, 142.

24. *New York Daily News*, September 29, 1932, 43; *Chicago Tribune*, October 1, 1932, 19.

25. *Chicago Tribune*, October 2, 1932, 21.

26. *St. Louis Star and Times*, October 3, 1932, 16.

27. *Chicago Tribune*, October 2, 1932, 22.

28. *Salt Lake Tribune*, October 3, 1932, 11.

29. *New York Sun*, June 28, 1932; in Lazzeri Scrapbooks.

30. *Des Moines Tribune*, June 29, 1932, 17.

31. *New York World-Telegram*, September 7, 1932, 14.

10. Pennant Drought

1. *New York Daily News*, December 20, 1932, 46–47.

2. *New York Daily News*, January 9, 1933, 37.

3. Quoted in *New York Times*, January 20, 1932, 22.

4. Quoted in *New York Daily News*, February 2, 1933, 38.

5. *New York Daily News*, March 24, 1933, 58.

6. *Brooklyn Times Union*, September 14, 1932, 13.

7. Quoted by John Kieran, *New York Times*, April 13, 1933, 24.

8. *Shreveport Times*, March 19, 1933, 6.

9. *New York Daily News*, January 8, 1933, 27.

10. The Burr interview, discussed in this and the following paragraph, is in *Brooklyn Daily Eagle*, March 19, 1933, 33.

11. In the bottom of the ninth inning of a 1–1 tie game between the Giants and Cubs on September 23, 1908, the Giants had the winning run on third while Merkle was on first base when Al Bridwell hit a single to apparently end the game. When the crowd rushed onto the field, Merkle ran toward the dug-

out without advancing to second. When Cubs second baseman Johnny Evers retrieved a ball—some argued that it was not the ball hit by Bridwell—and stepped on second for the force, Merkle was called out, and the game ended in a tie. After the two teams ended the season in a tie, the Cubs won the replay game and went to the World Series.

12. *New York Daily News*, April 26, 1933, 48.

13. *Louisville Courier-Journal*, April 27, 1933, 12.

14. *Arizona Daily Star*, April 28, 1933, 8.

15. *New York Times*, May 1, 1933, 11.

16. Nick Newton and Bill Minutaglio, *Locker Room Mojo* (1999); cited by Clay Smith, *Austin Chronicle*, June 4, 1999. https://www.austinchronicle.com/books/1999–06–04/522104/.

17. *New York Daily News*, October 1, 1933, 84.

18. *New York Daily News*, September 22, 1933, 65.

19. *Chicago Tribune*, July 6, 1933; *New York Daily News*, July 7, 1933, 44.

20. August 24, 1933; in Lazzeri Scrapbooks. "Nino" is a common Italian nickname for someone named Antonio. Since Daniel's reference to the nickname is the first I have seen regarding Lazzeri, it may have been initiated by Frank Crosetti when he joined the Yankees in 1932. Years later Bill Corum would write: "'Nino' is the pet name of the Yankees for the smartest player on their team." *San Bernardino Sun*, October 8, 1937, 21.

21. *Minneapolis Star Tribune*, September 15, 1933, 15.

22. *Brooklyn Times Union*, October 26, 1933, 15.

23. *San Francisco Examiner*, October 24, 1933, 23.

24. Quoted in *Pensacola News Journal*, October 27, 1933, 6. After eight seasons in the Majors, Byrd retired from baseball and became a pro golfer. He won six PGA tournaments between 1942 and 1945 and finished third and fourth in The Masters in 1941 and 1942 respectively.

25. *New York Daily News*, December 12, 1933, 54.

26. *Detroit Free Press*, December 15, 1933, 21

27. *New York Daily News*, April 15, 1934, 37.

28. *New York Times*, June 26, 1934, 24.

29. *Pittsburgh Press*, July 1, 1934, 16.

30. Greenberg, *The Story of My Life*, 101.

31. *Tampa Bay Times*, June 19, 1934, 8.

32. *New York Daily News*, September 20, 1934, 60.

33. Undated clipping in Baseball Hall of Fame Library files. St. Louis Browns shortstop Oscar Melillo was nicknamed "Spinach" when, as a treatment for his kidney ailment, doctors prescribed a diet featuring the leafy vegetable.

34. Green Hills Country Club Archives Facebook page. https://www.facebook.com/GreenHillsCountryClubArchives/posts/baseball-and-green-hills-country-club-baseball-players-are-interwoven-throughout/969385903129128/ (accessed November 17, 2019).

35. *San Francisco Examiner*, December 21, 1934, 26.

36. *San Francisco Examiner*, February 7, 1935, 23.

37. Green Hills Country Club Archives Facebook page. https://www.facebook .com/GreenHillsCountryClubArchives/posts/baseball-and-green-hills-country -club-baseball-players-are-interwoven-throughout/969385903129128/ (accessed November 17, 2019).

38. *San Francisco Examiner*, December 21, 1936, 21.

39. *The Sporting News*, February 7, 1951, 23.

40. Crosby hosted his first Pro-Am Championship—which featured a clam-bake—in 1937 at Rancho Santa Fe, California, with Sam Snead taking the title and the winner's prize of $500. In 1947 the event moved to the Monterey Peninsula, where it became the Bing Crosby Pebble Beach Pro-Am and later the AT&T Pebble Beach Pro-Am.

11. Snubbing Father Time

1. Frank Crosetti, telephone interview with author, September 4, 1998.

2. Quoted in Frank Graham, *The New York Yankees*, 222.

3. *New York Daily News*, March 3, 1936, 45.

4. *New York Daily News*, March 3, 1936, 47.

5. Barrow, *My Fifty Years in Baseball*, 173–74.

6. Frank Graham, *The New York Yankees*, 223.

7. *San Pedro (CA) News Pilot*, January 15, 1936, 9.

8. *Brooklyn Times Union*, April 21, 1936, 13.

9. *The Sporting News*, November 26, 1936, 3.

10. *The Sporting News*, April 30, 1936, 1.

11. *Philadelphia Inquirer*, May 25, 1936, 13.

12. *New York Times*, May 25, 1936, 24.

13. *New York Times*, May 24, 1936, S1.

14. *Washington Post*, June 1, 1936, X19.

15. *The Sporting News*, May 21, 1936, 3.

16. *Liberty Magazine*, July 4, 1936, 48. The reference to the "Purple Gang" is surprising in the context of this article since it was a predominantly Jewish crime organization that controlled bootlegging, hijacking, and other criminal activities in Detroit in the 1920s and 1930s.

17. *Baseball Magazine*, July 1936, 347.

18. *Baseball Magazine*, July 1936, 347.

19. Frank Graham, *The New York Yankees*, 226.

20. "Tony Lazzeri: A New Kind of Hero," May 26, 2016. https://1927-the-diary -of-myles-thomas.espn.com/tony-lazzeri-a-new-kind-of-hero-2d65a1504d18.

21. Harry Jupiter, "Lazzeri the Great," *San Francisco Examiner*, February 19, 1989, 6.

22. Graham quoted in *Waxahachie (TX) Daily Light*, February 5, 1943, 3.

23. *New York Daily News*, May 20, 1936, 58.

24. *The Sporting News*, June 4, 1936, 4.

25. Frank Graham, *The New York Yankees*, 226. When Jackie Robinson broke the color barrier in 1947, Chapman, who was managing the Phillies at the time, was one of Robinson's most vicious taunters.

26. *New York Daily News*, October 3, 1936, 34.

27. Some sources mistakenly reported that Elmer Smith had also driven in five runs in the game in which he hit the grand slam, but he drove in four.

28. *Philadelphia Inquirer*, October 3, 1936, 19.

29. *New York Times*, October 3, 1936, 1.

30. *Chicago Tribune*, October 6, 1936, 27.

31. The Player of the Year award would later be renamed the Sid Mercer Memorial Award, in honor of the writer who first proposed the idea. For more, see Bill Deane, "Awards and Honors," 272.

32. Quoted in Frank Graham Jr., *A Farewell to Heroes*, 78.

33. *The Sporting News*, February 11, 1937, 4.

34. *San Mateo Times*, December 8, 1936, 1.

35. *Altoona Tribune*, December 9, 1936, 8.

36. On page 3 of the same issue of the *Daily News* was the story announcing King Edward VIII's historic decision to abdicate his throne in order to marry American divorcee Wallis Simpson.

37. *Oakland Tribune*, December 9, 1936, 1.

38. *Oakland Tribune*, December 9, 1936, 1.

39. *Oakland Tribune*, December 16, 1936, 14.

40. Matt Lazzeri, interview with author, September 13, 2018.

12. Farewell to Pinstripes

1. *New York Daily News*, February 9, 1937, 46.

2. *The Sporting News*, February 11, 1937, 5.

3. *New York Daily News*, March 3, 1937, 61.

4. *Baseball Digest*, March 1939; cited by Votano, *Tony Lazzeri*, 145.

5. There was considerable disagreement over Gordon's selection as MVP in 1942, a year in which he hit .322 with 18 homers and 103 RBIs. That season Ted Williams won the Triple Crown (.356, 36 homers, 137 RBIs), yet finished second, twenty-one points behind Gordon.

6. Frank Graham, *The New York Yankees*, 233.

7. Quoted in Frank Graham, "Hitting Slumps," 341.

8. *Iowa City Press-Citizen*, September 29, 1937, 7.

9. *New York Daily News*, September 5, 1937, 34.

10. While I found no evidence of a fine being levied in the weeks following the event, in 1939 Tommy Holmes casually mentioned in a story in the *Brooklyn Daily Eagle* (March 25, 10) that Lazzeri was fined $400.

11. Frank Graham, *The New York Yankees*, 236.

12. *St. Louis Star and Times*, October 11, 1937, 19.

13. *Naugatuck (CT) Daily News*, August 14, 1944, 6.

14. Frank Graham, *The New York Yankees*, 236.

15. An otherwise undated 1937 column; in the Lazzeri Scrapbooks.

16. *Brooklyn Daily Eagle*, September 6, 1937, 12.

17. *New York Times*, October 16, 1937, 15.

18. *The Sporting News*, October 21, 1937, 1.

19. *Boston Globe*, October 16, 1937, 1.

20. *San Francisco Examiner*, October 18, 1937, 17-18.

21. *San Francisco Examiner*, October 18, 1937, 17.

22. *Chicago Tribune*, October 22, 1937, 9.

23. *Hartford Courant*, October 22, 1937, 17.

24. Quoted in *San Francisco Examiner*, October 29, 1937, 21.

25. Quoted in Frank Graham, *The New York Yankees*, 236.

26. *The Sporting News*, November 4, 1937.

27. *Cincinnati Enquirer*, November 15, 1937, 15.

28. *Chicago Tribune*, December 21, 1937, 23.

29. *Chicago Tribune*, January 13, 1938, 19.

30. *Brooklyn Times Union*, July 7, 1931, 15.

31. Quoted in *Chicago Tribune*, December 29, 1937, 17.

13. Twilight Trail

1. *Time*, June 26, 1939, 48-49.

2. *Oakland Tribune*, February 25, 1938, 28.

3. Quoted in *Chicago Tribune*, February 12, 1938, 21.

4. *Bakersfield Californian*, February 25, 1938, 15.

5. *San Bernardino County (CA) Sun*, April 4, 1938, 9.

6. Brown, "Gabby Likes It Hot," 244.

7. Grimm, *Jolly Cholly's Story*, 132.

8. Brown, "Gabby Likes It Hot," 244.

9. *Chicago Tribune*, June 11, 1938, 17.

10. *New York Daily News*, May 15, 1938, 9C.

11. *New York Daily News*, May 15, 1938, 34C.

12. *Chicago Tribune*, September 29, 1938, 1.

13. *Chicago Tribune*, October 26, 1938, 21.

14. *Los Angeles Times*, October 27, 1938, 31.

15. Quoted in *Brooklyn Daily Eagle*, March 13, 1939, 14.

16. *San Francisco Examiner*, December 11, 1938, 55.

17. Quoted in *Brooklyn Daily Eagle*, December 12, 1938, 14.

18. Quoted in *New York Daily News*, March 1, 1939, 54.

19. Honig, "Don Honig's Baseball Tapes," 35, 46.

20. According to a story in the *Pittsburgh Post-Gazette* (May 18, 1939, 16), Lazzeri had a choice to sign with the Dodgers for $10,000 with no ten-day firing clause or for $12,000 with the clause in the contract. He chose the latter, enabling the Dodgers to release him on a moment's notice.

21. *New York Daily News*, May 14, 1939, 84.

22. *Miami News*, March 18, 1939, 14.

23. *New York Daily News*, June 8, 1939, 52.

24. *Time*, June 26, 1939, 49. While the signing was publicly announced on June 12, Lazzeri actually signed with Toronto on June 11, the day before the first induction ceremony in Cooperstown.

25. *Ottawa Citizen*, June 14, 1939, 11.

26. *The Sporting News*, July 6, 1939, 5.

27. Quoted in *Rochester Democrat and Chronicle*, June 27, 1939, 18.

28. *Ithaca (NY) Journal*, August 18, 1939, 10.

29. "Our History," Association of Professional Ball Players of America web site: https://apbpa.org/about-apbpa (accessed January 8, 2020).

14. Final Years in Uniform

1. It was in this same Lakeside development, just a few blocks south of Ross-moor Drive, that Ellis and Henry Stoneson, immigrants from Iceland, built their personal mansions.

2. "Lakeside District," in OutsideLands.org, http://www.outsidelands.org /lakeside-district.php (accessed February 5, 2020).

3. Yogi Berra, telephone interview with author, February 17, 1999.

4. Dom DiMaggio, interview with author, July 7–8, 2002.

5. The ground floor of the apartment building was the site of Gus Suhr's Liquors. A friend of Lazzeri and fellow San Franciscan, Suhr played first base for the Pirates and Phillies from 1930 to 1940. He and his wife lived near the Lazzeris in the Millbrae Highlands.

6. Dario Lodigiani, interview with author, October 2, 2000. Unless otherwise indicated, all quotations from Lodigiani are from this interview.

7. Quoted in Votano, *Tony Lazzeri*, 166.

8. *Pittsburgh Press*, May 5, 1940, 30.

9. Quoted in *Baltimore Evening Sun*, April 27, 1940, 8.

10. *New York Daily News*, June 4, 1940, 47.

11. *Baltimore Evening Sun*, July 15, 1940, 17.

12. *Montreal Gazette*, August 26, 1940, 15.

13. *Windsor (ON) Star*, November 8, 1940, 31.

14. *Windsor (ON) Star*, November 26, 1940, 24.

15. Lazzeri did not officially sign a contract with the Seals until January 24, 1941.

16. *San Francisco Examiner*, June 12, 1941, 29.

17. Quoted in *San Francisco Examiner*, November 7, 1941, 25.

18. *Richmond Times Dispatch*, March 21, 1942, 10.

19. Lazzeri predictions and quotes in this and the following paragraph are in *Richmond Times Dispatch*, April 8, 1942, 16.

20. Quoted in *Richmond Times Dispatch*, June 5, 1942, 18.

21. *Salt Lake City Deseret News*, September 29, 1942, 12.

22. Quoted in *Staunton (VA) News Leader*, January 3, 1943, 6.

23. *St. Louis Post-Dispatch*, February 25, 1943, 20.

24. *Scranton Tribune*, April 5, 1943, 12.

25. *Scranton Tribune*, April 5, 1943, 12.

26. *Wilkes-Barre Record*, May 6, 1943, 14.

27. *Wilkes-Barre Record*, September 14, 1943, 17.

28. Quoted in Macht, *They Played the Game*, 292.

29. *Wilkes-Barre Times Leader*, September 21, 1943, 5.

30. *Wilkes-Barre Times Leader*, September 22, 1943, 7.

31. *Wilkes-Barre Record*, January 11, 1944, 13.

32. Quoted in *Knoxville News-Sentinel*, July 11, 1944, 10.

33. *Wilkes-Barre Record*, January 11, 1944, 13.

15. Life after Baseball

1. *Fresno Bee*, September 28, 1944, 26.

2. *San Francisco Chronicle*, June 11, 1944; in Lazzeri file in Hall of Fame Library; *San Francisco Examiner*, June 12, 1944, 18.

3. "Sudden Death of Popular 'Tony' Lazzeri Shock to Lakeside Golfers," *Olympian Magazine*, September 1946, 25.

4. Quoted in *Pittsburgh Sun-Telegraph*, September 10, 1945, 16.

5. Quoted in *Pittsburgh Sun-Telegraph*, September 10, 1945, 16.

6. *San Francisco Examiner*, August 8, 1945, 17.

7. *St. Louis Post-Dispatch*, July 19, 1991, 8D.

8. Quoted in *Pittsburgh Sun-Telegraph*, September 10, 1945, 16.

9. *San Francisco Examiner*, June 28, 1946, 18; June 23, 1946, 19.

10. In his biography of Lazzeri, Paul Votano, presumably drawing on the AP report, also cites the Millbrae home as the site of Lazzeri's death. Votano, *Tony Lazzeri*, 170.

11. Frank Graham Jr., *A Farewell to Heroes*, 260.

12. *San Francisco Chronicle* clipping in Lazzeri file in Hall of Fame Library.

13. *San Francisco Examiner*, August 8, 1946, 17.

14. Dr. Chad Carlson, email to author, April 10, 2020.

15. *San Francisco Examiner*, August 9, 1946, 16.

16. *San Francisco Examiner*, August 8, 1946, 17.

17. *San Francisco Examiner*, August 10, 1946, 14.

18. *Seattle Times*, May 23, 2013.

16. Legacy

1. For readers not familiar with the term, WAR is a method devised by analysts to quantify a player's value to his team compared to that of a theoretical replacement player—a Minor Leaguer or a Major League bench player—expressed as how many more wins he is worth.

2. "Doping the World Series," *Washington Evening Star*, September 15, 1926, 48.

3. Quoted in Lane, "A Great Natural Ball Player Is Tony Lazzeri," 305.

4. Quoted in *San Pedro (CA) News Pilot*, January 15, 1936, 9.

5. Quoted in *St. Louis Post-Dispatch*, September 16, 1979, 23.

6. *New York Herald-Tribune*, August 9, 1946.

7. *New York Times*, August 9, 1946, 29.

8. *Washington Post*, August 9, 1946, 12.

9. Bartell, *Rowdy Richard*, 279.

10. Angelo Giuliani, interview with author, June 8, 2001.

11. Harry Jupiter, "Lazzeri the Great," *San Francisco Examiner*, February 19, 1989, 6.

12. Quoted in *Chicago Tribune*, December 29, 1937, 17.

13. Barrow, *My Fifty Years in Baseball*, 147–48.

14. Quoted in Ritter, *The Glory of Their Times*, 229.

15. Gallico, "Reign of Terror," 251; Frank Graham, "Tony Lazzeri Was Like This," 57.

16. *The Sporting News*, June 7, 1969, 15.

17. Ford, *Few and Chosen*, 35–40.

18. In 1962 a rule was established requiring that a player must have been active during a twenty-year period prior to his election. Lazzeri was last active in 1939.

19. Bill Deane, email to author, February 20, 2020.

20. *San Francisco Examiner*, February 19, 1989, 5.

21. *San Francisco Chronicle*, March 5, 1991, D4.

22. Votano, *Tony Lazzeri*, 172, mistakenly identifies Kevin Johnson as a San Francisco restaurateur, apparently confusing him with Benedetti.

23. *San Francisco Examiner*, February 27, 1991, 35.

24. *Washington Post*, July 21, 1991, D1.

25. *Washington Post*, March 1, 1991, C1.

26. *New York Daily News*, February 27, 1991, 58.

27. Quoted in Henry Schulman, "Push for 'Poosh' Pays Off," *Oakland Tribune*, February 1991; in Lazzeri file in Hall of Fame Library.

28. From Hall of Fame transcription of the induction ceremony.

29. Marilyn Lazzeri, telephone interview with author, July 16, 2018.

30. Eig, *Luckiest Man*, 2.

31. *Miami News*, May 18, 1939, 14.

32. Lieb, "Baseball—The Nation's Melting Pot," 303.

33. Thorn, "Fight or Flight," 115.

34. *New York Times*, March 4, 1991, C5.

35. John Thorn, "Tony Lazzeri, A New Kind Of Hero," *The Diary of Myles Thomas* (May 26, 2016); https://1927-the-diary-of-myles-thomas.espn.com /tony-lazzeri-a-new-kind-of-hero-2d65a1504d18.

36. *San Francisco Examiner*, February 19, 1989, 6.

Bibliography

Alexander, Charles C. *Breaking the Slump: Baseball in the Depression Era*. New York: Columbia University Press, 2002.

Appel, Marty. *Pinstripe Empire: The New York Yankees from before the Babe to after the Boss*. New York: Bloomsbury, 2012.

Baldassaro, Lawrence. *Baseball Italian Style: Great Stories Told by Italian American Major Leaguers from Crosetti to Piazza*. New York: Sports Publishing, 2018.

———. *Beyond DiMaggio: Italian Americans in Baseball*. Lincoln: University of Nebraska Press, 2011.

Barrow, Edward Grant, with James M. Kahn. *My Fifty Years in Baseball*. New York: Coward-McCann, 1951.

Bartell, Dick, with Norman L. Macht. *Rowdy Richard: A Firsthand Account of the National League Baseball Wars of the 1930s and the Men Who Fought Them*. Berkeley CA: North Atlantic Books, 1987.

Bloodgood, Clifford. "Players You Ought to Know." *Baseball Magazine*, June 1926.

Brown, Warren. "Gabby Likes It Hot." *Saturday Evening Post*, February 11, 1939, 229–46.

Bryson, Bill. *One Summer: America, 1927*. New York: Doubleday, 2013.

Carmichael, John P., ed. *My Greatest Day in Baseball*. Lincoln: University of Nebraska Press, 1996. Originally published by G. P. Putnam's Sons, 1955.

Cinel, Dino. *From Italy to San Francisco: The Immigrant Experience*. Palo Alto CA: Stanford University Press, 1982.

Connell, William J., and Fred Gardaphé, eds. *Anti-Italianism: Essays on a Prejudice*. New York: Palgrave Macmillan, 2010.

Creamer, Robert W. *Babe: The Legend Comes to Life*. New York: Simon and Schuster, 1974. Reprint, New York: Penguin, 1983.

Daniel, Daniel M. "Viva Italia!" *Baseball Magazine*, July 1936.

Deane, Bill. "Awards and Honors." In *Total Baseball*, ed. John Thorn et al., 6th ed., 247–86. New York: Total Sports, 1999.

——— . *Award Voting: A History of the Most Valuable Player, Rookie of the Year, and Cy Young Awards*. Kansas City MO: Society for American Baseball Research, 1988.

Devinsky, Orrin. "Cognitive and Behavioral Effects of Antiepileptic Drugs." *Epilepsia* 36, no. 2 (February 1995).

Dobbins, Dick, and Jon Twichell. *Nuggets on the Diamond: Professional Baseball in the Bay Area from the Gold Rush to the Present*. San Francisco: Woodford Press, 1994.

Dorinson, Joseph. "'Poosh 'Em Up, Tony!'—Italian Americans and Baseball." In *Horsehide, Pigskin, Oval Tracks and Apple Pie*, ed. James A. Vlasich, 38–51. Jefferson NC: McFarland, 2006.

Eig, Jonathan. *Luckiest Man: The Life and Death of Lou Gehrig*. New York: Simon and Schuster, 2005.

Fleming, G. H. *Murderers' Row: The 1927 New York Yankees*. New York: William Morrow, 1985.

Ford, Whitey, with Phil Pepe. *Few and Chosen: Defining Yankee Greatness across the Eras*. Chicago: Triumph Books, 2001.

Gallico, Paul. "Reign of Terror." *Sport*, May 1951. Repr. in *The World of Sport: The Best from Sport Magazine*, ed. Al Silverman, 238–51. New York: Holt, Rinehart and Winston, 1955.

Gentile, Charlie. *The 1928 New York Yankees: The Return of Murderers' Row*. Lanham MD: Rowman and Littlefield, 2014.

Glueckstein, Fred. "Tony Lazzeri." SABR BioProject, sabr.org/bioproject.

Graham, Frank. "Hitting Slumps." *Baseball Magazine*, July 1937, 341–42.

——— . *The New York Yankees: An Informal History*. New York: G. P. Putnam's Sons, 1943.

——— . "Tony Lazzeri Was Like This." *Baseball Digest*, February 1959, 57–58.

Graham, Frank, Jr. *A Farewell to Heroes*. New York: Viking, 1981.

Greenberg, Hank. *The Story of My Life*. Edited and with an introduction by Ira Berkow. New York: Times Books, 1989.

Grimm, Charlie, with Ed Prell. *Jolly Cholly's Story: Baseball, I Love You!* Chicago: Henry Regnery, 1968.

Gumina, Deanna Paoli. *Italians of San Francisco, 1850–1930*. New York: Center for Migration Studies, 1968.

Holtzman, Jerome. *No Cheering in the Press Box*. Revised and expanded edition. New York: Henry Holt, 1995.

Honig, Donald. "Don Honig's Baseball Tapes." *Baseball Quarterly* 35, no. 2 (Winter 1977).

——— . *The October Heroes: Great World Series Games Remembered by the Men Who Played Them*. Lincoln: University of Nebraska Press, 1979.

James, Bill. *The New Bill James Historical Abstract*. New York: Free Press, 2001.

Kimball, Richard Ian. "Bringing Fame to Zion: Tony Lazzeri, the Salt Lake Bees, and Life in the Pacific Coast League." *NINE: A Journal of Baseball History and Culture* 14, no. 2 (Spring 2006): 40–58.

Lane, F. C. "A Great Natural Ball Player Is Tony Lazzeri." *Baseball Magazine,* December 1927.

———. "'Poosh-Em-Out' Tony Lazzeri and His Colorful Record." *Baseball Magazine,* April 1927.

Leavy, Jane. *The Big Fella: Babe Ruth and the World He Created.* New York: HarperCollins, 2018.

Levitt, Daniel R. *Ed Barrow: The Bulldog Who Built the Yankees' First Dynasty.* Lincoln: University of Nebraska Press, 2008.

Lieb, Frederick G. *Baseball As I Have Known It.* New York: Coward, McCann and Geoghegan, 1977.

———. "Baseball—The Nation's Melting Pot." *Baseball Magazine,* August 1923.

Linn, Ed. *The Great Rivalry: The Yankees and the Red Sox, 1901–1990.* New York: Ticknor and Fields, 1991.

Macht, Norman L. *Connie Mack: The Turbulent and Triumphant Years, 1915–1931.* Lincoln: University of Nebraska Press, 2012.

———. *They Played the Game: Memories from 47 Major Leaguers.* Lincoln: University of Nebraska Press, 2019.

Mackey, R. Scott. *Barbary Baseball: The Pacific Coast League of the 1920s.* Jefferson NC: McFarland, 1995.

Montville, Leigh. *The Big Bam: The Life and Times of Babe Ruth.* New York: Doubleday, 2006.

Mosedale, John. *The Greatest of All: The 1927 New York Yankees.* New York: Dial Press, 1982.

Notarianni, Philip C. "Italianità in Utah: The Immigrant Experience." In *The Peoples of Utah,* ed. Helen Z. Papanikolas, 303–31. Salt Lake City: Utah State Historical Society, 1976.

Pinelli, Babe, as told to Joe King. *Mr. Ump.* Philadelphia: Westminster Press, 1953.

Reports of the Immigration Commission: Emigration Conditions in Europe. Washington DC: Government Printing Office, 1911.

Reynolds, Quentin. "The Frisco Kid." *Collier's,* June 13, 1936, 22.

Ritter, Lawrence. *The Glory of Their Times: The Story of the Early Days of Baseball Told by the Men Who Played It.* New York: Macmillan, 1966.

Robinson, Ray. *The Greatest Yankees of Them All.* New York: Putnam, 1969.

Sillito, John. "'Our Tone': Tony Lazzeri's Baseball Career in Salt Lake City, 1922–25." *Utah Historical Quarterly* 72 (Fall 2004): 343–57.

Snelling, Dennis. *The Greatest Minor League: A History of the Pacific Coast League, 1903–1967.* Jefferson NC: McFarland, 2012.

———. *Lefty O'Doul: Baseball's Forgotten Ambassador.* Lincoln: University of Nebraska Press, 2017.

——— . *The Pacific Coast League: A Statistical History, 1903–1957*. Jefferson NC: McFarland, 1995.

Steinberg, Steve. *Urban Shocker: Silent Hero of Baseball's Golden Age*. Lincoln: University of Nebraska Press, 2017.

Steinberg, Steve, and Lyle Spatz. *The Colonel and Hug: The Partnership That Transformed the New York Yankees*. Lincoln: University of Nebraska Press, 2015.

Stout, Glenn, and Richard A. Johnson. *Yankees Century: 100 Years of New York Yankees Baseball*. Boston: Houghton Mifflin, 2002.

Thorn, John. "Fight or Flight." In *Chasing Dreams: Baseball and Becoming American*, ed. Josh Perelman, 112–23. Philadelphia: National Museum of American Jewish History, 2014.

Trachtenberg, Leo. "Tony Lazzeri." *Yankees Magazine*, August 4, 1983, 32–33.

——— . *The Wonder Team: The True Story of the Incomparable 1927 New York Yankees*. Bowling Green OH: Bowling Green State University Press, 1995.

Vellon, Peter G. "Italian Americans and Race during the Era of Mass Migration." In *Routledge History of Italian Americans*, ed. William J. Connell and Stanislao G. Pugliese, 212–22. New York: Routledge, 2018.

Votano, Paul. *Tony Lazzeri: A Baseball Biography*. Jefferson NC: McFarland, 2005.

White, G. Edward. *Creating the National Pastime: Baseball Transforms Itself, 1903–1953*. Princeton NJ: Princeton University Press, 1996.

Zoss, Joel, and John Bowman. *Diamonds in the Rough: The Untold History of Baseball*. Chicago: Contemporary Books, 1996.

Index

Kahn, James M., 200
Kallio, Rudy, 14–15
Kamm, Willie, 185, 262; and free baseball
  school, 258, 259
Keeler, Wee Willie, 234
Kemp, Abe, 133, 140, 244
Kieran, John, 100, 125, 136, 139; on
  Lazzeri, 109, 140, 144, 152
Killefer, Wade, 229
Kirksey, George, 214
Klem, Bill, 57, 236–37, 260
Knickerbocker, Bill, 201
Koenig, Mark, *fig. 5*, 59, 67, 110, 111, 124,
  131, 134–35, 138, 185; background of,
  48–49; with Cubs, 161–62; error in
  1926 World Series by, 68, 72; injury
  to, 102, 114; as Lazzeri advocate, 119,
  272; as Lazzeri double play partner, 58,
  100, 134; on Lazzeri seizures, 64; with
  Tigers, 135; Yankees' decision to start,
  49, 50, 57–58, 154
Krichell, Paul, 34, 35, 55
Ku Klux Klan, 40

La Guardia, Fiorello, 92, 205
Lajoie, Nap, 219, 234, 273
Landis, Kenesaw Mountain, 241
Lane, Bill, 20, 30, 36
Lane, F. C., 86
Lang, Jack, 273
Lardner, Ring, 96
Lary, Lyn, 100, 124, 136, 141, 156, 157, 158
Lavagetto, Cookie, 10
Lawrence, Frank, 245, 246, 249, 250
Lazzeri, Agostino (father), *fig. 2*, xv, 1,
  2, 5, 11
Lazzeri, David Anthony (son), *figs. 14, 19*,
  xiv, 155, 263
Lazzeri, Giula (mother), 1, 2, 245
Lazzeri, Marilyn (daughter in law), xiv,
  4, 65, 146, 263, 274
Lazzeri, Matt (grandson), xiv–xv, 4, 146–
  47, 208, 263
Lazzeri, Maye (wife), 41, 65, 113, 121, 155;
  death of, 274; and death of Tony, 260,
  261; divorce filing by Tony with, 206–
  8; and Hall of Fame, 7, 273–74; marriage to Tony, 17; personality of, 16–17;

photographs of, *figs. 14, 19*; stock market investments by, 146–47; and Tony's
  diet and preparations, 137–38, 151
Lazzeri, Tony (ballplayer): in 1922 (with
  Salt Lake City), 14–15; in 1923 (with
  Peoria), 18–19; in 1923 (with Salt Lake
  City), 19; in 1924 (with Lincoln), 21–23,
  27–28; in 1924 (with Salt Lake City),
  20–21, 28; in 1925 (with Salt Lake City),
  30–33, 36–39; in 1926 (with Yankees),
  51–56, 66–73; in 1927 (with Yankees),
  75–81, 82–86; in 1928 (with Yankees),
  103–5, 109–18; in 1929 (with Yankees),
  124–28; in 1930 (with Yankees), 133–
  38; in 1931 (with Yankees), 140–46, 151–
  52; in 1932 (with Yankees), 157–67; in
  1933 (with Yankees), 170–76; in 1934
  (with Yankees), 179–83; in 1935 (with
  Yankees), 186–89; in 1936 (with Yankees), 193–97, 201–2, 203–5; in 1937
  (with Yankees), 211–15; in 1938 (with
  Cubs), 224–27; in 1939 (with Dodgers),
  230, 231; in 1939 (with Giants), 232–
  33; in 1939 (with Toronto Maple Leafs),
  233–36; in 1940 (with Toronto Maple
  Leafs), 240–43; in 1941 (with San Francisco Seals), 244; in 1942 (with Portsmouth), 245–49; in 1943 (with Wilkes
  Barre), 249–53; Alexander strikeout
  in World Series, xii, 69–70, 71–73, 255,
  257, 269, 274–75; assessments of legacy, 267–70; awards, *fig. 13*, 205, 268,
  270; baserunning, 38–39, 266; batting stance and swing, 15–16, 19, 55,
  77, 171; with Brooklyn Dodgers, 229–
  32, 234, 295n20; with Chicago Cubs,
  fig. 17, 216–19, 221–28; clutch hitting,
  56–57, 118, 265–66; competitive fire,
  61, 84–85, 148, 244; considered over-
  the-hill, 161, 178, 193, 220; and DiMaggio, xi, 158, 190–92, 200–201, 269, 271;
  ejections, 47, 283n6; ethnic stereotypes
  and labels, 20, 22–23, 50–51, 53–54,
  80, 86–90, 111, 121, 156, 276; exhibition and benefit games, 98–100, 132,
  138, 183–84, 244; fielding, 20, 28, 80,
  85–86, 212–13, 266–67; Hall of Fame

season, 140–45; in 1932 season, 157–61, 165–66; in 1932 World Series, 161–65; in 1933 season, 170–75; in 1934 season, 179–83; in 1935 season, 186–89; in 1936 season, 193–97, 201–3; in 1936 World Series, 203–5; in 1937 season, 211–14; in 1937 World Series, 214–15; in 1938 World Series, 227; DiMaggio coming to, 190–92; double play combinations with, 58, 100, 134, 158; early history of, 47–48; hiring of managers by, 131–32, 138–39; Lazzeri purchased by, 36; Lazzeri's release from, 216; Murderers' Row with, 76–77, 81, 83–84, 95–96, 201, 278; Ruth's acquisition by, 48; salaries with, 75, 130, 133, 155–56, 169–71, 209–10; scouting of Lazzeri by, 33, 34–35; trade rumors about Lazzeri from, 143–44, 152, 153–54, 177–79, 193; uniform numbers of, 124–25, 154
Nichols, Malcolm, 93
Nuggets on the Diamond (Dobbins), 9

Oakland Tribune, 20, 99, 222
O'Doul, Lefty, *fig. 25,* 10, 33, 138, 185, 236, 243; career of, 29; and Lazzeri, 78–79, 133
O'Farrell, Bob, 68, 70
Ogden Standard-Examiner, 31
O'Leary, Charlie, 128
Olympic Club, 238–39, 255–56, 263, 276
O'Neill, Steve, 233
Orsatti, Ernie, *fig. 6,* 183

Pacific Base Ball Convention, 9
Pacific Base Ball League, 9, 10
Pacific Coast League (PCL), 12–13; history of, 9, 14. *See also* Salt Lake City Bees; San Francisco Seals
Palange, A. J., 94
Parker, Dan, 11
Partee, Roy, 248–49
Pearson, Monte, 196, 203, 204
Pegler, Westbrook, 49, 79–80, 138, 146, 154–55, 164
Pennock, Herb, 48, 55, 67, 76, 126, 128, 131; injuries of, 102, 114; Lazzeri on, 257
Peoria Journal Transcript, 18

Peoria Tractors, 16, 17–19
Perry, Gaylord, 1
Pettingill, Jayn, 16–17
Pettingill, Paul, 16
phenobarbital, 65–66, 284n55
Philadelphia Athletics: in 1927, 76, 79–80; in 1928, 103–4, 109–14; in 1929, 125–26; in 1930, 134; in 1931, 142; sell-off of players by, 174; Toronto Maple Leafs' affiliation to, 240, 241
Philadelphia Inquirer, 112
Philadelphia Royal Giants, 132
Picetti, Cookie, 12
Piedmont League, 245, 247, 249
Pinelli, Babe, 10, 87, 91, 185, 243, 286n29
Pipgras, George, 112, 115, 126, 135, 161
Pirrone, Joe and John, 99
Pittenger, Clarke "Pinky," 20
Pittsburgh Pirates, 226–27; in 1927 World Series, 82–83, 285n12
Pittsburgh Press, 180
Player of the Year award, 294n31; to Lazzeri, *fig. 13,* 205, 268
Poisall, Robert, 18, 63
Polli, Louis, 133, 289n3
"Poosh 'Em Up" nickname, 70, 84, 86, 91, 94, 154, 166, 214, 233, 256; Lazzeri opinion of, 51; origin of, 39–40, 42, 282n31
Portsmouth Cubs, *fig. 23,* 245–49
Povich, Shirley, 73, 268, 272–73
Powell, Jake, 202, 205
Powers, Jimmy, 242
Professional Baseball Players of America, 99–100
Quinn, John, 104

Ray, Robert E., 38–39
Raymond, Pete, 37
Reese, Jimmie, 100, 132
Reese, Pee Wee, 274
Reiser, Pete, 230–31
Rennie, Rud, 80
Reynolds, Carl, 161
Rice, Grantland, 72, 96, 275
Richmond Times Dispatch, 246–47
Rinetti, Cesare, 39, 41, 262
Rizzuto, Phil, 58
Roberti, Roberto, 62, 284n49

Printed in the USA
CPSIA information can be obtained
at www.ICGtesting.com
CBHW032314010424
6237CB00003B/171